# Think Like a Sheepdog Trainer

## A Guide to Raising and Training a Herding Dog

Kay Stephens, DVM and Beth Kerber

Publishing

Wenatchee, Washington U.S.A.

**Think Like a Sheepdog Trainer**
A Guide to Raising and Training a Herding Dog

Kay Stephens and Beth Kerber

Dogwise Publishing
A Division of Direct Book Service, Inc.
403 South Mission Street, Wenatchee, Washington 98801
1-509-663-9115, 1-800-776-2665
www.dogwisepublishing.com / info@dogwisepublishing.com
© 2022 Kay Stephens and Beth Kerber

Interior: Lindsay Davisson
Cover design: Jesús Cordero

Limits of Liability and Disclaimer of Warranty:
The author and publisher shall not be liable in the event of incidental or consequential damages in connection with, or arising out of, the furnishing, performance, or use of the instructions and suggestions contained in this book.

Library of Congress Cataloging-in-Publication Data

Names: Stephens, Kay, 1957- author. | Kerber, Beth, 1967- author.
Title: Think like a sheepdog trainer : a guide to raising and training a
    herding dog / Kay Stephens, DVM and Beth Kerber.
Description: Wenatchee, Washington, U.S.A : Dogwise Publishing, [2022] |
    Includes bibliographical references and index.
Identifiers: LCCN 2022036073 (print) | LCCN 2022036074 (ebook) | ISBN
    9781617813283 (paperback) | ISBN 9781617813290 (ebook)
Subjects: LCSH: Herding dogs--Training.
Classification: LCC SF428.6 .S74 2022  (print) | LCC SF428.6  (ebook) | DDC
    636.737--dc23/eng/20220829
LC record available at https://lccn.loc.gov/2022036073
LC ebook record available at https://lccn.loc.gov/2022036074

ISBN: 9781617813283

Printed in the U.S.A.

# More Praise for *Think Like a Sheepdog Trainer*

A comprehensive book on working dogs that also includes valuable information on sheep. A must have for beginners and experienced handlers alike.

**Michael Neary, PhD**, author, *Sheep for Sheepdogs: A Sheepdog Handler's Practical Guide to Sheep*

This book is a gold mine of information for those seeking to develop or improve their herding skills. It presents a thorough overview of learning theory, explained in understandable terms, which will help elevate the reader's knowledge and training skill. The first of its kind to apply behavioral science to the practice of herding, the book lays out a compelling reason for approaching herding with sound, proven training methods that both herding dogs and their handlers will find rewarding. The "real life" examples, offered by Dr. Kay Stephens, a pioneer in the field of evidence-based training, makes the book all the more readable and informative!

**Sarah Richardson**, PhD, CPDT-KA, CDBC, CSAT

# Dedication

This book is dedicated to all the dogs, people and sheep who increased our knowledge and skills on our sheepdog training journey—and to all those who have developed, selected, bred and preserved the working Border Collie.

# Table of Contents

# Acknowledgments

---

Dozens of people have helped make this book happen. First, we'd like to thank the sheepdog trainers we've worked with over the years, especially Linda and Bruce Fogt and Faansie Basson. We like to say that we stand on the shoulders of those who came before, and we feel very fortunate and humble to have worked with you over the years. Also, we thank the many dogs that worked with us in spite of our mistakes, helped us become better handlers and trainers, and taught us along the way.

A special thank you goes to all those who provided photographs for the book including Carol Clawson, Beth Murray, Joanne Hardy, Vernon Bewley and Libbeye Miller. Thank you to Joann Jozwiak for the illustrations and the laughs as she went the extra mile to follow Border Collies around and photograph them from above. Thank you to our readers, Carol Clawson, Beth Murray, Patricia McConnell, Brooks Watson and Joanne Hardy. A special thank you to Carol Clawson for all of the encouragement and assistance along the way.

Kay Stephens would also like to thank Marian Breland Bailey and Bob Bailey for teaching her and many others the science behind animal learning and as a result, revolutionizing modern animal training. She'd also like thank her husband, Mark Nevill, for his support during the multi-year endeavor—and for taking care of all the sheep and dogs while she traveled.

Beth Kerber also extends great appreciation to her writer's group and especially to Cathy Essinger for her continued support and nudging. Many other friends and family provided encouragement and support over the years. She'd also like to thank the pet sitters for keeping the animals, especially Dewey Kitty, alive during her travels.

# Introduction

This is the book we wish we had when we first started in sheepdogs. While there are good sheepdog training books available, almost all of them assume the reader has a basic knowledge of sheep and sheep behavior, the skill and experience to train a dog to do complex behaviors, the ability to figure out training steps on their own, and a clear mental picture of what a properly trained herding dog should look like. Of course, most newcomers to sheepdog training are lacking in at least some of these areas, so those books all have large information gaps for the novice. This book focuses on training Border Collies for United States Border Collie Handlers Association (USBCHA) type trials, but the information is applicable to all herding breeds and herding venues.

This book looks at the ancient art of sheepdog training through the lens of science-based learning theory and behavior analysis. It is designed to help you understand how and why a method works and to give you the tools for setting up and evaluating training plans and for approaching training problems in a logical, evidence-based manner.

This book covers several topics that will help you become a more successful sheepdog trainer. Here's what you can expect.

1. We discuss in detail how to train, manage and communicate with your dog before you take him to sheep. Without a proper relationship and training foundation, working stock with your dog is extremely difficult.

2. We introduce you to science-based learning theory and explain how it can be used to speed up and improve your ability to train your dog. We demonstrate how to evaluate and analyze training techniques so you can choose which ones work best for you and your dog.

3. We describe and discuss the physical and mental traits a sheepdog trainer must cultivate to succeed. People aren't born as excellent trainers; training is a learned skill that must be practiced and refined.

4. We explain the behavior and handling of sheep. Understanding and knowing how to properly control sheep is essential to your journey in the world of sheepdog training. Many newcomers to herding have no previous experience with sheep. We provide some basic sheep handling exercises to improve your ability to control livestock.

5. We offer detailed lesson plans that break down training sessions into very small and clearly explained steps that a novice handler can apply on her own. This should help you with developing a daily lesson plan, a goal for that day's lesson and a way to evaluate how you and your dog are progressing. You will discover that having a training plan and metrics to evaluate that plan will help you train faster and more efficiently.

6. Finally, we give you ways to think about training problems and how to approach and solve them in a logical, evidence-based manner.

Because people have been training dogs and herding with dogs for many years, some of the methods described here are similar to those found in other books and from other sources. We have chosen training approaches that are widely used, least aversive and easily understood and implemented by an inexperienced trainer. You will find our sources in the resources and recommended reading section at the end of the book.

Remember, sheepdog training is a lifelong journey. You will learn something new with every dog you train and with every competition that you enter. We hope this book will help make that journey a little easier.

## Can this book be used for other herding breeds and livestock?

While this book was written specifically for training Border Collies with the goal of competing in USBCHA trials, the science and training theory applies to all dogs. Breeds other than the Border Collie may need some modification in the application of the training steps. The working Border Collie has been bred to have a strong drive and motivation to work stock, to have some degree of "eye" or focus on stock, and to have a natural tendency to circle and to control stock. All these traits make their training somewhat easier. Breeds which lack the strong drive to work stock, or lack eye, or lack the tendency to gather will need modifications to the training approach. Other reinforcements, such as praise or food, may be necessary to motivate those dogs. A more incremental and mechanical set-up for training may be needed to compensate for the lack of instinct and natural stock sense. Finally, it will generally take longer and require more effort to train those dogs. The final goal, which for this book is competing in USBCHA Open sheepdog trials, will not be the same for the other dog breeds. Most herding breeds, other than the Border Collie, were developed for large flock work, for close at hand work, and for driving stock more so than gathering. The final product and the types of competition goals for other herding breeds will be different than what we are working toward in this book. That said, good stock work is good stock work. Regardless of breed, the dog still needs to be obedient, to gather and drive properly, to flank correctly and to handle stock humanely and quietly, all of which are covered in this book.

While this book does not address working other types of livestock, such as cattle, many of the same training methods and principles are going to apply. Many handlers who train their dogs to work other livestock, such as cattle, train their dogs first on sheep.

Two additional notes: For clarity and consistency, the handler in this book is referred to with the female pronoun, and the male pronoun is used for the dog. This is not to editorialize on whether males or females make better trainers or whether male or female dogs make better herding dogs. Both male and female handlers excel in this activity, and both male and female dogs also excel. And secondly, certain key words are bolded on their first use and included in the glossary at the end of the book.

*The Border Collie uses her "eye" to control stock. Photo courtesy of Vernon Bewley.*

# Part 1

## Skills and Knowledge for Handlers and Dogs before Working Sheep

# Chapter 1
# What is Herding?

*Beth Kerber and her dog, Mickey, pen the sheep. Photo courtesy of Libbeye Miller*

While **herding** is defined as the controlled movement of a group of stock, those who engage in herding may describe it as a magical partnership between dog and person, a necessary element of farm work and one of the most difficult human-dog activities to master. Sheepdog trainer H. Glynn Jones called it, "A Way of Life," while sheepdog trainer Faansie Basson points out that it is a "craft, not a sport."

Unlike most dog competitions, herding is based on a real job that still exists. A shepherd and her dog work as a team to gather sheep from hillsides, move them into different pastures or to the barn, sort sheep into groups, or move them into handling systems for hoof trimming and other care. A good herding dog saves the shepherd time, and often the need for another person. Just as importantly, the help of a good dog means less stress for the sheep.

## Is that dog herding? (Or what herding is not)
A herding dog controls and takes care of his stock or sheep. Just because a dog is in a field with sheep does not mean he is herding. As you watch dogs interact with sheep, keep these things in mind:

- Chasing sheep is not herding.
- Diving into a group of sheep is not herding.
- Grabbing a sheep and hanging onto it is not herding.
- A dog who spends time with the flock and barks at or chases off coyotes, stray dogs and people is not herding. He is a livestock guardian dog.

Sometimes a dog looks like he's herding but it is not. A dog performing obedience work while the sheep are following the handler is not herding. If the sheep are following the human, and the dog is following the sheep, look and see who is controlling the sheep's movements. If it's the person, then the dog is not herding.

## What is the role of the human?

The human is an essential part of the herding team. A dog may have the instinct to gather sheep, keep them together and even bring them to his handler, but that is only somewhat useful. The handler must teach the dog about pace (bringing them at a run is not good stockmanship), directions, pushing or driving, and other skills. These advanced skills allow the dog and handler to quietly and calmly move sheep to different fields, drive them into pens or trailers, or sort individual sheep from the flock.

A good handler must have:

- Concern for the mental and physical well being of both dogs and livestock;
- Patience and determination; and
- The ability to set long-term goals and work regularly toward those goals over a long period of time regardless of setbacks, training conditions and difficulties.

## How long does it take to develop a good herding dog?

This is a tricky question. Herding is a difficult activity because it involves so many variables: the sheep, the dog, the weather, the terrain, time of day and the handler. Most top handlers have 10, 20 or more years experience working with herding dogs and sheep.

A talented handler with experience working with herding dogs and sheep may be able to train a Border Collie to compete at the top or open level of USBCHA trials by age 3. However, that handler is still training her dog to perform more advanced skills. Someone who is starting out in herding may take years to teach the skills necessary to compete in sheepdog trials.

Most people who succeed at herding look at it as a long-term process. Each dog teaches them something new, and with each dog, they become better trainers. Most people who are successful at herding genuinely enjoy training and spending time with their dogs, learning new things and working with livestock. For many, these things are just as rewarding, if not more, than ribbons.

As you embark on herding, keep these things in mind:

- Herding is based on real farm work and good stockmanship. Sheep are living, sentient beings and must be treated with care and with the least stress possible. The care of the sheep is the cornerstone of all sheepdog training. All the things we teach the dogs to do are based on the behavior of the sheep and the best way to move and handle them. Understanding and taking care of sheep is essential for success. Anyone who allows a dog to harass, chase or "play with" the sheep doesn't understand herding and should take up a different activity with her dog.
- The dog controls the sheep—treating them kindly and with the least stress possible.
- The handler controls the dog—teaching the dog what is expected of him.
- Herding is a team activity involving both the dog and the human.
- Becoming proficient at herding, whether on the farm or in competitions, takes lots of practice, repetition and work.

## The magical moment between herding dog and handler

When all of the elements come together, herding can seem magical. The dog, handler and sheep seem to work in harmony—and no human or animal appears stressed. Here is a real-life example of a magical moment.

Several **ewes** in a four-acre field appeared sick, but the only way to know for sure was to give them a hands-on examination. Because the sheep were very wary of people, they would have to be coaxed to a holding area near the barn. A pond in the center of the field made moving them a challenge. If a person tried to move them, the sheep would certainly try to escape to the other side of the pond, and a game of ring-around-the-pond would ensue. This, in turn, would stress the sick sheep. A trained Border Collie who was agile and understood sheep was needed.

For the job, the shepherd selected Jack, a 10-year-old Border Collie who had been an accomplished competition and farm dog. Over the course of his lifetime, he had worked with ewes and lambs, sheep that challenged him, and sheep that tried to run away. Through training and experience, he became an expert at reading and moving sheep.

Jack ran in a wide arc around the sheep, and once on the other side of the sick ewes quietly walked up to them. An older ewe sized him up. From experience, the ewe knew she had many options: she could fight the dog, she could run, she could try to escape, or she could move away from the dog. Whatever decision she made, the rest of the group would follow. The dog's confident and authoritative movements made her dismiss the idea of fighting or escaping; he made her uncomfortable, but she did not fear for her life. She turned and walked toward the handler standing at the gate; the other ewes followed behind her.

Jack, too, was sizing up the situation. The ewes needed to move, but he sensed they were sick and handled them with care. Walking slowly and steadily would get the job done. He listened for the whistles from his handler and responded when the handler whistled for him to go right, to stop and to continue walking up on the sheep.

When approaching the gate, the ewe briefly considered darting to the left and escaping, but Jack sensed that. Without a cue from his handler, he stepped to the left and caught the ewe's eye. Instead of arguing, she continued moving through the gate opening.

Within minutes, the ewes were in a holding pen where they could be examined. None had moved faster than a walk to get there. None had been unduly stressed. The handler had given the dog very few cues—just a few directional cues so he knew where to take the sheep. It was a magical moment of herding at its finest, and those magical moments make the hours of training worth it.

## A Shepherd's Journey

When I first became interested in herding, I had been competing in obedience and agility competitions with my Shetland Sheepdog for several years. One of my early mentors, Red Oliver, allowed me to bring my dog to his farm and work sheep. He, too, had participated in obedience competitions with his Australian Shepherds.

Red Oliver was very encouraging, but he warned me right away that the "easy" ribbons we were used to in obedience competition did not exist in the USBCHA herding trials. He said that if I wanted to win ribbons, I should just stick to AKC (American Kennel Club) herding venues because the fields were a lot smaller.

He said herding was the most challenging dog sport because the stock's behavior varied so much from competition to competition and even throughout the day. Also, in USBCHA trials, the distance from the handler to the dog was so great, sometimes several hundred yards, that the dog needed both obedience and herding instinct. Both the dog and the handler have to have stock sense.

"It only takes about 15 years to become a decent open handler, if you work hard and are lucky," he told me.

I soon caught the herding bug and realized that if I wanted to herd sheep in larger fields, I would need a Border Collie. My first Border Collie was very natural and very easy to train (I wish I had her now that I know more). My second Border Collie was totally different and had a lot of **eye** (used her intense stare to control livestock). I needed help training her, and that's when I started working with my next mentor, Bruce Fogt. –Kay

# Chapter 2
# Choosing Your Herding Partner

While almost any dog can learn and perform basic levels of obedience and agility, the majority of dogs do not have the physical, mental and emotional characteristics to herd at a high level of proficiency. Before investing the time and energy into herding training, evaluate your herding prospect—whether it's a dog you own or one you're considering buying. It will be time well spent.

## The traits of a good herding dog

Over the centuries, herding dogs were bred for skills useful on the farm including a controlled prey drive, herding instinct, intelligence, athletic ability, trainability and a desire to cooperate with humans.

Most dogs have some **prey drive**—or the desire to chase, capture and kill prey like birds, rabbits, mice and sheep. But while some dog breeds have high prey drive, the herding dog's prey drive is truncated. The herding dog has the desire to stalk and chase, but less of the desire to kill and dismember. Training discourages the herding dog from harming his prey.

**Warning:** Because herding dogs have high prey drive, they should never be left unsupervised with poultry or livestock. They are not livestock guardian dogs, like Great Pyrenees, Akbash and Anatolian Shepherds, who live with the flock and ward off predators.

In addition to controlled prey drive, a good herding dog must have **herding instinct**—or the ability to group animals into a flock and move them as a group. Herding instinct is what makes a herding dog immediately react and bring an escaping ewe back to the flock. An obedient dog without herding instinct may be able to group sheep together if a skilled handler gives him directional cues. However, relying exclusively on obedience only works in smaller paddocks with well-behaved sheep. To herd in larger fields, a dog must have herding instinct.

The dog must be **biddable**, or willing to work with his handler—even when his prey drive and his herding instinct are telling him to do something else. The best herding dogs understand that herding is a team activity and they want to be part of that team.

While several different herding breeds developed over the years, the Border Collie—with its speed, endurance, athletic capabilities, biddable nature and working style, became the primary choice for working sheep.

## The ideal herding dog

The best herding dogs, whether working on a farm or competing at a sheepdog trial, have these characteristics:

- They are athletic, well-built and physically fit.
- They have herding instinct and a strong drive to work stock.
- They are able to work livestock in a serious and controlled manner.
- They are responsive to their handler when working sheep and around the farm or home.
- They get along with people and other dogs.
- They can settle down and relax when not working sheep and do not engage in obsessive behaviors like spinning, mindless barking and pacing.

**Note:** This book focuses on training to the level of USBCHA trials—considered the top level of the sport. It takes a special dog to succeed at this level. When selecting a dog for herding, you have to decide whether you are doing this for fun and are willing to work with a less capable dog, or whether you want a dog who will be competitive at the highest levels of sheepdog trials.

Getting a well-bred Border Collie from selectively bred parents who come from generations of dogs who have actively worked livestock on the farm or in trials can save you months or years of frustration. You can't win the Kentucky Derby with a Shetland pony, and you can't succeed at sheepdog trials with a dog who does not have the genetic potential to do the job. Because this is such a demanding sport, it pays to get a dog with the proper breeding. Look for a dog whose parents or close relatives have successfully competed at the USBCHA open level. This will give you the best chance of choosing a dog with the many qualities needed. A well-bred dog will have a lot of natural abilities that will make training faster and easier.

## Is my dog suitable for herding?

Many dog owners start their herding journey with a dog they currently own. However, not all dogs from herding breeds are good herding candidates. Before starting, evaluate your dog's physical capabilities, temperament and herding instinct. As much as you love your dog, it will save you and him much frustration if you are honest about his potential for this sport.

*Selecting a well-bred dog with natural abilities will make herding training easier. Photo courtesy of Carol Clawson.*

### Is the dog physically able to do the job?

A herding dog must have the stamina to work continuously, speed and agility. To determine whether your dog is physically up for the job, take a few minutes to assess your dog's weight, his physical fitness level, his conformation, his hearing and age.

### Is your dog fat, thin or just right?

Because they run long distances and work for long periods of time, herding dogs should look more like long distance runners and less like football linebackers. They should be lean and not overweight. A hands-on examination tells you a lot about your dog's condition. Because dogs, like people, can carry their extra weight in various parts of their body, examine several areas of your dog's body.

First, run your fingertips along his ribs. Ideally you should be able to feel them, but not see them from a distance. If you can't feel his ribs, he's likely overweight. If you can see them from a distance, he's likely underweight.

Next, run your fingers over his spine and hip bones. Ideally, you should feel a thin layer of fat covering the bones. If you can feel only fat and not bones, he's likely overweight. If you can feel the bones and no layer of fat, he's likely underweight.

Now stand your dog and look at him from the side. Do you see a tummy tuck? That indicates a good weight. If you can see no tummy tuck, he's likely overweight.

**Note:** The tummy tuck test is harder to view on a rough-coated, or long-haired dog, than on a smooth-coated, or short-haired dog. Look at your dog from above. Can you see an obvious waist? If not, he may be overweight.

When evaluating your dog's condition, remember these are guidelines. Your veterinarian can also help you determine whether your dog is of good weight and body condition.

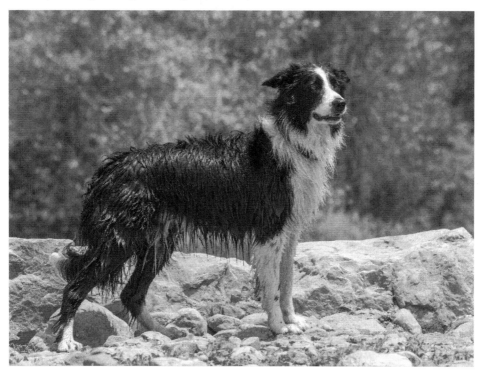

*To stand up to the rigors of herding, the dog must have good conformation. Photo courtesy of Carol Clawson.*

### How is my dog's conformation and fitness level?

Because herding is a physically demanding sport, dogs with severe conformation defects, like hip dysplasia, extremely straight shoulders and hocks or extremely long backs or flat feet, may not hold up for herding year after year.

Next, consider your dog's fitness level, and whether he has the aerobic fitness and muscle development for sustained physical work. Does your dog run for several minutes daily? Or does he take a quarter mile walk on leash and spend the day on the couch? A dog who is not physically fit is more prone to injury and unable to perform sustained herding work. While a dog will become fitter as he works at herding, the increased workload should be gradual, over the course of several weeks. As a handler, you should always pay attention to how your dog is handling the work physically.

Check his muscle tone. Feel the dog's upper front and back legs as well as his shoulders. Can you feel muscle? While your dog may not feel like a body builder, he should have good muscle tone and be neither flabby nor bony.

*This dog exhibits the muscle tone needed for a herding dog. Photo courtesy of Carol Clawson.*

## A few other physical considerations

Herding dogs often sprint to catch a wayward ewe or a flock of sheep. Being unable to outrun the sheep is no fun for the dog or the shepherd. If your dog is more of an ambler than a speed demon, herding may not be the sport for him.

Herding dogs need good eyesight so they can spot sheep that may be 300 yards away and avoid running into obstacles while working stock.

Herding dogs must also have excellent hearing. Unlike most other dog sports, herding requires the dog to work at a distance from the handler. Sometimes the dog cannot see the handler and must rely on voice or whistle cues. A dog with poor hearing may be able to compensate with visual cues for close-up herding maneuvers but will be unable to follow cues at a distance.

**Note:** Hearing issues are not always obvious. Herding dogs are masters at reading their human's body language and may compensate for hearing problems most of the time. If the hearing loss is in one ear, the dog may appear to have perfect hearing when he's facing you but struggle when he is facing away from you. Hearing issues often become obvious only when the dog is moving away from his handler or if he can't see his handler. If your dog has trouble responding to cues at a distance, have his hearing checked before blaming him for disobedience.

Finally, consider your dog's age. While you can teach an old dog new tricks, you have to consider whether you want to invest the time to do so. Training a herding dog can take years, especially if you are new to the activity. If you start training your six-year-old dog for herding, you may not advance far by the time he is ready to retire. On the other hand, if you have a good relationship with that six-year-old dog, you still may still learn a great deal from him.

If you have a puppy, plan on waiting until he is at least a year old before starting herding work. It is very risky to take young puppies to stock because they are more likely to learn bad habits, like biting, because they are not physically fast enough to control the sheep. Also, herding work creates a lot of stress on immature bones and growth plates; the chance of injury is high. It pays to allow the dog to mature mentally and progress at his own rate of learning, rather than to push a young dog before he is capable. While an experienced and skilled trainer may be able to evaluate and train a young dog, novice handlers should wait until the dog is older and more mentally and physically able to deal with training errors.

## A Shepherd's Journey

Social media seems awash with videos of young puppies being turned loose on livestock to show their herding instinct. This is a pet peeve of mine, as it's detrimental to a puppy. The puppy can't keep up with the sheep, so he chases and bites, learning bad habits. These unwanted behaviors of chasing and slicing will have to be untrained later on. His joints and growth plates are easily damaged at this age. On top of that, he can easily be run over, butted or kicked, and seriously injured. If he is frightened or injured, he can also develop a permanent fear of the sheep. Many pups go through fear periods between four and eight months of age and can develop stress-related behaviors if pushed to train at this age. The pup's herding behavior at this age is not much of an indicator of future herding talent. There is no benefit and a lot of risk in this practice. I don't recommend it. –Kay

### Is your dog biddable?

Herding requires a dog who is biddable, or readily listens for and obeys instructions. In herding, the dog is often required to perform cues that go against his instinct. Biddability can be trained to some degree, but it's a lot easier working with a dog who is naturally biddable. Biddability is a heritable trait and something to consider when buying a dog or puppy. Note that during a dog's adolescent stage, his biddability may go out the window. With consistent training, his biddability will return.

**Note:** If a dog with a biddable nature doesn't always come when called or starts missing cues, he may have a hearing issue.

### Does he have the herding instinct?

To succeed at herding, a dog must have the instinct to group the sheep into a flock and keep them together. Testing for this requires sheep, time and patience—as well as someone experienced with working herding dogs. When first introduced to sheep, a dog may not exhibit herding instinct. Some herding dogs require multiple introductions to and work around sheep before they show the herding instinct. If the dog fails to show herding instinct after several lessons, you will probably have to reconsider using him as a herding dog. At the very basic levels of herding and in smaller spaces, an obedient dog with little herding instinct may be able to perform some herding tasks. However, to perform in larger areas and with more difficult sheep, a dog must have the natural ability to keep the sheep together.

## Do all herding dogs herd?

The herding instinct is a trait that has been bred into—and out of—dogs. Today, only a small percentage of dogs from herding breeds actually do herding work. Dogs whose parents worked sheep are more likely to have the herding instinct, but it's no guarantee. Sometimes a dog can come from top herding lines and not have a strong herding instinct. Likewise, a dog can have parents who did not herd sheep, but he exhibits the herding instinct. While the herding instinct is a great trait if the dog has a herding job to do, it's not the best trait for a family pet. People tire of a dog who is trying to herd cats, chickens, other dogs and people. So herding instinct is often bred out of breeds that were used for herding in the past and are now pets.

# Chapter 3
# Acquiring a Herding Prospect

---

If you do not have a dog or your dog is not suitable for herding, you can choose a puppy or adult dog. Top handlers do both. Each has its advantages and disadvantages.

Some considerations when choosing an adult dog are the following:

- The dog may be through his puppy stage. While each dog is an individual, most herding dogs don't reach physical, mental and sexual maturity until they are anywhere from 18 to 36 months old.
- You know more about the dog's temperament, although it can change in different environments.
- The dog may or may not be well socialized with other dogs and people.
- The dog may or may not have obedience training.
- The dog may or may not have bad habits.
- The dog may or may not have herding experience.
- The dog is physically mature enough to start herding.
- The dog can be evaluated for herding instinct.
- It may or may not be more expensive than buying and raising a puppy.

Some considerations when choosing a puppy are the following:

- The puppy's lineage may or may not be known.
- Less is known about the puppy's temperament.
- The puppy's herding instinct is unknown.
- The owner can socialize the puppy with other dogs and people.
- The owner can teach the puppy obedience and house manners.
- The owner must wait several months before beginning herding training.
- It may or may not be more expensive than getting an adult dog.

Whether choosing an adult dog or puppy, take time and care in your selection, and plan on spending time bonding with and training your dog.

## Where can I find a puppy suitable for herding?
While there's no guarantee that a puppy will turn into a good herding dog, you can increase your odds by choosing a puppy whose parents (not just grandparents or great-grandparents) are working sheepdogs, either on the trial field or on a farm. If selecting a registered Border Collie, choose one registered with the American Border Collie Association. A well-bred, well-raised herding puppy can be hard to find, and not all breeders will sell a puppy to a person they don't know. A responsible breeder has spent many hours handling, socializing and caring for a puppy by the time the pup is ready to leave the litter. Expect to be quizzed on your dog experience, your housing setup and your training plans. Responsible breeders will be very cautious about placing a promising puppy in the right situation.

*A puppy's herding instinct is unknown. Photo courtesy of Carol Clawson.*

Likewise, you should question the breeder about the puppy. The dam and sire of the litter should exhibit good conformation, stable temperaments and be screened for and free from hereditary hip, eye and hearing defects. Puppies should be bright, alert and healthy, as well as friendly toward people. The breeder should have kept the puppies up to date on vaccinations and parasite control. When looking at a litter, pay attention to how the puppies have been socialized. Have they been handled by different people? Have they been raised with their littermates? Have they experienced new surfaces and experiences? Ridden in a car? You want puppies who have been exposed to different people and environments. Because this handling and socialization will affect your puppy's future herding success, be sure to ask about this. When you bring a puppy home, your socialization and training (but not on sheep) begins right away.

---

### The Four "S's" of Raising a Puppy

Raising a working-bred Border Collie puppy is a time-consuming and challenging project. You need to address the four "S's."

**Safety.** Keep the puppy safe from injury, escape or learning bad habits.

**Structure.** Have a predictable routine and expectations to help the puppy feel confident and secure.

**Social.** Spend time with the puppy daily and introduce the puppy to new people, noises, sights, sounds and objects in a careful manner so the puppy has control over his environment.

**Stimulate.** Have plenty of interactive toys for the puppy and teach the puppy to "learn how to learn" by teaching some basic obedience with a reward-based system.

---

## If I want an adult dog, what are my options?

Adult dogs may either have no herding experience, be started in their herding training or be fully trained. Each can have its pros and cons.

**An adult with no herding training.** An adult dog with no herding experience is usually the least expensive initially. Some people have found nice adult dogs through rescues, shelters and private sales. When doing this, take into account the dog's breeding. Border Collies are recommended for anyone considering advancing beyond herding in a small area. While registration papers do not guarantee the dog will have herding instinct, you can use them to determine whether the parents are active working dogs.

Herding instinct may not be evident the first few times a dog is exposed to sheep. However, you can temperament test an adult dog. The American Temperament Test Society offers temperament testing, but you may also feel comfortable temperament testing a dog on your own. For a more accurate temperament test, avoid testing the dog at its own home. Here are some things to look for:

- Observe how the dog behaves around people, both known and strangers. Ideally you want a confident dog who is not overly shy or aggressive.

- Observe how the dog behaves around other dogs. Ideally, he should be neither fearful nor aggressive.

- Is the dog attentive to his handler? Remember that you want a dog who is biddable and wants to work with you. While some rescue dogs have no history of working with people, this can be changed with training and time. You have to ask yourself whether you're willing to invest the time and training into the dog.

- Is the dog able to focus, or does he exhibit neurotic behaviors like spinning or uncontrolled barking? A dog with neurotic behaviors is more difficult to live with and train.

**Will a hyper dog make a good herding dog?** To be a successful herding dog, the dog must be able to focus on the task and listen to his handler. If the dog cannot settle and do this, his chances for success are diminished. In addition to being more challenging to train, a dog with frantic, uncontrolled energy is more likely to excite the sheep.

---

### A Shepherd's Journey

I started in the sheepdog herding world with a Sheltie and competed in American Kennel Club (AKC) and Australian Shepherd Club of America (ASCA) herding events. After watching Border Collies competing on large courses at USBCHA trials, I had a new view of herding. What the Border Collies did at USBCHA trials and what the herding dogs did at AKC and ASCA trials were two completely different things.

After seeing the Border Collies herding, I went out and bought a Border Collie puppy and trained her myself. Later, I bought Vic, a fully trained open dog, from Tom Wilson. That really advanced my herding journey. Vic showed me what a good dog was capable of—and set the bar for the dogs I trained after that. –Kay

---

**An adult dog with herding training.** Acquiring an adult dog with herding experience has its pros and cons, including the following:

- Some or much of the training has been done.

- The dog may have bad habits (such as not responding to cues or biting sheep).

- If the dog was trained correctly, the handler can learn how movements are supposed to look.

- A fully trained dog may be very expensive, and rightfully so. Hours and months have been invested in training him.

- The dog may or may not be a good personality match. For example, a slower, laid-back dog might not suit a handler that is quick and controlling, and a fast dog might not suit a careful, cautious handler.

When considering a dog with training, you'll still want to conduct a temperament test and evaluate his conformation, movement and fitness. You'll also want to evaluate his training level and skills. For the training evaluation, ask for the help of an experienced handler.

---

### Don't rely solely on videos

The best way to evaluate a herding dog is seeing it working in person, rather than watching a video. A skilled handler and videographer can make a dog look more skilled than he may be. For instance, a dog can look like he's pushing or driving sheep if barn-sour sheep are walking toward the barn and he is following behind. Also, it may have taken numerous tries to get a video of the dog working. If you must rely on a video, ask to see the dog gathering the sheep (leaving the handler's side, circling the sheep and bringing the sheep to the handler) with no cues. Also ask to see the dog holding sheep to a fence so that you can evaluate his natural ability and power. If you are inexperienced with herding, ask an experienced handler to help you evaluate the dog.

---

## Trained dog categories: started, open and retired open

**A started dog** is one that has had some training but is not running USBCHA open courses. The training, though, can range from performing 100-yard **outruns** to competing in lower levels of competition. If considering a started dog, some questions to ask include the following:

- What is the dog's level of training?
- Can he perform an outrun? At what distance?
- Has the dog worked in other locations or just at home?
- Has the dog started driving? At what distance is he driving from the handler?
- Does he know his **flanks** (or directions)?
- Can he complete a course?
- Has he competed in trials? At what level?
- What are his strengths?
- What are his weaknesses? All dogs, even the top herding dogs in the country, have weaknesses. It's important that the dog's faults are ones that you can live with.
- Why are you selling him? If the answer is that the person has too many dogs, ask why this dog is the one for sale.
- How old is he? Most started dogs for sale are ages 1 to 4. If they are older than this, it may indicate a problem with training. Or it could mean that life happened, and the handler just didn't have time to train the dog. Regardless, consider the dog's age. Most dogs are only able to work until 9 or 10 years old.

**A fully trained open dog** usually means the dog has competed at the open level of USBCHA trials. These dogs are usually the most expensive to buy. If considering a fully trained open dog, some questions to ask include the following:

- Has the dog competed? Where?
- How has he performed?
- What are his strengths and weaknesses?
- Why are you selling him?
- What is his age?
- Would he be suitable for a novice handler?

Some open dogs are top performers but may be unsuitable for a beginner. For example, a super-fast dog will be difficult for a beginner with slow timing. A sensitive dog may get frustrated with a handler with slow timing. A dog with a lot of eye or herding instinct may soon learn to do his own thing if a handler does not observe what the dog is doing and correct it effectively.

Paying a lot of money for a trained dog is risky. Some trainers are very good at hiding the dog's faults. It's best to ask several people for recommendations on a reputable trainer, and, if possible, have someone experienced go with you to look at a trained dog.

**A retired open dog** is usually 8 to 10 years old and has competed at the open level of USBCHA trials. These dogs are often less expensive and sometimes free because their owners are looking for a good retirement home for them. While they may not be up to running large open courses, they often are good for light farm work and smaller, lower-level courses. If you are willing to give a dog a retirement home (Border Collies can live 12 to 15 years), then this may be a good option for a novice handler. If considering a retired open dog, some questions to ask include:

- How is his health and does he have previous injuries? (Most older dogs have some arthritis, and previous injuries are common. Some extra health support is likely.)
- Would he be suitable for running smaller courses?
- Would he be suitable for a novice handler?
- What are his strengths and weaknesses?

**Will buying a trained dog lead to success?**
You can't buy success in the sheepdog world (although many have tried). It's a team sport. To become a good team, you have to work at it—and you have to be a good handler. At USBCHA trials, winning runs are often more the result of top handling skills than the dog (though the dog is talented, too). Many trained dogs may take six months or more before they are working well for their new owners. It takes most people years to become a good sheepdog handler.

However, a trained dog can help you in your journey to become a better handler or trainer. Many beginners struggle with having a clear picture of what a good outrun, drive or flank should look like. A well-trained dog helps give that clear picture. Also, a well-trained dog can give a novice handler the confidence to focus on the sheep as well as the dog.

---

### A Shepherd's Journey

After witnessing my struggle with an untrained herding dog, my mentor, Linda Fogt, gave me her retired open dog, Mickey. It was a win-win for both me and the dog. Mickey was still able to herd, but on a less physically demanding level. As a novice, I was still learning what ideal outruns, lifts, fetches, drives and flanks were supposed to look like. I often didn't know where the dog needed to be to impact the sheep.

Mickey was a patient teacher. When I gave her a cue, she did it, even if that meant pushing the sheep around the panels instead of through them. I made lots of handling errors when working her—and I also learned a lot. Thanks to her, I became more comfortable working around the sheep and a little better at anticipating what they were going to do.

A few times, all the elements fell into place, and we had some beautiful moments on the trial field, and even took home a few ribbons. Would I take that same route again? Definitely. Did I learn everything I needed to know from Mickey? Nope. That was the job of the next dog and the next one and the next one.—Beth

---

# Chapter 4
# The Other 23 Hours: Managing Your Dog When Off Stock

---

Most herding dog owners don't live on big farms or ranches where dogs work sheep for hours each day. If you are a part-time herder or have an off-farm job, you must find ways to manage your dogs when they are not working stock.

## Your dog is learning 24 hours a day!

Here's why the way you manage your dog or puppy away from livestock affects your dog's behavior on stock. Your dog is learning all the time, whether you are "training" him or not. This means that every time you interact with your dog, he learns what behavior is okay and what isn't. It also means he's learning even when you aren't around. What happens *with* your dog and *to* your dog off stock directly influences his behavior when on the sheep. If you allow crazy, frantic behavior around the house, you will get crazy frantic behavior on the sheep. If he is scared and nervous off sheep, he'll likely be scared and nervous when working sheep. Providing a calm, controlled, structured and predictable environment where the dog gets exercise, mental stimulation, training and play time, will help create a calm, confident dog when working sheep. Providing a good environment off stock takes work and planning—and is often more challenging than training your dog on livestock.

> ### A Shepherd's Journey
>
> I once bought a Border Collie that was described as crazy in the kennel. This dog fence-fought with any dog she was next to; she dug frantically in the kennel; she barked a lot in the kennel; and she grabbed the side of her kennel fence, breaking her teeth on it. This crazy kennel behavior spilled over into her sheep work, and she was wild and frantic on sheep. After observing her for a few days, I decided she was extremely smart, very high energy, very activated by visual stimulation, and did not like other dogs in her personal space. I moved her kennel away from the other dogs, put up a barrier so she did not have to watch other dogs, started running her a mile every day, and started feeding her in a Kong Wobbler or other puzzle feeding toy. In a couple of weeks, she was a different dog, staying quietly in her kennel; her sheep work got much quieter as well. –Kay

## Why socialization is important

A well-socialized dog is comfortable, calm and confident around people, other dogs, strange sounds, new places and new things—and he makes a better companion dog and better herding dog. Sheep respond better to a calm, confident dog, and for a dog competing in herding trials, socialization is a must. A competition herding dog must be able to ride in a car, stay in new places, work in new fields and work with different types of sheep. He'll also meet new people and new dogs. Some dogs are genetically more stable temperamentally than others, but all dogs benefit from well-planned socialization.

Whether you have a puppy or an adult dog, it is important to socialize him to different shapes and sizes of people, various kinds of dogs, car rides, new places, strange sounds and other environmental stimuli. Puppies have a critical socialization period before they are 16 weeks old. If not handled and socialized, they can develop "kennel dog syndrome" and be afraid of new people, places and situations their entire life. The key to good socialization is to keep exposing the dog to new things, but at the same time, making sure the dog feels safe and secure. When socializing a dog, keep three things in mind:

**1. Do not flood or overwhelm your dog.** Some people overdo socialization and drag their puppy into inappropriate and overwhelming situations. For example, taking a puppy or unsocialized dog to a dog park and forcing him to walk through groups of strange people and dogs is overwhelming. Doing this can cause a dog to learn to fear strange people, dogs and situations. When taking your dog out and about, watch your dog's body language to see whether he is feeling overwhelmed. If he's yawning, lip licking, raising the hair on his back, or tucking his tail, he's not happy. When raising a puppy, try to find a puppy training class that is carefully structured to avoid overwhelming puppies and which has an experienced instructor who does not allow puppies to bully each other.

**2. Socialize in a way where the dog has control of the environment.** If a dog can observe a new person or object and approach it at his pace, then you are giving the dog control of the environment. Doing this helps the dog build confidence. When visitors come to your home, put the dog in a safe place, such as a crate, where he can observe, but where he is not in the midst of the new people. Allow him to observe the visitors for several minutes or more, and then open the dog's crate or kennel. Let the dog approach the people when he's ready. Don't drag him over to meet people or corner him where he has no place to move away if he is uncomfortable.

---

### A Shepherd's Journey

I haul my puppies with me to herding trials from the time they are baby puppies. Yes, it is a lot of work. But they learn to ride in a car, to spend the night in car crates, to walk on a leash, to potty in strange places and to meet new dogs and people in a safe and controlled setting. By the time I'm ready to compete with these dogs in a trial, they may have hundreds of traveling miles already logged. They are already accustomed to the sights, smells and sounds of a herding trial. –Kay

---

**3. Use food to counter-condition a dog to enjoy new people and places.** Carry high-value, tasty treats, like chicken, with you when you and your dog are meeting new people and in new situations. While talking to the person, offer your dog some treats. This classical conditioning process will help your dog associate good stuff (food) with being around new people and things. Unless your dog is very confident, do not have new people offer your dog food. If the dog is shy and afraid of the stranger, he will be conflicted between wanting the food and being afraid of the stranger. This can lead to the dog being overwhelmed and possibly biting.

Socialization should be an ongoing process that should be practiced for the lifetime of the dog.

---

### Using Food as Reinforcement

Food is a powerful tool and there are many advantages to using it as a reward. Many sheepdog trainers are reluctant to use food as a reinforcement for basic obedience behaviors away from stock, but they shouldn't be. Food is a powerful primary reinforcement (meaning the dog must eat to live). You feed your dog every day anyway, so why not use it to train? Food is not only something dogs enjoy and will work for, but has a calming effect on most dogs. It's a waste of a valuable resource to not use food to train your dog away from the sheep. Also, refusing to take food (unless sheep are around) is a sign the dog is stressed and gives you an insight into the dog's mental state.

---

### Confinement: Where to keep your dog when he's not working sheep

Herding dogs, and especially Border Collies, are very smart, very active and easily stimulated by sights and sounds. When they are not working, they should be contained in a place that is safe for their bodies and their minds. One of the worst things that can happen to a young Border Collie is getting loose on stock unsupervised. He is likely to either chase or be chased, and the bad behaviors he picks up may affect his work for the rest of his life. He's also learning to work stock without you and that can permanently damage your working partnership.

Dogs, like children, need a safe, quiet, controlled space to relax and unwind. Dogs thrive in a structured, predictable environment. When considering confinement options keep these rules in mind:

- Keep your dog from getting killed or injured—by cars, other dogs, cows or horses, or by catching his collar and accidentally hanging himself.

- Prevent your dog from destroying things, like the couch, woodwork, doors, or anything else he can get his teeth on.

- Prevent your dog from learning bad habits such as crate fighting, mindlessly weaving, spinning or barking, fence running or working the sheep without supervision.

- Keep your dog occupied with appropriate toys or chews so he doesn't go crazy. This also means keeping sheep out of sight, so he's not working them in his mind.

*This puppy is kept in a securely fenced yard and has access to a rope toy. Photo courtesy of Carol Clawson.*

## Types of containment

A fenced yard allows the dog to move about. If leaving a dog in a fenced area, make sure the fence is dog proof with no holes the dog can crawl through. Keep in mind that Border Collies are athletic and hardwired to chase. Many are capable of jumping over a 6 foot fence and squeezing through a small hole in the fence. They are also excellent diggers and can excavate their way out of a yard quickly. Using wire or cattle panels along the bottom fence line can prevent digging escapes. Ideally, the yard should be set up so your dog can't see livestock, or that they are a long distance away.

If using a kennel, the same rules apply as to fencing. Also, pay attention to the flooring. While concrete is easy to clean and is dig proof, it can be really hard on the dog's joints and may contribute to diseases such as OCD (osteochondrosis dissecans) and hip dysplasia. If using concrete, consider using some type of padding, such as stall mats, to reduce the strain on the dog's feet and joints.

If you keep a dog in the house, you must have a crate or dog-proofed room to confine him when you can't watch him. This is true especially for puppies. If your puppy learns to chew on furniture or pee in the house, those habits last a lifetime. Prevention is the best way to avoid behavior problems. Dog proofing a room means removing or covering anything that might be chewed, including electrical wires. It means having an easy-to-clean floor, as accidents will happen.

## Sights, sounds and situations to avoid

When confining your dog, the best places are quiet, safe and free of exciting stimuli. Don't keep your dog in a place where he can see the sheep. Even if there is a barrier between the dog and the sheep, the dog will likely "work" the sheep, either by staring at them or running up and down the fence line. When he does this, he's learning to work the sheep without you, your instruction or your guidance. So, why should he work for you in a training session when he can work on his own?

Don't place your dog in a location where he can see cars, bicycles or other fast-moving objects. These movements can stimulate the dog to "work" or chase them. Once a dog learns to chase these things, it's difficult to stop him—and it's a dangerous habit. This type of frantic behavior in the kennel can affect your dog's overall attitude.

Be careful about crating or kenneling your dog with other dogs. Some dogs do not do well kenneled next to another dog, especially if one dog is barking or fighting at the kennel walls or fence. Barrier frustration can be a real issue and can cause your dog to have behavior and working problems. Placing a solid barrier between kennels gives the dogs more personal space and helps avoid dog-to-dog aggression.

Avoid leaving your dog tied out and unsupervised at home and at herding dog trials. A dog can get injured, tangled, choked and get loose. When tied out, your dog may not feel safe from people or other dogs and could become reactive to people and other dogs.

### A Shepherd's Journey

As a herding dog owner, you must be aware of your dog's environment. I placed a puppy with a family who kept him in the fenced backyard. The neighbor kids reached over the fence and teased the pup so he'd jump up at their hands. This quickly escalated to jumping up and biting their hands—and jumping up and biting other people's hands. –Kay

## Enriching your dog's environment

Herding dogs, and especially Border Collies, are very smart and very active. While they should be contained in quiet areas, free from exciting stimuli, they need an outlet for their mental and physical energy. Environmental enrichment gives your dog a healthy and safe outlet for normal behaviors. It also helps prevent behavior problems related to boredom such as obsessive pacing, spinning or barking. Some ways to enrich your dog's environment include offering chew toys, play toys and puzzle toys and allowing him to play with other dogs.

All dogs chew, and all dogs need to chew. It is a natural behavior. Chewing is a stress reliever and relaxes the dog. Giving your dog durable chew toys, cotton ropes and high-quality rawhides allows your dog to chew and relax his mind.

*Chew toys are an outlet for the dog's natural behaviors. Photo courtesy of Beth Kerber.*

Durable play toys that the dog can carry, squeak and toss also give the dog an outlet for his natural play behaviors. Feeding or puzzle toys, such as the Kong Wobbler, other Kong toys, activity balls and puzzle feeders slow the dog down when eating and give him a way to work his mind and mouth. You can also scatter kibble for your dogs to find. Tossing dog food in the grass teaches your dog to use his nose and keeps him mentally and physically occupied. It also forces him to eat more slowly. Don't be afraid of "ruining" your working dog by giving him play or chew toys. The dog needs them for mental and physical stimulation.

Most dogs also like the company of other dogs and will play with them. It is important to match up dog groups so they get along and no dog is being picked on or bullied. Because adult females are more likely to have fights and injure each other, be careful about matching up multiple females.

### Exercising your dog

Border Collies were bred to work sheep for many hours a day. Most people do not have that type of work for them, so the dogs must get their exercise in other ways. Ideally, you should plan to give your dog a long walk or run daily. Not only are long dog walks good physical exercise, but they're also great for the dog's mind. Being able to sniff, roll and explore allows the dog to decompress and express his natural dogginess.

While playing fetch or tug with a dog is a good form of exercise, it should be done with care. Many dogs get injured toes, shoulders and even torn ligaments as a result of playing fetch. For many herding dogs, playing fetch is over-stimulating. So, if playing fetch or tug, keep it in small doses and keep it calm and controlled.

Rather than playing fetch games, engage your dog in scent work. Teach your dog to locate toys or items marked with a particular scent, and then hide those items so your dog can find them. Dogs have a highly developed sense of smell and using their noses to solve problems and stay entertained is very satisfying and fulfilling to dogs. Joining a scent work class is a great way to spend time with your dog away from stock.

### A Shepherd's Journey

While I don't work my dogs on sheep every day, I make sure I take them on off-leash walks in the pastures at least once, if not twice, a day. I stuff my pocket with dog treats and let the dogs chase each other, hunt for rabbits and mice, roll and just be dogs. Sometimes I will practice recalls, but often, I just walk and let them be. Sometimes, like when it is 10 degrees outside and the wind is blowing, or when it is 90 degrees and the mosquitoes are biting, I'm unenthused about walking the dogs. I do it anyway. That 20-minute daily dog walk goes a long way toward preventing behavior problems and helping the dogs settle down in the house. –Beth

## Taking care of basic health needs

Herding dogs expend lots of physical and mental energy and should be treated like the athletes they are. Plan to feed them high-quality dog food designed for very active dogs. Do not try to save money by buying poor-quality dog food. It can result in decreased performance and predispose your dog to health problems. Finding affordable, high-quality food can be a challenge. (See the recommended reading list at the end of the book for some excellent resources on evaluating dog food.)

Check your dog's body condition at least once a month and adjust your dog's feed accordingly. Work with your veterinarian to determine what vaccinations are recommended in your area as well as in any areas where you are planning to travel with your dog. Also, work with your veterinarian to design an appropriate tick, flea and heartworm preventative program. Tick-borne diseases are a major cause of illness and disability in working dogs.

## Building the right relationship with your dog

To have precise teamwork with your dog in herding, you must develop a relationship with him away from the sheep. This means that you treat him in a respectful way, address his physical and emotional needs, treat him fairly and humanely, and be a consistent, confident leader. Therefore, the dog is tuned into you and responds quickly and reliably to your cues—and that the dog is happy and relaxed around you. The handler must guide and teach the dog the correct way to behave both when working sheep and away from sheep. If there is a relationship problem away from the sheep, the problem will be worse when adding sheep.

Newcomers to herding may make a few common mistakes with their dogs. Some may not try to establish any kind of relationship with their dogs; others may not have respectful relationships with their dogs.

Some people who take up herding are not really "dog people;" they are interested in herding only as another sporting event or competitive outlet. They only care about winning trials. They often don't pay enough attention to the dog or know enough about normal dog behavior to know whether he may be sick, lame, stressed or afraid. The dog may be afraid of this type of handler and obey out of fear or, because the dog will do anything to have access to sheep, the dog will tolerate a lot of abuse and may avoid contact with the handler. When things don't go well, these people will blame the dog and may say things like: "This dog is stubborn. This dog is stupid. This dog is being defiant." These types of handlers are all about the end result, not the journey. It's almost impossible for people with this type of relationship with their dog to succeed at the top levels of herding.

The super-permissive handlers are often pet owners who have never needed the precise control over the dog that is necessary when herding. Super-permissive handlers may not notice or realize that their dogs drag them on leash, lift their legs and pee on their coats, or aggressively lunge at other people's dogs. They often constantly chant cues without ever teaching dogs the meaning of the cues or following up to make sure the dogs comply. When herding, dogs with super-permissive handlers often ignore their handlers and do a lot of chasing or biting on the stock. These dogs haven't been taught that herding is a team event because their owners haven't taken the time to become part of the team.

Neither the "non-dog" handlers nor "super-permissive" handlers are successful at the top levels of herding. The consistently successful top sheepdog handlers are able to have precise and consistent control over their dogs and also enjoy and understand their dogs.

The good news is that you can develop a good relationship with your dog. Dogs are pretty straightforward: they do things that earn rewards and avoid things that are unpleasant. With planning, you can only reward behaviors that you want and avoid rewarding undesirable behavior. You don't need to "dominate" the dog to teach him to be obedient and well mannered. Physical punishment is not necessary to control a dog and has several undesirable side effects.

## How to build a better relationship with NILIF

One effective way to establish a mutually respectful relationship with your dog is the Nothing in Life is Free (NILIF) program, also called Learn to Earn. Developed by veterinary behaviorists, it teaches handlers a better way to interact with their dogs.

Any good relationship, dog or human, depends on one partner noticing and responding to the other partner's needs and actions. The goal of NILIF is to teach handlers to do exactly this: pay attention to the dog's actions and respond accordingly. The framework makes sure the handler pays attention to, asks for, and rewards calm, quiet behavior and does not reward undesired behaviors. It teaches handlers to "say what they mean and mean what they say" by consistently rewarding the dog when cues are correctly responded to in a timely manner, or when the dog offers desired behaviors. It also forces handlers to notice and interact with their dog multiple times a day. Additionally, this framework gives the dog a clear way to earn what they want by performing a behavior that is calm instead of learning to jump and lunge to get attention. NILIF requires the handler to close the economy on some things that the dog likes. For example, the dog may not get all-day access to toys, food, watching sheep, or other dogs. Access to these things is contingent on responding to the handler's cues.

---

### A Shepherd's Journey

In my animal behavior practice, I see many out-of-control pet dogs with loving owners. I recommend the Nothing in Life is Free program to many of my behavior clients because it is easy for even very inexperienced owners to understand and doesn't require much training skill to implement. It teaches the owner to ask for, notice, and reward good behaviors and to stop rewarding unwanted behavior. –Kay

---

## NILIF step by step

**Step 1.** Teach the dog a simple cue that you want him to perform quickly and reliably in any situation. For sheepdogs, "lie down" is a good one. Other people use "sit." It doesn't matter as long as the cue is for an action that is calm and easy for the dog to do. Teach the cue by pairing the desired action with a cue and a reward, (see Appendix A on teaching obedience for more details on how to do this) and practice it in various situations for at least 50 repetitions every day for several days to make sure the dog knows the cue well and can reliably do it in a variety of situations. If the cue is a word and you also use a hand motion (such as lifting up your hand for "sit" or a dropping your hand for "down"), decide whether you want to get rid of the hand motion before going to Step 2. If you want to use the verbal cue alone, make sure you can do 50 repetitions in various locations over several training sessions before going to Step 2.

**Step 2.** Make a list of all the things your dog wants, likes or enjoys. Note those that are high value to your dog. Some examples could be:

- getting fed
- getting petted
- getting to play/interact with another dog
- going for a walk

- getting on the couch
- going outside
- getting treats/toys
- getting a chew item
- getting out of the crate/kennel
- going through a gate
- getting access to sheep

**Step 3.** Now the dog getting these things is dependent on him performing the behavior you've trained on cue ("sit" or "lie down"). Everything on the list must now be "earned" by performing the behavior when requested. For this to be successful, the dog must be trained on the cue, and you must not allow access to the reward unless the dog performs the action on one cue or offers it on his own. Very important: You cannot force the dog to comply or repeat the cue multiple times.

For example, before the dog is allowed out of the crate or kennel run, he must lie down or sit on cue. As you stand in front of the kennel, give the cue to "sit" *one time* in a calm quiet voice. (Remember you've already taught and practiced "sit" dozens of times before this, so the dog is fluent with the cue.) If he does not sit, do not repeat the cue. Instead, walk away from the crate, wait a few minutes, come back and try again. If he sits, even imperfectly, open the crate. If he does not, walk away and try again in a few minutes. If the dog offers the behavior of sit, immediately praise and open the door.

Another example of the program is feeding time. After fixing the dog's food, cue the dog to lie down. If he lies down, feed him. If he just stands there, put the food away and ignore the dog for 30 seconds. Ignoring the dog means making no eye contact with him, not touching him and not talking to him. After 30 seconds pass, get out the food and cue the dog to lie down. If he lies down, give him the food. If he doesn't, put the food away and ignore him. This may take a few repetitions, but over several days, the dog will get the idea. Most times, a dog will start offering the action of sit or lie down even before you cue him. That's great because he understands how to get what he wants and is practicing some nice, calm behaviors!

## Using NILIF throughout the day

Throughout the day, if your dog approaches you and wants to be petted, give a cue for sit. If he sits, pet him. If he doesn't, actively disengage from him (don't look at, touch or talk to him) and walk away. Try again later and don't pet him unless he sits first.

Before opening and going through a gate, ask the dog to lie down. If the dog lies down, open the gate and let him out. If he doesn't lie down, don't open the gate. Instead, walk away from the gate and try again later.

With the dog on a long line, walk toward the sheep and ask for a "lie down." If the dog responds, keep walking toward the sheep. If he doesn't lie down, turn around and walk away with the dog from the sheep. Wait a minute and try again.

For this program to work, the handler must pay attention to what she is rewarding. Also, the handler should *not* help or force the dog to sit or lie down. Pushing the dog into position doesn't teach him to listen or take control of his behavior. If the dog is lunging and barking when you open his kennel door, you are rewarding lunging and barking. If you wait to open the door until he is sitting quietly, you are rewarding waiting quietly. If your dog knocks you down to get food and you feed him, you are rewarding that rough behavior. If you cue him to sit before you feed him and he sits, you are rewarding that behavior. If he continues to jump up on you, simply put the food away and wait a few minutes before trying again. Doing this is using positive reinforcement when the dog responds to the cue or offers a calm behavior and negative punishment (taking away what he wants) when he doesn't respond or tries an unruly behavior. If carried out consistently and correctly, it builds communication and a bond of trust and respect between the human and dog. It works without any physical pain or fear.

## A word about "dominance"

For many years, people believed that because dogs are descended from wolves, people had a wolf pack relationship with their dog. To control the dog, the person had to be the "alpha wolf." This belief caused people to do things like scruffing their dog as a mother dog might pick up her pups, biting their dogs' ears, doing "alpha rolls," pinning the dog to the ground and other various physical punishments to assert themselves as "alpha." This is all based on disproven and outdated ideas. These actions only make the dog afraid of the handler.

First, wolves do not have a dominance structure that involves beating up other wolves. This idea came from an early and flawed study on captive wolves. In reality, wolves in a pack work together as a team, and the only "alpha" is the pair that mates. Second, dogs are not wolves, any more than humans are chimpanzees. Basing dog behavior on wolves is like treating a child the way a chimpanzee would. Third, *humans* aren't dogs or wolves. The human-dog relationship is a relationship between two totally different species. Fourth, unlike wolves, dogs are not primary pack hunters. Feral dogs have a looser social structure and scavenge a lot. Fifth, methods like alpha rolls rarely happen between dogs (if you see a dog flip to the ground, it's because the dog is offering submissive behavior to the other dog, *not* that the dominant dog pushed him to the ground). Alpha rolls do not translate into the relationship between canines and humans and aren't necessary or helpful in training dogs.

To succeed in training and trialing herding dogs, you must have exquisite and reliable control over your dog's every move, even at great distances and in difficult circumstances. That level of control is achievable without using the traditional idea of "dominance" and without using harsh physical punishment.

### A Shepherd's Journey

I was working with a friend whose dog was frantically jumping up on her as we walked to the sheep. She commented that the dog was trying to dominate her and kept slapping the dog with her hat, to no avail. The dog was typically kept locked alone in the kennel for 23 hours a day and was so desperate for social contact that he was quite willing to be slapped with a hat to get any kind of attention. This wasn't a dominance problem. It was a sad case of a dog not having his basic social needs met. –Kay

# Chapter 5
# Good Trainers are Good Communicators:
# Talking and Listening to Your Dog

*"In order to really enjoy a dog, one doesn't merely try to train him to be semi-human. The point of it is to open oneself to the possibility of becoming partly a dog."* —Edward Hoagland

Good training starts with good communication with your dog. Understanding how humans and dogs communicate with each other and how a dog's emotional state impacts his learning will make you a more effective trainer.

## How humans and dogs communicate with each other

What are the best ways to communicate with dogs? Over thousands of years, dogs have evolved to live with humans. They're experts at interpreting human body language, facial expressions, vocal intonations and smells. Dogs communicate primarily through body language and smell, not vocalization. Humans, with a natural affinity for the spoken language, often forget that dogs do not have the same language system. To communicate effectively with dogs, you must adjust to their needs.

### Facial expressions

Dogs notice whether humans are smiling or frowning, and they quickly learn to identify an angry face. They also learn to offer eye contact with humans. Eye contact releases oxytocin in both dogs and humans, thus facilitating bonding. (However, making direct eye contact with a strange dog can be interpreted as a threat to the dog.) When a dog sees an angry face, he'll often offer appeasement behavior, such as tucking his tail and laying his ears back. This creates the illusion that the dog feels guilty for something he's done. He doesn't. The dog is just reacting to a facial expression and trying to avoid an aggressive act from the human.

### Body posture

Dogs learn to read and react to a person's body posture. Standing tall, with shoulders open and relaxed, and facing the dog directly shows confidence to the dog. When working with shy or frightened dogs, turning sideways makes you less of a threat and allows the dog to approach you if he chooses.

---

### A Shepherd's Journey

I was out in the pasture looking for a missing sheep and had all my dogs with me. I noticed that instead of running around and sniffing as they usually do, the dogs were all walking behind me, tails down, looking very worried. I realized I was stomping through the brush looking angry and frustrated. As soon as I relaxed my body and started walking normally, all the dogs went back to their usual run and sniff routine. –Kay

---

### Voice

Years ago, women were told they could not be dog trainers because their voices are too high pitched. While women trainers have disproved this, tone of voice matters. Using a calm, steady voice will help the dog relax. Using a deep or growling voice often intimidates a dog. Using a happy, high-pitched voice can make a dog feel more confident and willing to approach you. Using a screaming, hysterical or frantic tone is likely to upset the dog and cause tension and nervousness. The best trainers, male or female, give cues in consistent tones and volume. When training, handlers want the cue to be as consistent as possible. Because dogs are tuned into volume and tone, after a dog learns the cue, the handler can affect the dog's behavior by how she gives the cue. For example, if she says, "Lie down" in a hard, fast manner, the dog will respond quicker than if she says, "Lie down" in a soft, slow manner.

### Whistle tones

Patricia McConnell did some great research on different whistle sounds and how they affect dog behavior. In general, short, repeated notes induce action and movement in the dogs, and long, drawn-out notes result in the slowing or stopping of action.

### Touching and petting

People communicate with their dogs when they touch them. A firm and gentle stroking on the dog's side, shoulder or the side of the muzzle usually calms and relaxes the dog. A gentle massage at the base of the dog's ears, between the eyes, or at the base of the head can also be very calming to the dog. On the other hand, rubbing the top of the dog's haunches, slapping his rib cage or gently grabbing his muzzle is usually interpreted as an exciting or playful approach and will result in the dog becoming excited. Most dogs do not like being patted on the top of the head, and many dogs will duck or move away if someone tries to pat them on the head. Every dog is a little different, based on his personality and training history. Pay attention to how your dog reacts to your voice, face and body posture, and learn to use them appropriately. If you are a skilled trainer, you can change a dog's emotional state with just a touch, a glance or a word.

### Body space

Most herding-bred dogs have a large personal body space. Other breeds don't. For example, Labrador retrievers interact with both dogs and people with a lot of body slamming and jostling—their personal space is typically small. Most Border Collies prefer to keep a distance and do not appreciate being mauled or roughly handled by dogs or people unless they know them well and are in a playful mood. This body space issue is one reason humans can train Border Collies to move off sheep by simply using their bodies to block or push them away. Some Border Collies may require a little help, such as a feed bag slapped on the leg or the quick wave of a flag, but most move readily off a confident approach by a person. Many of the hunting or guard type breeds have no instinct to move away from a person and may actually consider the person approaching as a signal to play, bite or wrestle.

If you pay attention to how you interact with your dog, using your tone of voice, facial expressions and body language, you will find you can strongly influence your dog's attitude and behavior without using any vocal cues at all.

## What are dogs trying to tell you?

To become a good dog trainer, you must be able to "read dogs," or to correctly observe and interpret a dog's body language instantly. Misinterpreting or missing signs of stress or fear is a common and major flaw in beginning dog trainers.

*This dog is relaxed and eager to learn. Photo courtesy of Carol Clawson.*

When you are training your dog, it's important to watch his ears, eyes, mouth and tail. These body parts can tell you what your dog's internal emotional state is. Unless you know how your training is affecting your dog, you can't effectively modulate your training approach to that dog. You must learn to closely watch your dog; you must learn what each dog's physical cues mean; and you must be able to adjust your actions quickly based on what the dog is telling you. If you can't do that, you'll have a tough time training your dog.

While every dog is an individual in how he communicates, these are some general guidelines. Because dogs communicate with humans about 90 percent of the time through body language, you must understand what the ears, eyes, mouth and tail are saying.

*The dog on the left is offering a classic submissive posture to the other dog. Photo courtesy of Beth Murray.*

## Ears

When looking at the ears, take into account whether the dog's ear set is pricked, semi-pricked or floppy. Generally, when the dog's ears are pricked up, he is showing interest, excitement, curiosity or a willingness to participate in whatever is going on. If the dog's ears are naturally floppy, he may only have a slight forward set when he is interested or excited. A dog whose ears are pricked up is not necessarily friendly. An aggressive dog with pricked ears may be indicating he's ready to bite. A dog whose ears are tightly flat back against his skull is most likely showing stress, tension or fear. A submissive dog will also put his ears down, but with a relaxed softness to the ear. To become better at reading the ears, start with a dog you know. Then start watching the ears of other dogs while someone else is training them.

## Eyes

Border Collie owners are familiar with the Border Collie stare, a hard fixed stare with eyes slightly dilated. This indicates arousal and prey drive. Border Collies exhibit this hard stare or "eye" around sheep; when stalking other dogs, cats or other animals; and when fixated on toys. Squinty eyes while looking at a human usually indicates a submissive dog seeking attention. Eyes squinted or closed with the head averted indicates the dog is stressed or afraid and trying to avoid the situation; these are submission and appeasement gestures. This does not mean the dog is "feeling guilty;" he's just trying to avoid aggression from the human by showing appeasement. When a handler corrects a dog on stock, she should look for this type of body language to know that the dog is responding to her correction.

A "whale eye" with the whites of the eyes showing indicates a high level of arousal. This can be seen in dogs guarding food or toys, dogs before they fight or dogs which are terrified. Seeing the white of the dog's eyes usually indicates a problem, although when dogs play and get very silly, they may also show the white of their eyes. A dog who is afraid of the sheep may exhibit a whale eye or may close his eyes and avert his head when faced by a sheep.

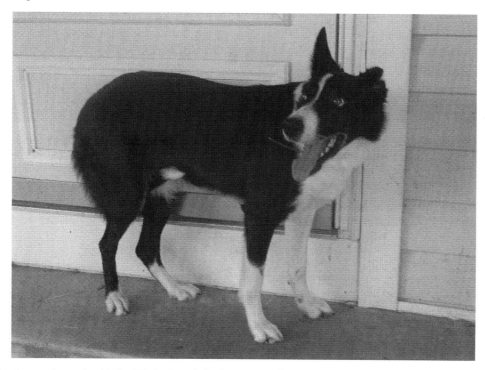

*A thunderstorm is stressing this dog. Notice the tucked tail, panting, wide eyes and flattened ears. Photo courtesy of Beth Kerber.*

## Mouth

A soft relaxed, closed or slightly open mouth indicates a relaxed dog. A dog whose lips are tight, or "pursed," is stressed or worried. A dog who is licking his lips is also showing stress. By watching the tension in the dog's jaw, you can often predict the dog's mental state. Obviously, a dog with his lips pulled back into a growl is showing fear or aggression. But a very submissive, scared dog can pull back his lips into a growl-type posture as well. Some dogs "smile" submissively to greet people. The soft, squinty eyes show that it's a greeting, not a threat.

## Yawning

A dog who is yawning is not bored or sleepy; he's most likely stressed. When training, if your dog yawns and looks away, he is likely stressed and trying to diffuse the situation with appeasement.

## Panting

Dogs pant to cool themselves, especially when it's hot or after exercise. But panting can also be a sign of excitement or stress. Panting associated with a lot of drooling is a sign of anxiety. If your dog is panting a lot during training (and he's not working hard nor is he hot), he is likely showing signs of stress.

*This dog is working in a relaxed, confident manner. Notice the relaxed tail. Photo courtesy of Carol Clawson.*

## Tail

The tail tells a lot—especially with Border Collies. As part of their stalking/prey behavior, Border Collies drop their heads and lower their tails when engaged with livestock. The most important thing about the tail is how much tension is in it. A relaxed, loose tail, hanging down between the dog's hocks is a sign of a relaxed and confident dog. A tail that is tightly tucked between the dog's hind legs indicates some tension or stress. A tail that starts to come up while the dog is working stock usually means the dog is excited or stressed and is probably about to jump into or bite the stock.

When away from livestock, a dog may carry his tail high or low. A wagging tail indicates interest or arousal. As with the ears pricking up, a wagging tail is usually a sign of friendliness. But if the tail is stiff and wagging, it indicates fear or potential aggression. A slow wag suggests a relaxed dog; a fast wag, an excited dog.

## Vocal communication

Dogs communicate vocally through whining, growling and barking. Whining is usually associated with excitement or distress. Growling is usually a warning that the dog wants to be left alone. Some dogs playfully growl during greeting or playing. The dog's body language tells the difference.

A dog's bark can indicate a number of things—and an experienced dog trainer can accurately interpret a dog's bark most of the time. Border Collies shouldn't bark when working stock. If they do, it's likely an indication they're playing or extremely scared. Border Collies will bark at other times, though. By listening to the cadence, tone and volume, it's possible to tell whether a dog is alarmed or startled, defending his territory, excited, bored, wants attention, or has learned barking as a stereotypical behavior from being kenneled too much. All of these barks are triggered by different circumstances and communicate different things.

Barking is a normal and hardwired behavior of dogs. When startled or alarmed, dogs are likely to bark unconsciously, much like a human might yelp when startled or hurt. For this reason, using an electronic collar that shocks the dog when he barks has the potential to cause anxiety and behavior problems in a dog. While electronic bark collars may seem convenient, their potential for harming the dog outweighs the benefits.

## A Shepherd's Journey

A friend had two dogs crated next to each other in the house. To keep one from barking excessively at the other, she put a bark shock collar on him. The dog with the collar was still barking when she opened the dogs' crates in the morning—and that dog attacked the other because he associated the shock with the other dog. She never used a shock collar after that. –Kay

# Chapter 6
## Your Dog Has Emotions and They Matter

Every action a dog does has at least three components: the action itself, the physical sensation the dog experiences while performing the action and the emotional state of the dog as he performs the action. When you start to train an action, you should keep all three of these components in mind. How, exactly, should each one be in the final product?

The first component, the action itself, is easy to observe. It's what the dog is *doing*. If lying down is the action, the dog is bending his elbows, lowering his rear end, bending his hocks and putting his belly on the ground.

The second component, the *physical* sensation the dog experiences, cannot always be observed. For many dogs, lying down feels very comfortable. For a dog with arthritis in his hocks, though, lying down may feel painful, and he may resist lying down. How the dog feels physically while doing the action impacts training. Dogs, like people, are reluctant or hesitant to perform acts that cause pain.

If you are having a training problem with your dog, it may stem from a physical or medical issue your dog has. If your dog shows resistance to perform a behavior or starts performing at a lower level, have him examined by a veterinarian.

### A Shepherd's Journey

One of my good open dogs started slicing, or cutting in toward the sheep, when circling in a counter-clockwise direction. I did all the usual training approaches to open his flank up but the slicing persisted. Although the dog was not lame, I decided to have an orthopedic specialist look at the dog. It turned out the dog had a partially torn cruciate ligament. We repaired the ligament, rehabbed the dog and sure enough, his flanks went back to being correct.—Kay

The third component, the *emotional* feeling the dog experiences while doing the action, has a big impact on his ability to perform reliably and calmly. A dog who feels fear or anxiety while performing a behavior is more likely to make a mistake or avoid performing that behavior than a dog who is relaxed and confident. Fear and stress interfere with learning new behaviors and can interfere with properly performing known behaviors. For example, imagine the difference between trying to balance your checkbook in the comfort of your living room versus standing in the middle of a busy road. Being comfortable and relaxed makes it easier to learn new things and to successfully complete previously learned tasks. The top human athletes work hard at learning to feel relaxed and confident when they perform in order to give their top performance. The same is true for our dogs. They will perform better when they are relaxed and confident than when they feel anxious or stressed.

### A Shepherd's Journey

Years ago, sheepdog trainer Red Oliver and I were comparing training methods. He used an ear pinch to get his dog to load into a crate, while I used a food treat as a reward. We decided to see who could train it faster. After a week, both dogs were loading quickly and easily. Then, we tested the method by closing, but not latching, the crate doors to see what the dogs would do. Red's dog frantically tried to get into the crate to avoid the ear pinch, then gave up and hid under the truck. My dog tried to open the crate door and kept trying to open the door until finally succeeding and jumping into the crate. Her tail was wagging. The difference in the two methods was the dogs' emotional state. –Kay

The emotional component of a behavior is an often overlooked but important factor in dog training. A dog who is lying down to avoid an electric shock, an ear pinch or a jerk on the choke chain is performing a totally different behavior from a dog who is lying down in hopes of earning a food treat or access to the sheep. The two behaviors may look the same to a casual observer, but to the dog they are emotional opposites. The dog wearing the shock collar is anxious to avoid the discomfort of the electrical jolt and feels great relief if he is able to avoid or stop that shock. This dog is on an emotional roller coaster. The reward-trained dog is enjoying the opportunity to get a treat, and then enjoys eating the treat or being allowed to work the sheep. For this dog, the whole situation is positive, and the training situation is enjoyable. He is looking forward to learning more.

A good trainer, regardless of the methods she employs, is always watching for and paying attention to the emotional component of the dog's behavior. A good trainer will make sure the dog is working in a relaxed and confident manner; if the dog shows significant stress or fear, she'll change the situation.

## A Shepherd's Journey

A friend wanted help with her dog who was slicing, or cutting in too close to the sheep, instead of keeping a consistent distance around them. As the dog started to slice in, I told her to stop the dog so we could change our position. As soon as my friend said, "Lie down," the dog tucked his tail, turned his back to the sheep, closed his eyes, took a few steps away from the sheep and then lay down. The woman had taught her dog to lie down by throwing a plastic water bottle full of pebbles at the dog. As a result, the dog learned that "lie down" meant to expect a bottle of rocks thrown at his head. Not only was the dog confused about what "lie down" meant, but the dog also had, understandably, a lot of anxiety when he heard the words "lie down." We had to go back and teach the dog that "lie down" was simply a cue for the dog to stop moving before we could use it in our training program. –Kay

# Chapter 7
## Better Training through Science:
## The Why and How of Training

*"Science is much more than a body of knowledge. It is a way of thinking. This is central to its success. Science invites us to let the facts in, even when they don't conform to our preconceptions."* – Carl Sagan

No dog trains himself. How well your dog performs depends on your ability to train him. Your ability to train depends on your understanding of, and your ability to apply, the principles described in this chapter. While it's true some successful trainers have never formally studied behavior, to really excel at training, a basic understanding of how animals learn is invaluable. Training a dog without a basic understanding of how animals learn is like building a house with no blueprint; you may get a finished product, but the odds of something going wrong are much higher, and the end result will vary with each attempt. To get consistently good results, you need a blueprint of training principles. This chapter provides that blueprint.

## Why bother with this science stuff?

Many of us know a dog or horse trainer who has never read a training book. Odds are, you aren't that trainer. While some people are able to figure out training principles on their own, it usually takes years of study with other trainers and years of trial and error. Using well-studied science to make training decisions will save you from those years of trial and error. It'll also save you from having to train 20 dogs incorrectly before you figure out a system that consistently works well.

People have been training animals for thousands of years. But it's only been since the 1940s that people began scientifically studying what works and what doesn't (also called evidence-based training) when training dogs. Keller and Marian Breland were students of the famous psychologist BF Skinner. They went on to take the principles of Skinner and apply them to animals of all species, thus revolutionizing training.

## What are the benefits of evidence-based dog training?

**You save time.** Behavioral scientists have extensively studied the pros and cons of different ways to train animals. By learning about their studies, you can save yourself years of trial and error. While the laboratory is not the same as real life, many discoveries in the behavior lab apply quite well to real-life dog training.

**You gain a common language.** Words matter. A universal definition of training methods gives us the tools to talk clearly with each other about training our dogs, and science provides this language.

**You're already using "science" to train your dog.** Chances are that the method you're using to train your dog has been tested. Learning about evidence-based training will help you know whether your method is the best approach for that situation. Science also describes very precisely how these methods should be applied for the best results.

**Using scientific language will improve your relationship with your dog!** Using science-based language takes the emotional/superstitious component out of training. We can talk about the dog's failure to respond to a cue, instead of saying the dog is stubborn or hardheaded.

Do not let some of the technical phrases in this chapter discourage you. Your dog will thank you for taking the time to learn how to train him more easily and efficiently.

## The ABCs of learning

Every action your dog takes has three steps. First is what happens *before* the action. Trainers call this the antecedent, or cue. Second is the behavior, an observable action by the dog. Third is the consequence or result of the action. This third part, the result or consequence of the action, determines what the dog will do in the future.

All behavior/actions of your dog are driven by the consequences or results of that action. If your dog touches an electric fence and is shocked, that shock is an undesirable result or consequence, and he is less likely to repeat that action. If your dog jumps up on the table and gets a tasty bite of roast chicken, that's a desirable consequence, and he's likely to do that behavior again in the future. *Thus, if you control the consequences, you control the dog.*

The sequence is:

1. Cue/Antecedent
2. Action/Behavior
3. Result/Consequence
4. Future actions based on previous result/consequence

This principle is the basis for all animal training: *All normal behaviors/actions of your dog are the result of your dog trying to escape or avoid things he finds unpleasant, or the result of your dog trying to obtain or keep things he finds pleasant. It's a simple concept, but applying it correctly is not easy.*

From this concept come four ways to change your dog's behavior. Each method depends on controlling the consequence of the dog's actions, and thus changing his future behavior. Broadly speaking, we use four types of consequences. Thus, comes the concept that there are four ways to change your dog's behavior. Each way, or method, has advantages and disadvantages, and each must be applied correctly to work. If you take the time to understand how each method works and when to properly use each one, you'll have a well-stocked toolbox for training your dog.

## The four methods to change a dog's behavior

The four methods to change a dog's behavior are:

1. Positive reinforcement (reward)
2. Negative reinforcement (escape/avoidance)
3. Positive punishment (aversive/correction)
4. Negative punishment (reward removal).

These terms are used by behavioral scientists (and not terms we made up). Each method has its pro and cons—and all four have been used in training herding dogs. The terminology can sometimes be confusing or intimidating, but it shouldn't be. Just think of add or subtract and increase or decrease. Think of them in terms of math. In this terminology the *positive* refers to adding something (good or bad) to the dog's environment. *Negative* refers to removing something (good or bad) from the dog's environment. Think of positive and negative in math terms, adding and subtracting, rather than good and bad. *Reinforcement* means we increase the dog's action/behavior. *Punishment* means we decrease the probability of the action or behavior. Contrary to popular lay usage, it does NOT necessarily mean doing anything aversive to the dog.

|  | **Behavior Increases** | **Behavior Decreases** |
|---|---|---|
| **Stimulus Added** | Positive Reinforcemnt | Positive Punishment |
| **Stimulus Removed** | Negative Reinforcemnt | Negative Punishment |

*The four methods of changing an animal's behavior.*

|  | **Behavior Increases** | **Behavior Decreases** |
|---|---|---|
| **Stimulus Added** | Positive reinforcement: When the dog lies down, he is *given* access to the sheep, *increasing* the likelihood of him lying down again. | Positive punishment: When the dog chases sheep, the handler *adds* a hat slap, *decreasing* the likelihood of the dog chasing sheep. |
| **Stimulus Removed** | Negative reinforcement: When the dog lies down, the handler moves *away* from the sheep, *increasing* the likelihood of the dog lying down again. | Negative punishment: When the dog chases sheep, the handler *takes away* the sheep from the dog, *decreasing* the likelihood of the dog chasing sheep again. |

*How the four methods are used in sheepdog training.*

## What must I know for these methods to work?
For any of these methods to work, the trainer must:

- Know what the dog considers worth getting/keeping and what the dog considers worth avoiding/escaping.

- Be aware that what the dog wants enough to work for and what the dog dislikes enough to avoid will vary with each dog's inherent temperament, his genetic makeup, with the environment or setting you are training in, the dog's training history/experience and the dog's internal state during the training session.

- Be able to see even a small change in the dog's behavior and body language and respond to the change quickly by applying one of these four methods.

- Be able to provide the consequence for the behavior quickly enough during or after the behavior for the dog to associate the consequence with the selected behavior. Or use an event marker, such as a clicker, to mark the behavior. (See the Appendix A for more information about clicker training.)

- Be aware that in real life, all four of these methods may blend together.

## How to use the four methods

### 1. Positive reinforcement

The *positive* part means the trainer is *adding* something to the animal's environment, or often in layman's terms, is rewarding the dog. The reinforcement part means the animal's behavior is increased or strengthened.

Here are two examples of **positive reinforcement**:

- The dog sits and you give him a piece of food. You added food to the dog's environment after he sat. He becomes more likely to sit in the future as he learns that sitting increases the likelihood that he will get food.

- The dog lies down and then you open the gate to allow him access to the sheep. The dog becomes more likely to lie down at the gate, as he has learned that the action of lying down earns the reinforcement of being allowed to work sheep.

For this method to work, the reward/reinforcement must occur during or immediately after the desired behavior. This helps the dog link the behavior with the reward. One second or less is ideal. Any longer and the dog won't know what he did that earned the reward.

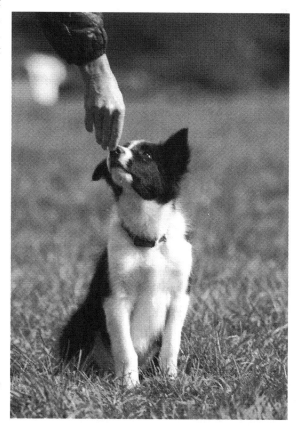

*Positive reinforcement is used to teach the sit. The dog receives food when he sits. Photo courtesy of Carol Clawson.*

This method requires that the reinforcement be something the animal is willing to expend energy and effort to acquire. Research has shown that dogs will work harder for higher value rewards, so it pays to know what your dog values. Also, what the animal considers reinforcing depends on the situation. At home with no distractions, your dog might do all kinds of tricks for a piece of kibble. Around sheep, he might spit out kibble, caring only about getting to the sheep. At that point, access to sheep is the reinforcement.

**Advantages**: Positive reinforcement is the best way to train an animal. By making the process pleasant and rewarding, the dog develops a positive emotional response to the trainer and the training process. This positive emotional response is very important because it means the dog will enjoy and feel safe doing the behaviors trained with positive reinforcement. This emotional component is just as or even more important than the physical components of a behavior.

For well-bred, working Border Collies, the highest value reinforcement is access to the sheep, or being allowed to work the sheep. Generations of selective breeding has modified the brain chemistry of the working Border Collie. The brain's reward center and the release of brain chemicals such as dopamine and serotonin are linked to access to the sheep. This is a huge advantage for herding dog trainers because they can use access to the sheep as positive reinforcement to increase desired behaviors in the dogs. For example, you can ask for the dog to lie down and reward the behavior by then allowing the dog to interact with the sheep. Keep in mind that the exact reinforcing aspect of the sheep varies with each dog. For some dogs, it's just staring at the sheep. For some, it's making the sheep move. For others, it's stopping or blocking the sheep. You'll need to know what action your dog finds rewarding and use it to reinforce the behaviors you want. Remember: timing is still important. The timing must be close enough that the dog connects the action of "lie down" with earning access to sheep.

**Disadvantages**: Setting up the animal to earn a reward takes some planning and preparation. You must make sure the reward you use is of more value than something else in the environment (or have previously conditioned the reward to be of great value). When using this method on sheep, make sure the dog's access to the sheep is predicated on him performing a behavior you want. This can require some skill, planning and careful manipulation on your part. You can't just turn the dog loose on sheep and start yelling at him. You have to plan ahead.

## 2. Negative reinforcement

Negative reinforcement is stopping, removing or taking away something the dog doesn't like in order to increase a behavior. Examples are common in horse training. A rider applies leg pressure and releases when the horse moves away. The rider pulls the reins and releases when the horse gives to her hands. A person chases a horse in the round pen and stops the chase and walks away when the horse slows or stops.

Some other examples of **negative reinforcement** are the following:

- When you get in the car and start moving, the seat belt beeper beeps until you fasten your seatbelt. The *stopping* of the beeping reinforces you for fastening your seat belt; you stop/remove the annoying beeping by performing the task of buckling up.
- Retriever trainers often teach a "forced retrieve." They will pinch the dog's ear and keep applying the pinch until the dog takes the object in his mouth. The dog stops the painful ear pinch by grabbing whatever they've been asked to retrieve.

Over time, you learn to avoid the seat belt beeper by buckling up as soon as you get in the car. The retriever learns to avoid the ear pinch by quickly taking any object offered in his mouth. This is why negative reinforcement is often referred to as "avoidance or escape" training and being able to escape is a very powerful emotional drive for dogs.

**Disadvantages**: The big problem with negative reinforcement is that positive punishment, or at least a mild aversive, is often part of the picture. In order to remove something the animal does not like, that thing has to be applied in the first place. So, to stop the seat belt beeping, it first has to beep; to stop the pinch, the dog first has to be pinched. The problem is that whatever the animal is doing at the moment the aversive is applied may be positively punished. This means if your dog was looking at you when you pinched his ear, you've punished him for looking at you. For this reason, this method is risky and can sometimes backfire. Also, by using aversives too much, you risk losing the positive associations and may even create a negative association with the trainer or the training environment. Because sheep are such an intense reward for Border Collies, herding dog trainers sadly may be able to get away with using aversives more in their training than in other dog sports.

The timing must be excellent for this method to be effective. The instant the seat belts are buckled, the beeping stops. The instant the dog reaches for the dumbbell, the ear pinch must stop. Also, as with using punishment, the thing the animal wants to stop must be suitable. For example, the car beeping must be annoying enough to make the person buckle the seat belts. If it's too quiet, she might drive around all day unbuckled. If it's too loud and upsetting, she may find a way to disable the beeper or get another car. The same is true for the dog. The annoying thing the dog wants to work to get rid of must be strong enough to motivate the dog to stop it, but not so upsetting that the dog is frightened or too stressed to learn. This will vary based on the dog's personality, the situation or environment, and the dog's learning history.

**Advantages**: Negative reinforcement is frequently used in sheepdog training. The most common example is blocking the dog from access to the sheep. When a dog is too tight or close to the sheep, the handler applies pressure (positive punishment) by moving toward the dog and blocking the dog from the sheep. The handler releases the pressure, changes her body position by moving away (negative reinforcement) when the dog gives ground, shows submission or changes his attitude from frantic to thoughtful. The release of the body pressure teaches the dog what the desired behavior is. The dog learns that he can control and avoid the application of pressure by performing correctly.

A sheepdog trainer can also apply pressure (something the dog wants to avoid) to the dog using her voice (growly or scolding) or making noise, such as slapping a hat against her leg. The trainer applies the aversive/pressure (positive punishment) when the dog is wrong, such as too close or chasing, and releases or stops the aversive when the dog stops or gives ground (negative reinforcement). The working Border Collie tends to have a natural instinct to move away from body pressure. Such a method would be less likely to work in some breeds, such as terriers and Labradors, who do not have the genetic predisposition to avoid approach.

For this method to work, the timing of both the application of the pressure and the release of the pressure must be closely associated with the start and end of the unwanted behavior. The pressure or punishment must be of a level the animal will work to avoid, but not of a level that scares or stops the animal from trying to work. Because negative reinforcement requires at least a mild punishment to be present, all the same issues involved with using punishment can also occur with negative reinforcement, so care is needed to apply this procedure correctly.

### 3. Positive punishment
Positive punishment is adding something unpleasant to the dog's environment to decrease or weaken a dog's behavior or action.

Some examples of positive punishment are the following:

- Your dog barks and you hit him with a rolled-up newspaper.
- Your dog jumps up on you and you step on his back toes.
- Your dog chases the sheep and you throw a stick and hit him.

In each case, something unpleasant has been added to the dog's environment in order to decrease the frequency of a behavior.

As with positive reinforcement, successful punishment requires that the timing of the punishment must occur during the unwanted action or within a second of the action. Also, the punishment must be of the correct level of intensity. This can be very tricky. The punishment must be aversive enough that the animal will work to avoid it. If the punishment is too mild and doesn't affect the behavior, then the level of punishment must be increased—and this can lead to the dog learning to ignore the punishment and to a very high, inhumane level of punishment being implemented. This is what behaviorists call a punishment callus. On the other hand, if the punishment is too severe, the dog may be so afraid or stressed that it interferes with his learning and performance.

**A Shepherd's Journey**

I was working dogs with a friend whose dog was constantly chasing the sheep down the field while he yelled and growled at the dog. The dog never slowed down. He commented that his dog was ignoring his corrections.

My thought was that to the dog, the yelling and growling weren't corrections. They were just noise. My friend needed to change what he was doing if he wanted to get the dog to change what the dog was doing. Remember, punishment is only punishment if it decreases the likelihood of the dog repeating the behavior. –Kay

**Advantages**: Punishment using the correct intensity and timing can very effectively stop an unwanted behavior. If applied correctly, it works quickly and will cause minimal side effects. The dog will associate the action with a correction and stop the action immediately. If the unwanted action is associated with the dog being in a hyper aroused state, a properly timed punishment not only stops the action but will change the animal's emotional state to a more submissive one. It's also very satisfying for the trainer to see an unwanted behavior stop almost instantly. This is why people use this method so often, even when better methods are available.

**Disadvantages**: There are many.

1. Punishment creates a negative *emotional* association between the punisher and the dog/person being punished. This negative emotional state means the dog's view of the training is colored by fear of the punishment. Fear creates stress and tension and interferes with learning. For example, evaluate your emotional state the next time you see the lights of a police car in your rear view mirror.

2. To be truly effective in stopping the unwanted behavior, punishment must be applied consistently—that is every time the action occurs. That can be difficult. Just think about how many people continue to drive over the speed limit if there are no police present. Or think about how often you let your dog jump up on you when you're wearing farm clothes and then punish him for jumping when you're wearing dress clothes.

3. The payoff for the behavior must not be bigger than the punishment. If your dog gets attention for jumping up on you, he may decide having his paws stepped on is worth the attention.

4. The level of punishment used must be very carefully chosen. Punishment that is too extreme will cause fear and stress and will stop the animal from learning at all; the animal may shut down, quit working or become aggressive. Punishment that is not enough to stop the behavior makes the animal more resistant to the use of punishment in the future; this can lead to escalation of punishment.

5. As with any training method, timing of the punishment must happen during or within one second of the unwanted behavior to be effective. For example, if you arrive home to find your dog has gotten into the trash earlier in the day and punish your dog, the dog will not know why he is being punished. Sometimes even if the timing is perfect, the dog may not know which behavior he is being punished for or may associate the punishment with something else. This is especially true with shock collars that shock for barking. The dog may think the shock is related to what caused him to bark, such as a strange noise or a squirrel, rather than the action of barking. As a result, he may develop anxiety or an aversion to those things.

6. If the dog is punished for an unwanted behavior that is the result of fear or anxiety, (for example, the dog barking at a scary person), then the fear and anxiety will increase, even if the barking stops. This can lead to fear and anxiety being expressed in other ways, such as biting.

7. Punishment provides no information on what you want the dog to do. While it may stop the unwanted behavior, the dog has no idea what you want him to do. *The most important part of training is always teaching the animal what the correct behavior is, and then reinforcing that.*

## Why is positive punishment popular in dog training?

Positive punishment is popular in training dogs and, to some extent, in teaching people, because the punishment usually stops the unwanted behavior immediately, at least temporarily. That's very rewarding to the person doing the punishing. It feels like you've really accomplished something (your behavior is being negatively reinforced). However, although you've stopped the behavior, you haven't taught the animal what you consider to be the correct behavior. In the meantime, you have created a negative association between you and the animal. The use of too much positive punishment or the incorrect use of positive punishment can cause a dog to work frantically, to lack enthusiasm, to be tense or to quit and leave the sheep. The more you avoid the use of positive punishment, the better for your training program and for the animal's well being.

## 4. Negative punishment

Negative punishment is subtracting something from the dog's environment to decrease or weaken a behavior. In other words, you take something away to stop him from continuing an unwanted behavior.

Here are some examples of **negative punishment**:

- Walking away when a dog jumps on you. This takes away attention (what the dog wants) to decrease his jumping behavior.
- Taking the dog away from the sheep if he is not working correctly. A handler stops the training session if the dog is working rashly.

Just as with the other methods, the timing must be such so the dog associates the removal of the desired object or activity with the unwanted behavior. For example, if your dog jumps up on you, and you stand there, allowing him to jump for a few seconds before walking away, then the dog has already been rewarded for jumping up (getting to touch you). Walking away at that point is unlikely to change his behavior. If, however, you walk away as soon as his front paws start to come up off the ground (before he touches you), he will associate jumping up with you leaving (taking the attention/payoff away).

*The handler uses negative punishment and walks away as the
dog starts to jump. Photo courtesy of Beth Murray.*

**Advantages**: For attention-seeking behaviors such as jumping, whining or barking, removing attention can be very effective, if the timing is correct. This method stops the animal from getting rewarded for unwanted behaviors. This is especially effective if you combine negative punishment with positive reinforcement for an alternative behavior.

**Disadvantage**: As with positive punishment, it does *not* teach the dog what he should be doing or what you would rather have him doing. And that's not fair to the dog. Most dogs want your attention. Why not teach them more appropriate ways to ask for attention, such as teaching them to sit in front of you and then pet them for doing so?

When training your sheepdog, you'll use all four methods to change behavior. While positive reinforcement and negative reinforcement will be used most frequently, take the time to learn and understand each method, as well as its advantages and disadvantages. Knowing how each one works, why and when they work and don't work, gives you the power to use each one appropriately. Understanding these four methods will give you more tools to train your dog in the most efficient and best way possible.

## Can you use only positive reinforcement for herding training?

An animal training revolution has happened in the past 40 years. Long gone are the days of using choke and prong collars to jerk dogs into compliance for obedience competitions. Thanks to people such as Karen Pryor, Bob and Marian Bailey, Ian Dunbar and Jean Donaldson, science-based training using mostly positive reinforcement has become the standard for teaching dogs basic manners and training them for obedience, agility and many other dog sports. Nowadays, most pet dog trainers use positive reinforcement with food, toys, and environmental control. Fortunately, the use of harsh methods has become rare. Today, most dog owners would never dream of hurting or scaring their dog in order to train it.

With so many wonderful training techniques available, there is no reason to use aversive methods in pet dog training. One reason the author, Kay Stephens, started her pet dog training and behavior business in 1992 was to provide people with modern, positive alternatives to the rather rough methods available at the time.

Herding dog training, though, presents dog trainers with a unique set of circumstances that make it difficult to use only positive reinforcement.

First, the dog is interacting with sheep. Sheep are living, sentient beings who feel fear and pain, just like humans and dogs. They are not dog toys. As a shepherd, your job is to protect the sheep from injury and to handle the sheep in ways that create the least amount of stress and fear. A good shepherd does not allow the dog to chase, grab, bite or harass the sheep.

Second, Border Collies have been selectively bred to have a strong focus and desire to interact with the sheep. This means the reinforcement or reward for the herding dog is not praise, toys or food, but is being allowed to interact with the sheep. Thus, controlling the dog means controlling access to the sheep. It also means that in times of excitement, herding instinct can easily progress to prey drive—and you cannot let the dog harm the sheep.

Third, we can't train the dog to correctly interact with the sheep without sheep. In other words, you cannot train herding behaviors without livestock. Some people try to teach herding behaviors without the stock but doing so does not teach the dog how his actions affect the sheep.

Because of these factors, when training the herding dog, you have to do three things: protect the sheep and handle them humanely; use access to the sheep as a reward for the dog; and use some type of correction, usually a combination of a mild punishment and negative reinforcement, to stop or prevent unwanted behaviors by the dog.

This does not mean you have to hurt or scare your dog. In fact, we advise against that and suggest avoiding trainers who imply this is necessary. One of the main reasons for writing this book was to promote gentler and more effective methods of training the herding dog. We do not advocate harsh or physical corrections. The best trainers follow the least invasive, minimally aversive approach and use the least amount of aversive to get the job done. But, because you must protect the sheep, some verbal or other types of corrections may be necessary. This could include slapping a rolled-up feed sack against your leg to startle the dog or stepping quickly toward your dog or even, in extreme cases, chasing the dog away from the sheep. The dog must be attentive to and responsive to the handler, and the dog must treat the sheep kindly. If you are not willing to use at least some type of effective correction on your dog, then herding training may not be for you.

# Chapter 8
## Using Corrections Correctly:
## Maximize Success and Minimize Distress

When training your sheepdog, he will perform some unwanted behaviors. He may bite the sheep; he may chase them. This chapter looks at ways to stop unwanted behaviors, and how to use corrections effectively in sheepdog training. It also addresses how to minimize your use of corrections.

## How to use corrections in sheepdog training

Understanding the why, what and how of corrections are some of the most difficult concepts and skills for novice handlers to master. Because corrections are rarely used in other dog sports nowadays, this can also be a controversial and emotional topic. For this book, corrections are defined as the minimal effective aversive to change a dog's behavior.

## Why are corrections used in sheepdog training?

When so much of modern dog training can be accomplished using management, positive reinforcement and negative punishment, many people question why corrections are used in sheepdog training. As was discussed in more detail in Chapter 7, the reasons that corrections are used in sheepdog training are:

- The mental and physical well-being of the livestock must be protected at all times.

- Border Collies have a strong, instinctual drive based on predatory and hunting behavior that may be difficult to control.

- For a working Border Collie, access to the sheep activates the reward circuit in the brain and is the most powerful reinforcement available. They will choose to work sheep over praise, sleep, pain or any other reinforcement. Thus, if we control access to the sheep, we control the dog.

- It's not always practical or possible to control herding behavior by managing the surrounding environment as might be the case in other dog training venues.

- In herding, the dog is often far away, commonly at distances over 400 yards away.

- A herding dog should be working in "pack" mode, working with the handler as a team and the handler as team leader.

- Finally, and most importantly, a good herding dog must learn to control sheep properly even when not directed by the handler. Unlike other sports where almost all the dog's actions are contingent on handler cues, a working sheep dog must not only obey cues but understand how to move sheep in a calm and controlled fashion without cues. Correcting the dog for improper handling of the sheep teaches the dog what is and what is not allowed even when cues are not being given or the dog is out of sight or hearing of the handler.

## What is a correction?

**Corrections** mean different things to different trainers, and the term "correction" is not a well-defined or scientific term. In this book, we define correction as the least aversive yet effective action to change a dog's behavior. Our definition of correction does not mean scaring, injuring or abusing the dog. A correction used in sheepdog training will typically consist of one or more of the following actions:

- Often, but now always, stopping the dog first.
- Usually, a positional change by the handler.
- Sometimes, applying an aversive or positive punishment (*adding* something the dog wants to avoid).
- Often, applying a negative punishment (*taking away* access to the sheep from the dog).
- A negative reinforcement (release or removal of punishment/ pressure) when the dog's attitude, position or behavior changes.
- Often, but not always, stopping the dog again if the dog has started moving to reset the scene.

A properly executed correction is a complex maneuver with a lot of moving parts and variation in the application. (See Chapter 7 for more on the science behind training). What makes properly executing a correction even harder is that it often happens very quickly. Moreover, a dog will often respond completely differently to a correction from an experienced, confident clinician than they do one from their hesitant or unsure owner. A dog will also respond differently to a stranger than his owner with whom he has an established relationship and a long reinforcement history.

## An effective correction does the following:

1. Stops or interrupts the unwanted behavior. It does not allow the dog to rehearse the wrong behavior.

2. Decreases the likelihood of the unwanted behavior in the future by applying a well-timed and effective punishment (something the dog wants to avoid). Remember, this punishment may be very mild and doesn't need to hurt or scare the dog.

3. Rewards the dog for the correct behavior by removing the punishment when the dog's behavior changes. The timing of the release is just as important as the timing of the pressure.

4. Accomplishes these three goals with the least amount of stress for the dog while being effective enough that it does not need to be repeated multiple times. If a correction is given multiple times with no change of behavior, then it is not effective, and the trainer should change what she is doing.

Using corrections effectively is complicated and learning to properly time and apply a correction is difficult. Understanding how and why corrections work or don't work will help you use corrections effectively.

If your corrections are not working, it is likely that:

- You are applying them too long after the unwanted behavior and the dog isn't associating your correction with the unwanted behavior.
- Your position relative to the dog and sheep is wrong. Many novice handlers try to correct the dog from too far away from the sheep.
- Your intensity of correction is wrong for the dog or wrong for the situation.
- Your body language is frantic, unclear or hesitant.
- You have made too big of a jump in your training and multiple things are going wrong at the same time. This means you should go back and break your training into smaller steps.
- The dog has an underlying issue such as fear or confusion that needs to be addressed.

## Training aids used for corrections

To perform effective corrections, you may need training aids. Your goal is to apply some punishment/aversive or pressure to the dog that he finds unpleasant and will want to avoid. The aid used will vary with the dog and the situation. The aid should be both easy to use and not dangerous to the dog, handler or sheep. Here's a list of commonly used training aids as well as a description about how they are used:

- **You**. Your body posture, facial expression, where you are standing and how you move can convey an aversive to the dog. You can apply a correction by leaning forward, taking a full-frontal approach, stomping on the ground, making direct eye contact, rapidly approaching the dog or spreading your arms as you approach. You can clap your hands or slap your hands on your leg for noise. A skilled trainer can quickly change her body posture and her voice to threaten the dog, and then switch back to calming the dog with a relaxed posture and soft voice. Pay attention to what you are doing with your body when you train. If you aren't sure what you are doing, then have someone video you while you train.

- **Your voice.** Your voice can be loud, growly or angry. Yelling at a dog is usually a punishment for the dog. For many dogs, a loud voice alone is a correction. Yelling can also be a predictor to the dog that you are going to apply an aversive such as stepping between him and the sheep. Be careful, though, if you start yelling at the dog but do not follow up with a positional correction, he may learn to ignore your verbal corrections.

- **Your position**. When you stand directly between the dog and the sheep you are taking possession of the sheep away from the dog and telling him he can't have them. Backing away from the sheep or turning your back to the dog tells the dog he may work the sheep again and releases pressure on the dog.

*This is an example of a good correction. The handler is full frontal to the dog and applying pressure to the dog's head area. The dog's ears and body posture show that the dog is responding to the correction by showing appeasement and moving away from the sheep. Photo courtesy of Beth Murray.*

- **Baseball cap**. This is a great aid in terms of convenience and effectiveness. A baseball cap is usually slapped against the handler's leg to make a noise that'll startle a dog. It can also be tossed at the dog. Select one with Velcro instead of metal buckles, because metal can leave bruises on your leg. A baseball cap is easy to store on your head when not in use—and can be worn to sheepdog trials as well.

- **Tightly rolled-up feed sack**. Take a 50-lb. dog food, grain or cat food bag, fold it in half, and then tightly roll it up and tape it into a roll with duct tape. Usually a handler will slap the bag against her leg to startle the dog. It makes more noise than a ball cap. It can also be thrown at the dog.

- **Long line**. The line is used to catch or stop a dog if necessary. In most cases, a 20-ft. biothane line is recommended.

- **Lunge whip or stick with flag on the end**. These can be popped or slapped against the ground as a correction and to block the dog. For some dogs, this movement adds excitement and anxiety, and it can be counterproductive. If using these aids, watch for this side effect.

- **Water bottle half filled with pebbles or pennies**. Water bottles with thicker plastic usually last longer. The handler can shake the bottle to make noise and startle the dog. It can also be tossed toward the dog. Be careful about using these, as this type of correction is strong and will scare or overwhelm many dogs.

- **Stock stick**. Some trainers use a stock stick to slap the ground and correct the dog, and some trainers will throw the stick at the dog. We don't recommend either. Because you will use a stock stick with penning and shedding, you don't want the dog to fear the stock stick. Throwing a stock stick at the dog is dangerous and can seriously injure the dog.

When selecting training aids, start with the least aversive, yet effective correction.

## Four elements of a successful correction

For corrections to be effective, they must:

- Take place at the proper time
- Be in the right location
- Be of the correct intensity
- Be released

After a correction is given, the correction should be *evaluated* for effectiveness. Did it stop or decrease the unwanted behavior without overwhelming the dog? If it did, it was effective.

**Timing**. In an ideal situation, we must react *to the dog as he starts the incorrect behavior, or no later than 1 second after the incorrect behavior, by either correcting or stopping the dog*. While you may not be able to correct the dog at the exact moment he is wrong, you should at least stop the dog at the moment he is wrong. By stopping him, you prevent him from rehearsing the wrong behavior. It also gives you time to reposition yourself to apply a correction. To be able to react to the dog as he starts to be wrong, you must closely watch the dog and know his body language. If the correction is late, the dog may not understand why he is being corrected. Often, a dog who is going to grip or slice in will show tension in his mouth or tail before diving in. If you watch closely you can apply the correction as the dog starts the wrong behavior. A dog that dives in, grips a sheep, and then doesn't get punished for the gripping until several minutes later will likely not understand what he is being punished for.

One way to improve your timing is to rehearse your corrections away from your dog before your dog training session. Ask yourself questions such as, where is the dog likely to be incorrect? How am I going to respond to that? Videoing your training sessions is another way to evaluate your timing.

**Location**. Corrections should take place where the incorrect behavior happened. This means that in many cases, you will have to *stop* your dog before applying a correction. Stopping your dog does three things. First, it interrupts the wrong behavior. Second, it keeps the dog (and hopefully the sheep) in the place where the wrong behavior happened. Third, it allows you to get in the best position to make an impact on your dog. The handler should always move between the dog and the sheep because taking control of the sheep away from the dog is a key component of this maneuver.

Often, after stopping your dog, you will likely have to reposition yourself before making a correction. The handler's position is relative to the dog and the sheep, and often between the dog and the sheep. Almost always, the handler will be in a direct line between the sheep and the dog and facing directly at the dog in a full-frontal position. The handler may step forcefully toward the dog, scold the dog or slap a feed sack on her leg. This applies a positive punishment (threat from the handler) to the dog and a negative punishment since it also takes the sheep away from the dog. In other words, the dog feels uncomfortable pressure from the handler's approach and dislikes losing control of the sheep.

Because of the distance involved and the sheep, applying corrections is very tricky. It is usually not possible to be in the right place (usually between the dog and the sheep) when the dog makes a mistake. In these cases, stopping the dog allows you to move into the correct position to apply the correction. However, when you do that, you lose the ideal timing of the correction. This is one reason training herding dogs is so challenging.

Here's another thing to keep in mind. Because you will often stop a dog before correcting him, you should make a point to randomly stop the dog at other times during training, and then reward him for stopping (this is often done by letting him go back to working sheep) so that being asked to stop does not become a predictor of a correction.

**Note**: At sheepdog trials, you may see a handler standing at the post, giving her dog a verbal correction—and the dog responding to the correction by changing his behavior. The reason this works is because the trainer has practiced this skill hundreds of times on the practice field and moved to the location of the incorrect behavior.

Through repetition, the dog learned what that correction means and responded to it. The verbal correction has become a predictor of a correction because of training.

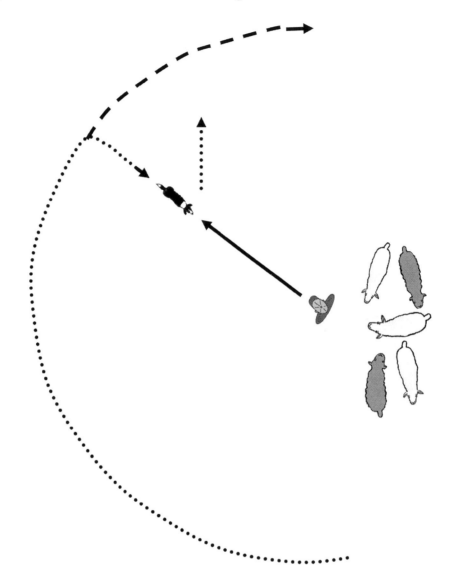

*An example of a good correction. The correct actions include:*

- *The handler is close to the sheep.*
- *The handler is between the dog and the sheep.*
- *The handler directly focuses on the dog's eyes and head.*
- *The handler is blocking the dog from the sheep.*
- *The handler can prevent the dog from interacting with the sheep until the dog changes his position or attitude.*

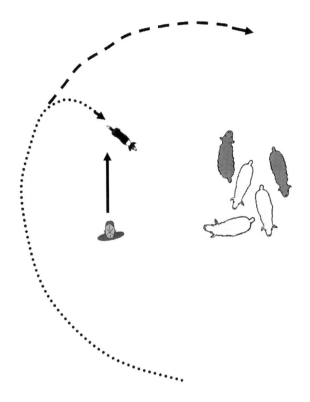

*An example of a poor correction. The incorrect actions include:*

- *The handler is too far from the sheep and too close to the dog.*
- *The handler is not positioned between the dog and the sheep.*
- *The handler is facing the dog's side and hindquarters and will likely speed the dog up.*
- *The handler does not have control of the dog nor the sheep.*
- *The handler is out of position and too slow. The dog will likely dive into the sheep unless the handler can stop the dog and reposition.*

**Intensity**. Corrections come in all levels—from quietly saying "Ah-ah," to slapping your hat against your leg, to running toward the dog. No corrections should involve physically hurting your dog, and you should avoid any trainers that suggest otherwise. Choosing the level of intensity depends on the dog *and* the mistake.

There are generally considered to be three levels of corrections:

- **A mild or instructional correction**, also called an "oops" correction, lets the dog know that is not what you wanted. It is usually a quietly delivered "ah-ah," followed by a lie down so you can reset the situation. This correction is often used when teaching directional cues such as flanks when you want to inform the dog that he is going the wrong direction. It also might be used for an action that is wrong for that situation, but not wrong for all situations. For example, if a dog circles between you and the sheep when teaching balance work.

- **A moderate correction** usually involves moving between the dog and the sheep and slapping your cap on your leg. This is used when the dog does something you don't want, but it is not endangering livestock. You'd use this if a dog was tight on his outrun or sliced a flank.

- **A hard correction**, such as yelling and running directly at the dog, is given for a behavior that you never want, such as chasing or biting the sheep. The other time a hard correction would be appropriate is if the dog's attitude is wrong. The dog should be working cooperatively with his handler, what some would call "pack drive." If the dog is in "prey drive" and only interested in chasing and biting the sheep instead of tuning into his handler and making her part of the picture, then a hard correction can be used to change his attitude. In a good training program, a hard correction should be extremely rare. Never give a hard correction after lying the dog down. It's a sure way to ruin your dog's lie down cue. A hard correction should be done, if possible, while the dog is doing the unwanted behavior. Remember this type of correction should seldom, if ever, be needed if the proper foundation of a working relationship and basic training is in place.

To further complicate matters, your correction intensity is going to vary depending on the dog. A very intense, high-drive dog might need a strong correction, such as being chased off the sheep, while a very sensitive, low-drive dog might only need a light verbal correction for the same infraction. This is where reading the dog's body language is important.

Corrections must be strong enough to change behavior—but not so strong that the dog doesn't want to or is afraid to work. Dogs are experts at reading body language, so movement, body position and posture are key. A handler makes a big impact when she is close to the sheep, calm and confident, stands upright and squarely in front of the dog, looks the dog directly in the eye and steps forward. Being frantic, uncertain or half-hearted confuses the dog and increases tension. You will also need to be an expert in reading dog body language so that you can tell if your correction had the desired effect.

**Release**. Forgetting to release the pressure and letting the dog have the sheep after a correction is a common novice trainer mistake. By trying too hard to prevent the dog from being wrong, some trainers never let the dog have the sheep. This creates either tension or depression in the dog.

The release or releasing pressure, after a dog responds to a correction, is vital to the training process because it rewards the dog. The handler must release the pressure and allow the dog to go back to working the sheep. This can be done by stepping away from the sheep, turning away from the dog, speeding the dog up, doing some balance work, or calling the dog off and resetting the situation.

Failing to release the pressure means the dog is not rewarded for changing his behavior. It may result in a slow, confused, unenthusiastic dog or one that is frantic to regain control of the sheep.

---

### Don't use cues as corrections

This is easy to do—and most handlers are guilty of doing this at one point in training. For instance, when a dog doesn't lie down when asked, the handler may follow up with a growling, yelling command: "LIE DOWN." The more effective response is saying, "Ah-ah" (telling the dog he is wrong), running toward the dog and blocking the dog from the sheep. Then, after the dog tunes you in, repeat the "lie down" cue in a quiet, firm tone.

If cues are consistently loud or angry, the dog learns to ignore cues in the normal voice, as the dog learns that loud, angry cues are the important ones. Once the cue (information) gets confused with a correction (punishment), the dog's response to the cue often becomes erratic. The dog may also avoid the cue or command by performing other stress-related, unwanted behavior such as spinning or eating sheep poop. For these same reasons, use your dog's name to get his attention, not to correct him.

Verbal cues let the dog know what is wanted. As a handler, aim to give the cues quietly, clearly and confidently—and leave the emotion and excitement out of them. Easier said than done, but it can be achieved with practice.

## Evaluate your corrections

When giving a correction, you must evaluate its effectiveness. Here are some questions to ask and things to look for:

- Does the dog's body language show signs of appeasement, such as ears back, tail down, head down, eyes averted, moving away from you or lip lick? Effective.
- Did the correction stop or decrease the unwanted behavior? Effective.
- Did it increase the desired behavior? Effective.
- Is the dog's attitude correct? Is he keen to work, yet focused on you? Effective.
- Is the dog trying to get past you to the sheep, eyeing the sheep, leaning into the sheep or have his head or tail up? Ineffective.
- Is the dog tense or excited? Ineffective. The correction either took place at the wrong time or at the wrong intensity.
- Does the dog want to leave the field, eat sheep poop, quit working or seem afraid? Ineffective. The correction either took place at the wrong time or at the wrong intensity.

The training exercises in this book include information for correcting specific behaviors. To be effective though, you should have a clear understanding of how to give and evaluate corrections. Remember, a good correction does the following:

- Stops an unwanted behavior.
- Decreases the behavior in the future.
- Rewards a change in the dog's behavior.
- Provides clear, unambiguous information to the dog.
- Achieves the above results with the least stressful, least aversive means.
- If your corrections are NOT working, review the timing, position and intensity with a video or having an experienced trainer watch you.

While using corrections may be a necessary part of sheep dog training, remember the old saying that: "The best trainers use the least amount of force."

## Some examples of corrections in sheepdog training

Below are some common mistakes that dogs make in training and how a handler would correct for them:

- A dog dives into the sheep as he circles them, scattering the sheep. The handler slaps a ball cap on her leg and chases the dog away from the sheep.
- A dog starts to cut in on the outrun. The handler stops the dog, moves to position herself between the dog and the sheep, steps at the dog, then stops the dog again and resends the dog.
- A dog doesn't lie down on command but continues to chase sheep. The handler gets between the dog and the sheep and blocks the dog's access to the sheep until the dog responds to the cue.
- A dog takes the wrong flank. The handler quietly says "ah, ah," stops the dog, repositions herself and then repeats the cue.

## Minimize your use of corrections

While some uses of corrections are needed, a good trainer wants to use positive reinforcement as much as possible and use any type of correction as little as possible. By setting the dog up for success and teaching the correct behaviors, you'll save training time and minimize the use of corrections.

These are the steps to minimize your use of corrections:

1.  Pick a different behavior that is not compatible with the unwanted behavior. Some off-sheep examples are sitting instead of jumping up or walking by your left side instead of pulling on the leash. Some on-sheep examples are, if the dog is slicing or cutting in on a flank, set him up with your position to make his flank a circle around the sheep. If your dog is chasing sheep, show him how to properly handle sheep. If he is **gripping**, or biting, the sheep, teach him how to move sheep without a grip. Just punishing the dog without first setting him up for success is unfair to the dog and will make your training take longer as the dog struggles to figure out what you want him to do. The more you set the dog up to work correctly, the more that working correctly will become a habit, and the less often you'll need to apply a correction.

2.  Use positive reinforcement to teach the dog the new behavior so that the dog likes doing the new behavior and enjoys it.

3.  Practice and reward many hundreds of repetitions of the new behavior so that it becomes strong, automatic and reliable.

4.  Use negative punishment any time the dog offers the wrong behavior. Take away what he wants. If your dog jumps on you, actively disengage from him and don't look at him, talk to him or touch him. Don't walk forward if the dog is pulling on the leash. Block access to the sheep if he is working rashly. Be consistent. If you allow the bad behaviors occasionally, the behavior will persist. (In fact, because you have now put the bad/unwanted behavior on a variable reinforcement schedule, the behavior may increase and the dog may become very resistant to retraining. Similar to gambling, the dog keeps trying as he knows occasionally you will reward the behavior.)

5.  Use the positive punishment and negative reinforcement part of training (applying an aversive) carefully and sparingly, being careful that the aversive is of the appropriate level and knowing that some negative side effects are possible.

6.  Remember that the key to success is to notice and respond to the dog's behavior quickly and appropriately. Timing, timing, timing.

7.  Any behavior the dog performs consistently is either being rewarded unintentionally or fulfilling some innate need that the dog has. If you are struggling to change a behavior, consider what the underlying motivation is for the dog and address the motivation.

together, and rather harshly, to control the dog. I knew from my work in behavior modification and from working with sophisticated animal trainers that this approach was neither necessary nor desirable. Since then, I've been searching for effective methods that avoid the use of harsh corrections.

To minimize how much or how often you have to correct your dog on stock, I have found these things very effective:

- Develop a strong relationship and partnership with your dog off stock so that he is tuned in to you.

- Manage your dog so he does not constantly watch or chase stock when not training. This keeps his reactivity level lower and makes sure that working the sheep is something he does WITH you.

- Have a reliable obedience framework off stock so that he can more easily adapt to responding to you quickly and reliably on stock.

- Always set the dog up for success in early training sessions with the right sheep and the right environment to ensure success. Don't let your dog practice being wrong.

- Go slowly and progress the training in small steps to avoid introducing mistakes and overwhelming the dog.

- Select a dog with the proper breeding and temperament to meet your goals. A hard truth is that not all dogs have the traits necessary to become a good trial or working dog. Choose a dog whose working style and temperament mesh well with yours.

–Kay

## A painful truth: shock collars should not be used in sheepdog training

Shock collars, sometimes called electronic collars or anti-bark collars, deliver an electrical stimulation to the dog's neck. Some are controlled remotely, while anti-bark or no-bark shock collars are triggered by the vibration of the dog's vocal cords. They are often marketed as a quicker, easier way to train dogs. They claim to use a mild pulse or stimulation and even claim to not cause pain. That is ridiculous. If the shock were not painful, it would not affect the dog's behavior.

Several countries ban the use of shock collars. All the major dog training and veterinary behavior organizations strongly discourage their use. Top sheepdog trial winners in both the United Kingdom and the United States don't use them for training. Most of the top dog trainers would never dream of using them on their dogs. We do not recommend using shock collars for training nor using anti-bark shock collars in the kennel. However, because they are still being used by some stock dog trainers and by some dog training franchises, we are commenting on their effects.

### Here's why you should never use shock collars

Shock is a very strong aversive, especially when applied to the delicate structures of the throat area. Don't believe it? Put a shock collar snugly around your neck with the prongs on your windpipe as is done with dog shock collars. (Do not place it around your arm, as that is totally different nerve sensitivity.) Give a friend the controller and have her apply the shock. How does it make you feel? Even at very low settings, shock collars can make dogs fearful or anxious. When a dog is fearful or anxious, he has a tougher time learning and may develop anxiety related behavior problems.

It's also very easy for an animal to develop the wrong association with the shock. For example, let's say you shock a dog when it barks. But when the dog is barking, he is also looking at a person walking down the street. The dog may associate the shock with the person and become fearful or aggressive to the person. And to make matters worse, if you are handling the remote and your timing is off (most people are too slow), the dog is now being shocked at the wrong time or for the wrong behavior. This results in a multitude of serious training or behavioral issues.

Also, every action your dog takes has an emotional component. If a dog is trained to lie down using a shock collar, he'll likely associate lying down with fear and anxiety over avoiding the shock. He'll likely be stressed, and thus, more likely to make mistakes and perform poorly. Fearful, anxious dogs have more difficulty learning and are more likely to make mistakes than relaxed, confident ones.

The working Border Collie has been selected for generations to work cooperatively with humans and to respond to human direction. Using a shock collar on a well-bred Border Collie is like using a sledgehammer to drive a thumbtack. If people start selecting for Border Collies that tolerate the use of a shock collar, the breed's sensitive and cooperative nature will be lost.

### A Shepherd's Journey

I purchased a dog who had been kenneled with an anti-bark shock collar, as had all the dogs in the kennel. Although I never used a shock collar on this dog, for the rest of his life he would duck and flinch whenever another dog barked. He associated another dog barking with being shocked. This may have been because when another dog in the kennel barked, he responded with a bark and was shocked. It also may have been because some shock collars are sensitive enough to be triggered by nearby vibrations, and this dog was being shocked every time the neighbor dog barked.

Barking is an inherent part of a dog's nature. Dogs bark to express excitement, fear and anticipation. They often bark instinctively, especially if startled. Using a shock to stop this natural behavior, while convenient for kennel owners, is cruel to dogs. I've had people tell me that they use shock collars all the time and never see adverse effects. My response is that just because they don't "see" side effects doesn't mean that they aren't there. Often the fallout from using a shock collar is a subtle, generalized anxiety that is overlooked or misinterpreted by the owner as poor temperament, shyness, obsessive-compulsive behaviors, or aggression.

In my 30 years as a pet dog trainer and behaviorist, I've worked with dozens of dogs who had shock collars used for barking or training. I can't recall a single dog who did not have some type of fallout from the use of a shock collar. –Kay

# Chapter 9
## Dogs Don't Speak English:
## How to Add a Verbal Cue

---

During the training section of this book, you'll teach your dog actions or behaviors, such as lie down, flank right, flank left or walk up. After your dog can successfully perform these actions in a reliable manner, you'll link the action or behavior with a verbal or whistle cue, commonly called a command.

### Adding a cue

When training, start by shaping the action or behavior. Without using verbal cues, get your dog to perform the behavior. For example, use your body positioning to make the dog flank, or walk with the dog to get a "walk up" or "drive," or step toward your dog to get a "steady" or "take time." First, get an approximation of the behavior. Then, refine the behavior until it looks like the final product you want. Finally, practice the behavior so it is 80 percent correct on multiple sessions. *Only after getting the behavior correct 80 percent of the time do you add the cue (verbal or whistle) for the action.*

### Why should you teach the behavior first and then the cue?

Once you add the cue, the dog associates the word or whistle with the action he is currently doing, whether the action is correct or not. For example, when a dog learns his flanks (circle to the left or circle to the right), he often must be taught the correct shape. A dog who is just learning may be flanking too tight or close to the sheep or slicing or cutting in toward the sheep. If a cue is added at this point, the dog will associate that word, such as "come-bye," with a tight or sliced flank. By waiting to add the cue until the action is correct, the dog associates the cue with the correct action, not the incorrect one.

### The sequence

When adding a cue, the sequence is as follows:

1. Verbal (or whistle) cue.
2. Pause (count to two).
3. Physical prompt for the behavior that the dog already knows.

**The cue predicts the physical prompt**. The verbal or whistle cue must be clear, obvious and occur *before* the physical prompt. If you give the cue at the same time as the physical prompt, the dog is likely to notice only the physical prompt and to think the verbal cue is background noise. Plan on giving the cue, and then the physical prompt, dozens of times. Eventually the dog will realize the cue predicts the old physical prompt for the behavior and start offering the behavior on just the cue. Once he responds consistently to the verbal cue, the dog "knows" the cue.

**Note:** Because it's very easy to develop the habit of giving the physical prompt and cue at the same time, the trainer must focus on the sequence of giving the cue, then the prompt. Taking the effort to make sure the cue predicts the physical prompt will help your dog learn more quickly and with less confusion. Since we use the physical prompt first, and the dog has been reinforced for responding to it, the dog is likely to focus on it. It's easy for the physical prompt to overshadow the new verbal cue. That's why we put a lot of effort into teaching the verbal cue cleanly and after we have the behavior we want.

**If you give the verbal cue and your dog does the correct behavior, allow him to continue to work.** This is his reward for doing the correct behavior. If appropriate for the dog and the situation, also give a little verbal praise. You can also reward the dog by stepping away to release pressure, or if teaching flank cues, making a shh-shh noise to speed up the dog.

**If, after a few dozen repetitions of the verbal cue, count to two and physical prompt sequence, your dog is not doing the correct behavior after the verbal cue, then give a mild ccorrection such as slapping your hat against your leg, after the verbal cue and pause.** At this point, you don't want to be harsh. Instead, you want to give the dog information (oops, that was wrong). Remember: dogs don't speak English. Repeating the cue or making the cue louder doesn't teach the dog what the cue means. Only pairing the cue with the desired action will do that.

**If you give a cue, pause, and then the dog makes a mistake, then stop the dog.** Pause, reposition and give the cue and pause sequence again. Depending on the dog and the situation, you might add a mild verbal correction or slap a hat or feed bag against your leg as the dog gives the wrong behavior.

**The goal is for the cue to result in the correct behavior every time.** If it does not, then you are making the cue weaker and even possibly turning that cue into an aversive.

### After several repetitions, shouldn't my dog know it?

It's very common for people to get frustrated with their dogs when they don't respond correctly to a new cue. Sometimes, a handler may say, "My dog *knows* this," or "my dog is blowing me off" or "my dog is being hardheaded."

**There is no way to know what your dog is thinking.** You only know what he's doing. Theorizing about why the dog is not performing the cue is a waste of time because you can't know for sure. Instead, accept what you see: the dog is not performing the correct action as a response to the cue. It's most likely because he is confused, overexcited or lacks training. The solution is to go back and set the dog up for success again. Remember, dogs communicate primarily through body language, so discriminating between different spoken words is not a natural behavior for them. It helps your dog if you pronounce the verbal cue the same way each time. It also seems that whistles are easier for the dog to learn to differentiate, perhaps because they are clearer and more discrete than spoken words.

**A note about keen dogs:** sometimes people call very keen dogs hardheaded. Often, these dogs are just so excited or focused on the sheep, they have trouble concentrating on anything else. It may take a little more effort by the trainer to make sure the dog keeps the trainer as part of his mental picture.

*Keen dogs, like the one above, are often so focused on sheep that they have trouble also paying attention to the handler. Photo courtesy of Carol Clawson.*

## Does your dog take his cue 80 percent of the time? Proof the cue

Once the dog learns the cue, you have to keep using it. Good responses to cues are the result of many repetitions, lots of practice and keeping the consequence of the behavior in place (the reward or correction). If you don't respond to the dog's mistakes, they will become habits. For instance, it's common at sheepdog competitions to hear a handler say "Lie down" again and again, and the dog does not lie down. Most likely, in training, the handler did not stop and correct the dog every single time he didn't take that cue. The dog learned that taking the cue was optional.

> ### The three 'D's' of generalizing a behavior
>
> When training the herding dog, you will teach an action and then, once the dog learns it, work on the three D's: distance, duration and distractions (or difficulty). Distance is how far away you are from the dog when he performs the behavior; duration is how long you ask the dog to perform the behavior without extra cues; and distractions/difficulty is the environment and situation in which you are asking the dog to perform.
>
> It's best to take an incremental approach and work on each "D" separately. Work on duration of a behavior first. Once that's well established, add some level of difficulty or distractions. Add the distance factor last, after the action is pretty well trained, because at a distance, it is much harder to help the dog or add a correction if needed. It's best to have the dog pretty solid on his training at hand before adding distance. If you increase more than one "D" at a time, you are lumping the pieces of the behavior together and increasing the chances of errors in the dog's action.

To proof the cue, gradually start giving the cue in more difficult situations. Work on the three D's, distance, durations and distractions, separately. For example, if you are teaching the "away-to-me" cue, the dog must learn that "away-to-me" means go right, even if the sheep are running in a different direction or even if it's near a fence or a person is standing nearby. Good trainers will continue proofing cues for the life of the dog. Remember what to do if your dog doesn't take the cue in a challenging situation. Stop the dog, set it up again, give the cue, pause and then give a physical prompt. The cue should be information to the dog that tells him what you want him to do. It should not be a correction.

When switching dogs from verbal cues to whistle cues, you'll use the same process. First, give the whistle cue, then pause and either give the verbal cue (if it is well trained) or give a physical prompt by your body positioning. After several repetitions, the dog will realize the whistle predicts the verbal cue and start working off the whistle alone.

### A Shepherd's Journey

When I competed in obedience, a common saying was, "A 'sit, sit' is a no, no." That means repeating the cue only teaches the dog to wait for you to give the cue again or to say it louder. Do not fall into the bad habit of chanting the cue over and over again. If the dog misses a cue, either prompt or correct him, but do not nag him. –Kay

# Chapter 10
# Developing Good Training Skills

Good training skills are more important than the training method used. A trainer with excellent training skills can make a bad method work, at least some of the time. A trainer with poor skills can't make even the best methods work. Most of these skills are habits that can be learned, practiced and perfected. Developing these skills will make you a better trainer. Here are the top 20 skills that lead to great dog training.

**1. Always have a plan for each training session.** What are you going to train? Where are you going to train? How are you going to train? More details about planning a training session are included chapter 11.

**2. Have your training plan clear in your head.** Always know what you will start the session with, what each step in the training process will be, how you will know whether the dog is ready to progress and what the final behavior should look like. Have a clear mental picture of what you want. Make it as detailed and be as precise as possible.

**3. Set your training session up for success.** Training depends on the dog performing the action correctly and repetitively—and of the dog developing a mental and physical habit, or muscle memory, of the correct action. Allowing the dog to be wrong will only teach him to perform incorrectly. Don't let your dog practice mistakes. The best way to do this is to set up the training environment to help the dog make the right choices. Later, after the dog has learned the behavior, you may want to "proof" the dog's learning by making the environment more challenging. During the teaching phase, though, always set up the dog for success.

**4. An ideal training session is like a good story.** It's interesting for the learner; it has a beginning, middle and end; and it leaves the learner wanting more.

**5. The first few minutes of the training session are the most informative.** What the dog does when he first goes to stock will tell you where his training level really is. Once he's warmed up and has worked a few minutes, he's more likely to be correct. When judging your dog's progress, look at what the dog does when he's fresh. The first few minutes are also when the dog's mind is most ready to learn, so plan to work on new or difficult exercises early in the session.

**6. Know your dog.** Every dog has a different temperament, inherent ability and history. The final goals for each dog may be the same, but the path to get there will be determined by what works for each dog you train. Good trainers are flexible in their methods but firm in their goals.

**7. Watch your dog.** You must keep your complete focus on the dog (and sheep) while training so that you can quickly notice and react to any change in the dog's actions and to changes in his body language. Good training depends on the trainer giving the dog feedback constantly and quickly. You can't train what you don't see! You must stay focused on the dog in order to train him.

**8. Timing is everything!** A good trainer who is closely watching the dog can tell what the dog is going to do even before it happens. That gives the trainer the opportunity to react as the dog starts the unwanted behavior and interrupt the behavior. You must see and react to what the dog is doing within a maximum of 1 second of the dog's action in order for the dog to effectively understand and respond to your reaction. A slow or late reaction by the trainer makes it impossible for the dog to learn.

### A Shepherd's Journey

I learned timing by training chickens. In the mid-1990's I was lucky enough to do a series of animal training seminars with the founders of modern animal training, Marian and Bob Bailey. In those seminars, we learned to train chickens to do a variety of complex behaviors. We had to become skilled with the chicken training before we were allowed to work with the dolphins. Chicken training requires exceptional observational and timing skills because they are small, very fast and change behaviors very quickly. Training a chicken also tends to remove the thoughts we often ascribe to dogs (such as saying he's being stubborn, stupid or hard-headed). Among other things, we had to teach a chicken to peck a dot in the middle of a bar. This was the first step taken to teach the chicken to roll the bar through a tunnel in a straight line. Anticipating where the chicken was going to peck and rewarding only pecks closer to the center of the bar was quite a challenge. –Kay

**9. Be consistent.** It's unfair and confusing to the dog if you insist on the correct behavior sometimes but not others.

**10. Give the dog a lot of information.** If you watch great trainers, they are constantly communicating with their dogs through body positioning, movement and voice. The more information you give your dog, the faster he can learn. This does not mean chattering away for no reason, but rather giving your dog timely and meaningful feedback.

**11. Don't just stand there.** Do something. If you aren't moving, you aren't training; you are watching. You can move away to give the dog his sheep as a reward or follow up a command or verbal correction with a change in your body position if the dog doesn't respond. Remember, if you control the consequence, you control the dog.

**12. Pay attention to what the dog is actually doing.** Don't try to guess what the dog is thinking.

**13. Stay calm and analytical.** Good trainers don't get angry or emotional when training. If you lose control over yourself, you lose control over your dog.

**14. Train each part of a behavior separately.** Break each training item into small pieces and teach each piece before combining them. For example, if teaching a flank, teach the shape of the flank, the speed of the flank, the direction of the flank, and the cue for the flank in separate steps. After the dog has mastered the behavior, then teach the three D's, distance (from the dog), duration (how long the dog has to perform) and difficulty/distractions, in separate steps.

**15. Train in small steps or with "just noticeable differences."** In other words, the difficulty or complexity of the training increases in such small increments that the animal barely notices the change. This has some big advantages. Small increases mean less chance for the dog to be wrong and make a mistake. It's faster to train in small steps because there is less chance of leaving a hole or skipping steps in the training. It's more time consuming to go back and fill in a training hole than to get it right the first time.

**16. Know when to progress, when to continue at the same level and when to drop down and make things easier for the dog.** If the dog is correct 80 percent of the time or more, he's ready to move on to the next step. If he's only correct about 50 percent of the time, he isn't ready to progress and needs more practice at that level. If the dog is correct less than 50 percent of the time, chances are he's confused, and you will gain more by dropping back a step in your training program and helping the dog.

**17. Three mistakes and you'd better fix it!** If the dog makes the same mistake three times in a row, you've failed to teach the dog what you want. You need to drop back a step in your training and fix that mistake before it becomes a habit. Or, you need to change what you are doing and help the dog make it right. Practicing a mistake only makes the mistake more likely to continue.

**18. Keep notes on your training sessions.** This prevents you from forgetting or skipping steps in your training. It lets you know whether the dog is progressing at a normal rate of learning or not.

**19. Analyze yourself constantly.** Be self-critical. If possible, video your training sessions or have an experienced trainer watch you. Pay attention to your timing, your consistency, and your body position and language. We all fall into bad habits if we don't constantly evaluate our performance.

**20. Keep learning and stay open to new ideas and information.** You will never learn all there is to know about training herding dogs. Keep an open mind and always look for new ways to train and enjoy the journey.

## Tag yourself as you train

Targeted Acoustical Guidance (TAG) is a useful method for teaching humans. Here's what it involves. When a desired action occurs, it's marked with a sound, such as a click, that tells the person when they are correct.

While you can't really click yourself, you can use the WOOF approach to help you stay focused on what you want you or your dog to do correctly in that training session. WOOF stands for What do you want you or your dog to do, an Observable action, and One action that you can describe in Five words or less. For example, for the dog, tell yourself that you will focus on the dog stopping on the first cue. For yourself, you might focus on "walking quickly when driving." Using these specific, clear reminders can help your training stay on track.

# Chapter 11
## Good Trainers are Good Planners

The second part of this book includes detailed training plans for teaching the herding dog to perform balance work, outruns, lifts, fetches, driving, shedding and penning. However, it's impossible to include every scenario you'll encounter on your herding journey. To successfully train your herding dog, you'll need to learn how to develop and set up training sessions.

## The overall plan: it starts with a picture

Before developing a training plan, have a clear, detailed picture of the final product. For example, if you want to teach your dog to shed, or separate one or more sheep from the group, have a clear image of what the finished product should look like. Start by watching videos of top handlers shedding and write down all the details of the shed. Does it happen quickly or slowly? What is the dog's body language when he comes between the sheep? What is the handler doing? What is the dog doing? Does the dog come between the sheep in a straight line to the handler or does he turn toward the sheep? Does the dog hold the sheep apart or does he chase the shed group away? The more detailed picture of the finished product that you have, the more detailed training plan you can make.

## Break your plan into parts

Once you know what the final picture should look like, break it into small, discrete steps. Be as detailed as possible about what each step should look like.

**What is it that you are going to work on?** What is the most important part of the behavior or action? Start by teaching that. For example, if you want to teach your dog to drive, or push the sheep away from you, the most important part is the dog confidently and quietly moving the sheep away. Teaching the dog to push to the left or the right, or in a perfectly straight line, are things you will teach later. Be sure to break what you are teaching into the smallest parts possible that you can easily observe. For example, plan to have the dog take five steps while you walk next to him in the beginning of driving. Then increase it to 10 steps, then 20 steps and so on.

**Next, ask yourself, "How can I set this up so the dog can learn to do it with the least amount of stress or struggle?"** Your goal is for the dog to do the basic part of the action with the least amount of confusion. In this example of driving, you might start with having sheep that are amenable to driving, having the dog drag a long line for control, or using a fence line to help cover the pressure while the dog learns the behavior.

**Where are you going to train?** Set the stage for success by having the right stock and the right pen or pasture available. Make sure the training area is as free of distractions as possible. Noises, smells and visual stimulations can confuse and distract the dog (and the trainer).

**When are you going to train?** Try to avoid doing beginning training in difficult circumstances such as extremely hot temperatures, high winds or heavy rain. Give yourself and the dog the opportunity to focus on the training process in the beginning. Don't train if you are upset or in a bad mood. It's better to skip a training session than to have to go back and fix something you did wrong because you did a poor job of training it.

**How often and how long should you train?** It's important to spend some time with your dog every day. Serious training sessions are only needed four or five times a week. Young dogs often benefit from a break of a day or two between sessions. In fact, research indicates that dogs learn more quickly when trained every other day or so. For most young dogs a training session should not need to be more than 20 minutes. Longer sessions are fine for older dogs, and they can help build mental toughness and stamina. Remember the first few minutes of a session are the most valuable in evaluating the dog's progress.

## Set your dog up for success and repeat

Dogs learn by many successful repetitions of the correct behavior. Once you've picked the most important part of the behavior, think of a way to get the dog to do that action or behavior. If teaching flanks, you could use your body position to help create the correct shape or path the dog takes. If you can get your dog to perform the correct behavior the first time and to repeat it, he is going to learn faster.

Dogs are like people and remember the way they first learned a behavior. Under stress, they usually revert back to the way they first learned it *even if you've changed the behavior since then.* That's why you shouldn't let puppies play with and chase sheep. It's also why it's so important the dog performs the behavior correctly the very first time. When lesson planning, think about how you can set your dog up for success, and then plan to perform it dozens of times. If the dog repeats the correct behavior 50 or more times, that muscle memory and behavior pattern is well started.

### Don't practice failure

One of the hardest—and most important—skills to learn is to stop when a dog makes a mistake. You don't want the dog to develop a motor pattern of doing an incorrect behavior, such as slicing a flank. When training, if the dog does something wrong, stop.

Stopping the dog's motion and body stops his thought process as well. When stopping the dog, you interrupt the unwanted behavior, reset the situation and help the dog be correct. Next, evaluate what happened and what you should do next. Your goal is to set up the situation so the dog is correct. Remember: if things are going wrong, stop and evaluate.

## The daily training plan: write down the details

Before going to the pasture to train your dog, plan your daily session. A daily training log is included in the back section of this book. You can use it for your lessons.

As discussed earlier, start with a detailed, overall final picture of what you'd like to teach. Next, break it into small steps. For your daily training session, focus on one of those steps. Set up the lesson so the dog is most likely to do the action correctly the first time, and then repeat it successfully. To plan your lesson, then, start with your goal, and then set up your beginning, middle and end.

**The Beginning:** Start each training session with something easy that the dog already knows; this gets the dog in the right frame of mind. After the dog has learned the outrun, lift and fetch, also called the gather, many trainers will start the training session with a simple gather and a little balance work. Doing this also gives you a chance to evaluate the sheep and determine whetnher they are appropriate for the lesson you want to teach that day.

**The First Few Minutes:** Dogs (and people) are often freshest and are the most open to learning during the first few minutes of the training session. So, after the dog has done his warm-up (often the gather), focus on the main actions you want to teach. Don't wait until the dog is tired or hot to start teaching new material.

**The Middle:** The main part of your training session should be the new material you want your dog to learn. Plan for many correct repetitions. The length will depend on the dog, the weather and other factors. Younger dogs or dogs just beginning herding training may not have the attention span that a more experienced dog does. Remember, you want to stop while the dog is still eager to learn. Pay attention to the dog and how he responds to what you are doing. He should show small improvements quickly. If he isn't, stop and evaluate. Don't practice failure.

**The End:** Finish the training session with something the dog likes to do. This helps keep the dog fresh and eager to learn. If you can't do that, at least stop before the dog starts making mistakes or is mentally exhausted.

### The setup and equipment

Before starting the training session, think about the sheep and the equipment you'll need. Are you going to train in a large field or a small pen? What number and type of sheep are ideal for that situation? Are you going to need a long line or a rolled-up feed sack (used for slapping on your leg to startle your dog)? How can you set up the lesson so the dog does the exercise right the first time? Because you want to teach your dog during those first few minutes of training, have your equipment and sheep in place before you start working your dog.

### Don't use your dog to set up the lesson

Because you want to train your dog during those first few minutes of a training session, do not use the dog you're training to set up your lesson. If at all possible, use another dog—or, though it may take longer, set up the sheep and training situation without using a dog.

### Evaluate your daily session

After you've completed your training session, jot down the behaviors you worked on, the number of repetitions and the percentage of correct responses. Note the distances, durations or distractions for each behavior, as well as the corrections or rewards used. Also evaluate your handling skills, what went well and what needs improvement. Then, make plans for the next session.

# Daily Training Log

**Dog:** *Rocky*

**Plan/Goals for Today's Training:** *Improve momentum on the drive*

**Date:** 8/3/21

**First 2 Minutes Plan:** *Quick balance work, then walk with him driving*

**Time of Day / Weather / Length of Session:** *Morning / 75 degrees / 20 minutes*

**Equipment Used:** *Drag long line*

**Location /Stock:** *Long pasture away from barn, 10-head of quiet sheep*

**Behaviors worked on / Number of Repetitions / Percentage of Correct Responses:**

**1.** *Started with balance—good*

**2.** *Walk with dog on drive—focused on keeping moving. Had to encourage him by patting my leg. Able to get 50 ft. of solid driving.*

**Comments:** *Getting better. Need more speed.*

**Distance / Duration/ Distractions for Each Behavior:**
*Able to drive about 50 ft. while walking with him.*

**Corrections Used / Rewards Used / Effectiveness:**
*Clucking and patting my leg for momentum*

**Handler skills / focus / timing / consistency / clear commands / corrections/what I did well / what I need to improve on:**
*I need to walk faster myself and not hesitate*

**What is going well:**
*Driving getting better*

**Need solutions for:**
*Sheep sometimes break away*

**Plan / Changes / Ideas for Next Training Session:**
*Try using a different set of sheep next time*

# Chapter 12
## Is It You or the Dog?
## 10 Common Training Mistakes

When training, you'll run into roadblocks. Sometimes the problem is the dog. Usually it's the handler. If you're stuck in your training, ask yourself if any of these errors belong to you.

**1. Are you staying focused?** Do you find yourself talking to someone nearby, talking on your cell phone or watching birds? Are you watching your dog all the time? Sometimes a person watches her dog for a few minutes, then zones out and completely misses what the dog is doing. You can't train what you don't see. Focus is essential.

**2. Are you giving the dog enough information to learn?** Is your dog working stock but receiving no direction as to what he is doing, right or wrong? Do you hope your dog does the right thing, but often find yourself unprepared to tell the dog one way or the other? Are you just a bystander, hoping things work out? Ideally you should be correctly applying pressure when the dog is wrong and releasing pressure when the dog is working correctly. The more feedback you give your dog, the faster the dog can learn. Don't leave the dog in the dark wondering. A good handler doesn't just stand there, she does something.

**3. Is your timing quick enough to give the dog the correct information?** Dogs learn by association. Chasing the dog and yelling at him minutes after he's bitten a sheep or sliced a flank may scare or upset the dog, but it doesn't teach him to connect his behavior with your correction. The dog may look scared or sorry or guilty, but he has no clue as to what to do the next time. Timing is everything. You must stop, reward or correct the dog *just as he* performs the behavior, or within 1 second, to be effective. (The training chapters explain how to do this when the dog is at a distance from you.)

**4. Are you upsetting your dog or yourself by being too emotional?** The trainer's job is to help the dog learn the right way to work and to prevent or correct the dog when he is wrong. A good trainer is calm, clear, confident and consistent. If the dog is wrong, it's up to you to calmly and logically fix the problem. Getting upset or angry does not teach the dog anything.

**5. Are you keeping a clear picture of the final product and the steps leading up to it in your head?** If you aren't sure what the dog should be doing, then the dog will never know. This is a common problem with novice handlers because they often don't know what the correct behavior looks like. If you don't have a clear picture of what the correct behavior is, then watch videos or get help from a more experienced handler. Have a stepwise training plan and follow it. Are you consistent in your expectations? When you ask the dog to lie down, do you follow through and make sure he does? Or do you let things "slide" until it's a problem? Know what you want and make sure you follow up and get what you want.

**6. Are you failing to "set the stage" so you and the dog can succeed?** Do you put the dog in a situation that's much too difficult for his age or level of training? If you do, then you're allowing the dog to fail. When the dog fails, he learns bad habits or that he can't control the stock, or he loses confidence. If your dog isn't ready yet for a particular stage of training, wait on Mother Nature and give him some time to mature physically and mentally. Often waiting a few weeks or months can dramatically change a dog's response to training.

**7. Are you trying to teach too many things at one time?** You should teach one step of a behavior at a time and make sure each step is correct before moving on. Make each step a small, achievable progression from the last step. Your training will actually progress much faster this way than if you try taking big jumps ahead. By taking small steps, you won't have to backtrack and fix problems.

**8. Are you confusing the dog with mindless chatter?** Dogs don't speak English. If you want them to respond to your cues, you must make sure the cues are salient and relevant. That means if you give a cue, follow up to make sure the dog responds. Endlessly commanding and talking without following up teaches the dogs that your cues are meaningless. Say what you mean and mean what you say.

**9. Are you mistaking stress (like eating sheep poop, working slowly or mindlessly diving into the sheep) for disobedience?** People often misinterpret a dog showing fear, stress or avoidance as being stubborn or stupid or blowing them off. Learn to read dog body language.

**10. Are you guilty of anthropomorphism?** When someone says the dog is "cheating on me, or hardheaded, or doesn't respect me," she is applying human values, thought processes and mind reading to a species that does not think or behave as humans. Better to evaluate what you actually see. Occam's razor applies: the simplest explanation is the most likely. *If the dog isn't doing what you want, it's probably because you didn't train him.*

For a flow sheet on solving a training issue, see Appendix C.

---

### A Shepherd's Journey

I was helping a woman with her young dog when he started diving in and chasing sheep. She yelled his name, and kept yelling his name, getting louder and louder. I noticed that every time she yelled his name, he would look at her but continued chasing the sheep.

After a moment, I said, "Why don't you tell him what you want him to do?"

The next time he dove in and started chasing sheep, she yelled, "Lie down." The dog immediately stopped and lay down.

Just screaming the dog's name isn't a command, and you don't want the dog's name to be the correction either. For me, the dog's name just means, "pay attention to me." If you want your dog to do something besides just pay attention to you, you have to tell him what you want. –Kay

# Chapter 13
## How to Evaluate Training
## Methods and Herding Clinics

There are as many different ways of teaching a dog as there are dogs. When you go to herding clinics and trials, you will see and hear a wide range of opinions on how to train something or how to fix a problem. Sometimes you will receive suggestions that contradict each other; sometimes a clinician or trainer may tell you her method is the best or only way to teach or fix something. It can be overwhelming and confusing.

## Evaluating a training method

First, keep in mind there are many good ways to teach something. Likewise, there are many bad ways to teach something. Learning how to evaluate a training method or idea can help you decide if a suggested method is worth trying. These 10 steps will help you evaluate a training method.

**1. Evaluate the source.** Has this person offering advice trained a number of dogs to a high level of performance? Do you like the way this person's dogs work? Does the person have a good relationship with her dogs? If a clinician, does this person have students who are successful and progressing? Truly good teachers enjoy seeing their students do well and even beat them at herding trials.

**2. Does the method make logical sense?** If the person giving advice can't clearly explain what she is suggesting, then take a step back and think about it. Training should be a clear logical progression that provides a consistent framework for training each dog. If the trainer or clinician can't present it that way, she is probably lumping too many steps together—and that will confuse you and the dog.   Alternatively, a poor teacher may not have a clear idea of how and when to help you and your dog progress. If you are doing the same exercise lesson after lesson without much change, it is a sign your teacher is unable or unwilling to help you reach the next step.

**3. If someone says, "I don't know why this works," be very cautious.** A good teacher should have a least a minimal understanding of how animals learn and why her method works. Avoid trainers who use a lot of vague, non-scientific or emotionally loaded terms to describe the dog or the training method. Applying words like hardheaded, stupid, stubborn, bossy, weak or lazy to dogs or energy, aura or dominant to people are warning signs that the teacher may not have a good understanding of how animals and people learn.

**4. Does the method set the dog and handler up to succeed?** The method should break the final product into smaller pieces. It should show the dog the right way to do something before adding a correction. If the clinician advises to just "give a harder correction," training steps are likely missing. Dogs do not make mistakes on purpose, especially if they are being corrected for them. If the dog continues to make mistakes, it's an indication that either the correction is poorly timed or applied, or that the dog does not really understand what you want and how to avoid the correction. Teach him instead of correcting him.

**5. Does this method make you or your dog stressed out?** All learning is stressful. But training done properly in small steps should not cause the dog to leave the field or you to feel overwhelmed. Yes, sometimes a handler must really "get in the dog's face" if the dog is abusing the sheep or completely ignoring her cues. But this type of situation usually means some basic training or relationship work was skipped, and the handler needs to go back and address it. Good trainers follow the concept of using the least aversive technique that gives results.

**6. Does the training method show small, steady improvements almost immediately?** If someone tells you it takes a year to train something, then reconsider the method. Sure, it might take a year to get to the final product but some improvement steps toward that goal should be quickly apparent.

**7. If the dog leaves the field or quits working, reconsider the approach.** Typically, dogs quit when:

- They are asked to learn too many variables at one time (lumping of criteria).

- They are corrected too harshly for their temperament or the infraction.

- They have not been taught the correct behavior so that they can avoid a correction.

- They have been given "non contingent" punishment, meaning the correction was so poorly timed, the dog doesn't know what action caused the punishment.

- The trainer did not release the pressure when the dog responded to the correction.

While some dogs have a more sensitive temperament than others, a good training method should allow for variations in temperament. *If someone suggests you keep correcting your dog without first teaching the dog the correct way to perform and that your dog should "figure it out," that is not a training method. That is just punishing the dog and hoping the dog eventually guesses what he should do. Such an approach results in a lot of dogs failing the program.*

**8. Is the teacher willing to share the entire training progression with you?** If someone tells you that she won't tell you the next step in the teaching process, it is a red flag that she may not know what it is.

**9. Avoid any and all trainers who recommend the use of a shock collar.** The risk of serious damage to your dog's temperament is not worth the benefit, if any, that a shock collar might give.

**10. Is your teacher a student?** Sheepdog training is one of those endeavors where "the more you know, the more you know you don't know." Someone who is truly a student of the craft will always continue to study other handlers and dogs, seeking new insights and new ways of thinking about problems. *A good teacher knows there is always more to learn.* Sheepdog training is a lifelong pursuit and no one knows it all. A good teacher is also willing to admit mistakes, or say, "Let's try a different approach for this dog." You will also hear good teachers crediting their mentors.

## How to get the most out of a herding clinic

Herding clinics can be a great opportunity to advance your training skills as well as your dog's skills. As in a personal lesson, the handler will work with the clinician one-on-one. Unlike in a lesson, though, other handlers will be observing each lesson and learning from it. To get the most out of a clinic, follow these steps:

**1. Find a clinician who has trained multiple dogs to be successful at the open level of USBCHA trials.** Someone without that experience is unlikely to know all of the many details that go into producing and running a top-working open dog.

**2. Find someone who is willing to share their knowledge and ideas with clinic goers in a frank and open fashion.**

**3. Find someone who enjoys working with dogs and who enjoys teaching people.** The person should be kind and patient with dogs and humans alike. There are enough good clinicians out there that you shouldn't accept verbal abuse or humiliation from anyone.

**4. Be honest with the clinician.** Be open about what problems you are having and what you have done to address them. Be honest about how long the problem has been present and describe the problem in clear, concise terms. Don't spend a lot of time trying to come up with reasons why the problem exists, just explain *what* the problem is.

## A Shepherd's Journey

I've attended many training clinics over the years, but one of the most memorable ones was with Faansie Basson, a nationally recognized clinician and sheepdog hander. I had recently acquired an 8-year-old, fully trained Border Collie who had competed in and won open trials. I, though, was fairly new to open level competitions. During the clinic, Faansie stood with me at the handler's post and explained what I should be doing, looking for and anticipating during each section of the course. Then, he had me explain it to the other clinic participants. I am not sure how many times we practiced turning the post that weekend, but I came home from the clinic with a clear picture of what I needed to work on and a better understanding of my role in the herding partnership. My expectations, my handling skills, and my scores all went up after that clinic. —Beth

**5. Go to the clinic with the intent to learn something.** Going to a clinic with the intent to learn something is a very vulnerable thing to do. It requires admitting there is an issue you need help with; it requires you standing up in front of other people while addressing the problem. It can be very intimidating and stressful. Many people don't have the courage to put themselves in a position to make a mistake or to try something new. Some people go to clinics with the intent to visit with people; some go in hopes of showing off their dog or themselves; some go and spend most of their time telling the clinician their opinion about dogs or dog training. If you are going for these reasons, realize that you will not learn as much as if you go with the intent to learn.

**6. Take notes and pay close attention to what the clinician says and even closer attention to what she *does*.** For example, note where she is standing and moving, what she is saying and what she is doing while working with a dog. Some clinicians do things so naturally that they aren't aware of doing them and may not think to tell people what they are doing. If you observe closely, you will often see small changes in position or situation that make a big difference in the dog's reaction, even if the clinician does not mention it.

**7. Watch all the participants in the clinic, not just your dog.** You will find that watching other people and their dogs will often teach you more than your own lesson. It is easier to see someone else's mistakes than your own. Also, someone may be working on an issue that you will deal with later in your dog's training.

**8. Take a notebook and write down what the clinician says.** When you get home, review your notes. You will find it is easy to forget what happened at a clinic if you do not study what was covered.

**9. When you apply what you learned at the clinic, remember that in familiar surroundings with the same sheep and the same setup, it is easy for you and your dog to fall back into old habits.** It requires special effort and attention (and possibly a change of sheep or environment) to maintain your new skills and your dog's. Also, remember it requires many, many repetitions of a new or changed behavior to make it a habit for you and the dog. Just trying what the clinician told you to do a few times will not make a change that will last. Plan on at least 50 successful repetitions of the new skill to make a lasting change in your or your dog's behavior.

Also remember that at clinics, it is often impressive to see a skilled clinician make a big change in a dog quickly and easily. Remember that the dog has no reinforcement history with the clinician and may be a little afraid or surprised when a new person applies a confident and quick correction. The dog may show a rapid change in behavior as a result. When you try it at home, you may find you need to make bigger moves or progress more slowly to get the same changes.

**10. Be careful about going to many different clinicians and changing your training methods after every clinic.** While it is great to go to a variety of clinicians and see different methods, it is often confusing for your dog when you keep switching methods. It's a good idea to stick with a method you are comfortable with until you have completed the basics on that dog.

# Part 2

It's All About the Sheep

# Chapter 14
## Basic Sheep Information

Those getting into sheepdog herding come from various backgrounds. Some have sheep and want a dog to help them out; some have experience with horses or other livestock; some have dog experience but no livestock experience. This chapter focuses on basic sheep information, care and sheep breeds as well as general farm etiquette.

*A ewe tends to her lambs. Photo courtesy of Carol Clawson.*

### Sheep and humans share a long history

Sheep were domesticated about 10,000 years ago, after dogs but before many other animals. Today, most sheep are raised for their wool and meat. Some are raised for vegetation control. Some are kept for milk. Some are kept as pets.

While the weight of sheep will vary, depending on their age, breed and diet, a mature sheep generally weighs 150 to 300 pounds. That's large enough to seriously injure or, in rare cases, even kill a human or a dog. Most sheep reach sexual maturity before their first year, and the gestation period for a ewe is about 5 months. Their average life span is 10–12 years.

**A Shepherd's Journey**

When I got into herding, I did not think of it as a dangerous sport. I think differently now.

I've been knocked down by sheep multiple times when working dogs. Once, I fell and broke my wrist. Once, an aggressive ram charged me and knocked me flat on my back. I know many people who have been hurt by sheep.

I've learned to be a lot more careful in choosing sheep for dog work. I never trust or turn my back on a ram, no matter how friendly people say he may be. I'm also careful around ewes with young lambs, as they can be very aggressive toward people and dogs. –Kay

## A few terms you should know

Below are some common words people use to describe sheep:

**Wool sheep**: Sheep that grow wool fibers and must be shorn annually. Some common wool breeds are Rambouillets, Merinos, Dorsets and Cheviots.

**Hair sheep**: Sheep that have hair fibers and shed naturally. They are raised primarily for meat. Common hair sheep breeds include Katahdins, Dorpers and Barbados.

**Lamb**: A male or female sheep younger than a year old.

**Ewe**: A female sheep.

**Ram**: An intact male sheep.

**Wether**: A castrated male sheep.

## What sheep eat

Sheep are herbivores, eating mostly grass, clover (or other legumes like alfalfa and vetch) and forbs, or broad-leafed plants. Sheep can be selective grazers, opting for legumes and forbs over grass. They'll also eat hay and grain. Sheep do not have upper incisors. Instead, they have a dental pad that enables them to gather a large amount of vegetation.

Sheep, like cattle, are ruminants and have specialized, four-chambered stomachs that break down plant-based food through fermentation. During grazing, primarily in the mornings and evenings, sheep take in large amounts of vegetation. After a few hours of grazing and usually in the heat of the day, they'll lie down and ruminate, regurgitating the food, also called the cud, and chewing it again. This grazing and rumination pattern is why sheep are often "heavier," or slower to move during the heat of the day.

While sheep can adjust to different diets, the change must be gradual, slowly over the course of a few weeks, to give the rumen microflora time to adapt. Because sheep require diets low in copper, they shouldn't be fed most horse and cattle feed, as this could cause copper toxicity. Sudden changes in a sheep's diet can cause death. Sheep are also susceptible to bloat, a condition caused when gases build up in the stomach and can't escape. This can happen when sheep move from dry forage, or hay, to a lush pasture with legumes. Bloat and overeating disease, a condition where clostridia bacteria cause acute sepsis, are two of the most common causes of death in otherwise healthy sheep. Sheep must also have water and should have minerals and salt available.

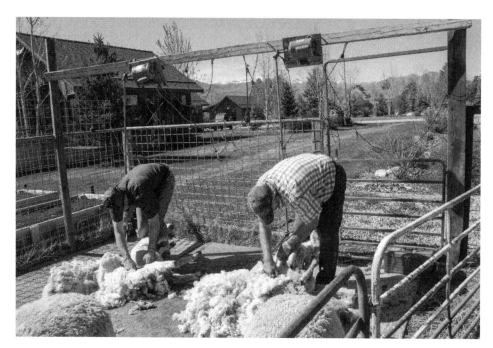

*Wool sheep should be shorn annually. Photo courtesy of Carol Clawson.*

## Caring for sheep

In addition to food and water, sheep need vaccinations, hoof trimming, protection from the weather and other care.

All adult sheep should receive vaccinations annually. Most veterinarians recommend the CDT vaccine for protection against *Clostridium perfringens* type C and D (overeating disease) and *Clostridium tetani* (tetanus). Other vaccinations may be recommended depending on where you live and your management system. Lambs, too, must be vaccinated. In addition to vaccinations, young lambs may need their tails docked (very common with wool breeds); male lambs are often castrated. If raising a wool breed, the sheep should be shorn annually.

Sheep have cloven hooves that usually require periodic trimming. The trimming schedule will depend on whether the sheep wear down their feet. Sheep that spend their time on softer pasture surfaces require more frequent trimming than those that wear down their hooves by walking on sandy, gravelly or rough surfaces.

Foot rot is a contagious disease that can cause lameness in sheep. Prevention is easier than treatment. Avoid buying sheep from an infected flock and quarantine all new animals for several weeks and check their hooves before introducing them to the flock.

Sheep are susceptible to and can die from parasitic infections. Parasites and parasite resistance to most deworming products are huge problems for sheep producers in the southern United States. This is a major factor for the decline of sheep production in some areas. Shepherds just can't keep the sheep alive. Shepherds try to keep parasitic infections under control through pasture management (rotational grazing). They monitor the sheep closely for parasites through fecal egg counts and checking for anemia by examining the eyelids for paleness, and only deworm the affected sheep. They also judiciously rotate deworming products and select stock that exhibit parasite resistance.

Sheep need protection from the weather. The type of shelter, or protection from the weather, varies throughout the country. For more detailed advice on your area, contact your state's Extension Service. In general, most sheep need shade during warm months. Sheep are not very heat tolerant and during warm afternoons, they'll seek out shade rather than graze. If hot from the weather or exercise, they'll pant like dogs. Like dogs, they do not sweat.

In colder climates, sheep need some type of windbreak or shelter, such as a barn or a three-sided shelter. If keeping sheep in a barn, they must have adequate ventilation. In the colder months, ewes giving birth to lambs and recently shorn sheep should have the protection of a barn.

In many parts of the country, predators, including coyotes, bobcats, stray dogs, birds of prey, wolves, bears and cougars, are a major cause of sheep deaths. Good fencing and a good livestock guardian dog, llama or donkey may be necessary to protect the sheep. Sheep in flocks that have been attacked by predators may become aggressive or very fearful of dogs, and thus become unworkable for herding training.

As a shepherd, you should check your flock daily. Look for sheep that may be limping or showing signs of sickness, such as not eating, looking depressed, exhibiting signs of diarrhea, acting lethargic, coughing or separating from the flock. You'll also want to check fences and the water trough. It's not uncommon to find feces or a dead bird in the water. In most cases, the shepherd vaccinates, trims and provides medical care for the flock. Quite often, the value of an individual sheep is less than the cost of a vet visit. So, you'll need to become savvy in a variety of medical and husbandry procedures yourself.

*Hair sheep, like these lambs and ewe, shed naturally and don't require shearing. Photo courtesy of Carol Clawson.*

## What breeds of sheep are common in the United States?

Dozens of different sheep breeds are raised in the United States. When selecting sheep, consider your climate—some sheep perform better in more arid climates while others do well in cooler, wetter areas. Also, consider your purpose for raising sheep. Many people who raise sheep for meat prefer the hair sheep breeds, such as Katahdins and Dorpers, because they require no shearing or tail docking. On the western rangelands, fine wool breeds like Rambouillets and Merinos are favored. Other common wool breeds include Hampshires, Suffolks, Cheviots, Dorsets and Southdowns. If raising sheep for fine wool or spinning, you might consider Merino or Icelandic sheep. Romanovs and Finn sheep are smaller breeds and tend to have multiple offspring.

When considering sheep for use in sheepdog training, remember that how sheep behave is influenced by their genetics and how they are managed. Katahdins and Cheviots are prone to be flightier than Dorpers and some other wool breeds. Western range sheep tend to flock very strongly and can be hard to shed or keep apart. Their survival depends on flocking from predators. Because they have been exposed to predators, range sheep may also be aggressive toward the dogs. Other breeds or Eastern farm flocks may be easier to shed or separate from the group, unless, of course, they've been shed so much they are wise to it and stick together like glue.

Southdowns are a heavy breed and don't move as well from the dog. For that reason, they aren't recommended for sheepdog training. Likewise, Suffolks are rarely used for sheepdog training because they don't flock well and tend to be aggressive to dogs. Usually white-faced wool breeds are preferred for sheepdog training.

---

### A Shepherd's Journey

When I first bought sheep for dog training, I knew nothing about sheep behavior. As a veterinarian, I had treated them, but never thought much about how they would respond to a dog. I found a newspaper ad for inexpensive Barbados lambs near me. I brought them home and discovered they ran like the wind if they saw a dog even 100 yards away. They would easily jump over my head if I tried to catch them. My little Sheltie could not even get close to them. I was advised to buy Southdowns because they were slow and gentle. More like small Sherman tanks, they stood solidly ignoring my poor dog. I called in an experienced sheepdog handler to help, but she and her experienced Border Collies failed to move them. She told me the Southdowns were harder to move than the cattle she normally trained her dogs on. I finally found some dog-broke Finn sheep that suited my needs. –Kay

---

Hair sheep and wool sheep respond to dogs differently. Hair sheep can see further behind them so respond more quickly to a dog flanking. Wool sheep often have wool on their heads that blocks them from seeing very far around to the side. Sometimes the wool on the sheep's head will block his forward vision as well. If extreme vision blockage occurs, a sheep is called wool-blind. Because of the wool on the sheep's face, the dog has to flank further around for the sheep to see and respond to him.

*Because of the wool on the sheep's face, the dog has to flank further around the sheep for a response. Photo courtesy of Carol Clawson.*

## Looking at the world through sheep eyes

Sheep, unlike dogs and humans, are **prey animals**. They are the hunted, not the hunters. As prey animals, they must be hyper-aware of their surroundings and potential danger. Like other prey animals, sheep's eyes are positioned on the side rather than the front of their heads. Their horizontal, rectangular pupils give them a great range of vision as they graze, and they can see most everywhere except directly behind them. In addition to their sight, sheep rely heavily on hearing and will react to loud, unusual and sudden noises.

As prey animals, a sheep's first reaction to danger is flight, or to run away. They then may flock and, as a group, turn and face the danger. As flock animals, sheep do what the others in the flock do. If one runs through a gate, then they all do. If one jumps a fence, they all do. *When they are running, do not stand in their way.* They could run over you. Handlers and dogs have both been seriously injured by running sheep. It is something to keep in mind as you embark on this journey and caution is advised. Remember that sheep panic easily and act as a group. To them, danger means run or fight.

*It's not uncommon for range sheep to charge a dog. Photo courtesy of Carol Clawson.*

There's another characteristic of flock animals that you need to know. Being removed from the group causes them to panic—and a panicked sheep will run into fences, people or dogs. Moving a single sheep is difficult and dangerous. If a sheep separates from the flock, move the flock to it rather than trying to move the single animal to the flock.

Remember that a scared sheep is a dangerous sheep. When working around sheep, pay attention to their body language. If a sheep has her head up, snorts, stomps, or stops and urinates, she is showing signs of fear or stress. When chased, extremely stressed or sick, a sheep may resort to "playing dead" and just lie down and refuse to move. When working sheep, watch their ears. Most sheep will cock their ears backward when a dog is behind them but hold their heads up. If you see a sheep with a lowered head and drooping ears, it's probably sick. A sick sheep may drop out of the flock or turn and charge the dog.

Weather also affects sheep. Sheep are spookier if it's windy, and they don't like to move in the rain. On hot, sunny days, they prefer to seek shade.

## Reading sheep body language

To successfully train and trial your dog, you must understand and "read" sheep. Sheep's response to people and dogs is based on their personal history with dogs and people, with their age, breed and sex, and with different weather conditions.

Start at the top: A sheep's head indicates where she is going to go. She will point her nose in the direction she is heading. If her body points one way and her head another, she is going where her head points. A sheep with its head held high is on alert, considering whether to run or fight.

A sheep's ears indicate where her attention is focused. If her ears are forward, she is focused ahead. If her ears are cocked backwards, she is focused behind her. A sheep with her head held low or her ears drooped may be sick. The lead sheep in a group is often the one holding her head higher than the other sheep. Pay attention to the lead sheep, as the others will follow her. The dog must firmly control the lead sheep to control where the group goes.

A sheep snorting indicates alarm. A sheep stomping its front foot is threatening to charge. A sheep will usually drop its head and face the dog before charging. A ewe stopping to urinate indicates stress.

Discharge from the sheep's eyes or nose often indicates a sick sheep. A sheep's tail, if undocked, can indicate the sheep's health. A healthy sheep has a tail that hangs loosely. A sick sheep's tail is often tucked or clamped. A sheep with an arched back or looking "humped up" is likely sick. A healthy sheep will have a full, round abdomen. A sheep with sunken flanks is sick, dehydrated or off feed. A sheep with a very full tight bulging flank may be bloating or overeating rich grass. Sheep stool should be dry, firm pellets. Manure on a sheep's rear end or loose stool indicates illness, parasites, or over feeding. A healthy sheep will have a tight full fleece or shiny hair coat. A fleece that is loose or patchy indicates disease or poor nutrition. Hair sheep with bald spots may have skin disease, poor nutrition or parasite problems.

Pay attention to any sheep standing with her head lowered while the rest of the flock is grazing or chewing their cuds. A sheep hanging back from the rest of the group as the dog moves the flock is usually weak or sick. Trying to push a weak sheep or sick sheep to keep up with the flock will often cause it to turn and fight or lie down and refuse to move. Sick or weak sheep must be handled slowly and gently. The dog must stay back and not stress these sheep.

## A few things to keep in mind when visiting sheep farms

Many people starting out in sheepdog herding do not own their own sheep and must go to farms to work their dogs. Some people may rent their sheep for herding dog training. Some may not charge. Regardless, if you'd like an invitation to come back, follow these etiquette tips.

**Respect the sheep.** Sheep farm owners have a lot of time and money invested in their flock. Most care about their sheep and don't want to see them bitten or chased. Sheep are living, sentient beings, not dog toys.

**Pay attention to your dog and keep him under control.** Many farms also have barn cats; some may have free-ranging chickens, dogs and other animals. Most farm owners don't take kindly to having their animals chased or attacked. Keep your dog in a crate or on a leash until told otherwise.

**Ask to enter pastures.** A livestock guardian dog or ram may be in with the flock. It's better to ask permission to enter pastures than risk a dog bite or being hit by a ram.

**Close gates.** If you open a gate, close it.

**Offer to help.** Keeping a farm and sheep is a lot of work. Moving hay, cleaning stalls, repairing fences and caring for animals are part of farm life. Working your dog on a sheep farm is a privilege, not a right.

**Practice biosecurity.** Sheep diseases, especially foot rot, can be carried from one farm to another. If you visit a farm where there have been diseases or foot rot, disinfect your shoes and clothing.

# Chapter 15
## Selecting Sheep for Dog Training

The sheep make sheepdog herding one of the most challenging dog sports. To succeed, you must understand sheep. The top sheepdog handlers aren't just good at working with dogs; they're good at working with sheep. They can quickly size up sheep and know how to move them—both with and without a dog.

*Dogs must learn to work wool sheep, like these Rambouillets, as well as hair sheep. Photo courtesy of Carol Clawson.*

### Think like a shepherd
Sheepdog trialing started when sheep farmers or shepherds got together to test their dogs' skills on sheep. The people competing at these early trials were shepherds first, and dog trainers second. Nowadays, many people come to sheepdog training and trialing through other dog sports, and they often have limited experience with handling livestock and sheep. With practice, you can learn to think like a shepherd.

The first rule of shepherding is *taking care of your sheep*. Unlike toys and agility equipment, sheep are living, sentient beings that eat, drink, and experience fear and pain. A good shepherd, or stockperson, looks out for the sheep's well-being. In addition to making sure they have food, water and shelter, the shepherd also handles them in the calmest, least disruptive way. Rough handling, stress and excessive running can lead to weight loss and injury in sheep—and as a good shepherd, you should try to avoid this kind of handling. Rough handling will also change the way the sheep react to a dog and can make them unusable for dog training. Don't buy sheep from someone whose dogs chase and abuse the sheep.

Practicing good stockmanship and taking care of your sheep will also make you a better dog trainer. When training, *the dog must learn the sheep are yours and must be treated well*. Consistently taking care of the sheep and treating them well during training leads to consistently doing it in trial situations. Sheep learn by the same principles that dogs do and respond to pressure from the dog and handler and release of pressure from the dog and handler.

## Understanding the flight zone

The best sheepdog trainers understand sheep and know where the dog needs to be to move them. They've acquired these skills by observing sheep and how they behave and react to situations. They've spent countless hours working with sheep.

Sheep, like other prey animals, have a **flight zone**, or an area around them that, when encroached, will cause them to move. *The flight zone area varies with different sheep and in different situations.* Think of a sheep's flight zone as its personal space. When you or a dog steps into it, they react by moving away or fighting. When you step out of it, most sheep will slow or stop. The zone varies with the animal and the situation. Just as you may not be worried about a smiling stranger who is 20 yards away, a sheep may not be worried about a person who is walking in the next pasture. However, a scowling stranger with a menacing posture might worry you and cause you to turn and walk in another direction. Likewise, a stranger marching toward sheep may make them run before he is 20 yards away.

**Flight Zone**

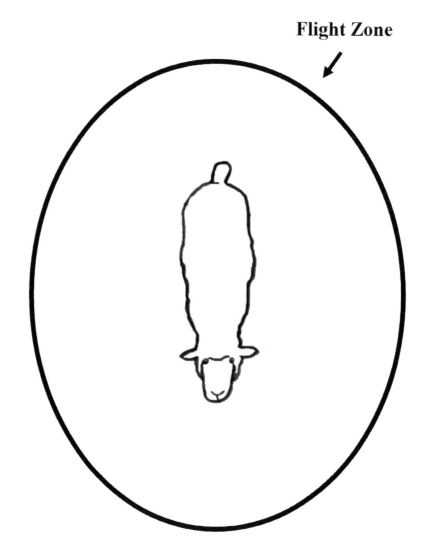

*A sheep's flight zone is the area around it where, when encroached by humans or other animals, the sheep will move or flee.*

Factors impacting a sheep's flight zone include perceived threat and past experiences. The perceived threat varies with the sheep. If sheep see people daily and are handled kindly and frequently, they'll often allow people to come quite close. Their flight zone might be very small, such as a few yards, or nonexistent. Sheep that live on the range and seldom see people are more likely to be wary of people. Their flight zone from people might be 20 yards or more. Sheep that live on the range may also encounter predators, which could make them afraid or aggressive with dogs.

As you work with different sheep, you'll discover the size of their flight zones differs with people and dogs. Some sheep may let people get closer to them than dogs; others may have smaller flight zones with dogs than they do with people.

The sheep's age impacts how she behaves. Lambs are unpredictable, especially when grouped together. They have no clear leader and may split from the flock, jump in the air or run into fences. They may also be curious and approach the dog. Older ewes usually will have a clear leader and follow her cues. Ewes with young lambs may be very protective or aggressive. Rams may be very aggressive. Again: never turn your back on a ram.

You can increase or decrease the sheep's flight zone by how you approach them; your speed, posture, any use of noise or stock stick impacts their behavior. For example, a brisk or sudden approach increases the flight zone. A person who approaches slowly and sideways is less threatening than one who comes toward them fast and straight on. Range sheep are very sensitive to movements, and even a very small motion can startle them.

Sheep also remember past experiences. If they've been handled kindly in the past, they likely will allow people to come closer than if they received rough treatment. Most sheep that have experienced being dewormed or vaccinated move away from a person leaning or reaching toward them.

Weather, too, can impact sheep's behavior and flight zone. Windy days can distort sounds and smells, often making the sheep flightier. If sheep are moved to an unfamiliar location, they're more wary than they are at their home farm. Also, sheep tend to avoid tight spaces, shadows and dark places. If barns, gates or pens are unfamiliar, they will often balk at them.

Sheep separated into small groups will behave differently than sheep in a larger group. Generally, the smaller the group, the more excitable and more difficult to control the sheep become. Sheep are flock animals and become panicked when separated from the rest of the flock.

When working with sheep, remember that as prey animals their best defense is often flight. They tend to do what the others do. If one sheep bolts, they may all bolt. If one steps into a trailer, they may all follow. This is why you'll often see a "Judas" goat at livestock sale barns. A Judas goat has learned to go into pens or stalls. Because sheep will follow a leader, workers use this goat to move sheep around the sale barn. Smart shepherds use the sheep's natural instincts and behaviors to help move them.

## What kind of sheep are best for dog training?
One of the hardest parts about training dogs on sheep for the novice trainer/handler is finding the appropriate sheep. Good sheep for dog training can be either hair or wool sheep.

The best sheep for dog training are used to dogs and people, but not too much. They should flock fairly well and respond to the dog honestly, meaning they move when the dog pushes them and not when the dog doesn't. They shouldn't be really hard to move, or heavy, nor should they be too flighty.

Typically, young to middle-aged ewes or wethers that are white-faced wool or hair sheep breeds and that have been lightly worked by dogs are best. They should be healthy and in good physical condition. Ideally they should be medium to small-sized so they are less likely to hurt you. Sheep that are uniform in type tend to flock better. If buying sheep, try to buy them from someone who has worked them in a calm and proper manner with their dogs.

Avoid using these types of sheep:

- Knee knockers and bottle babies
- Flighty sheep
- Ewes with lambs
- Rams
- Sour or abused sheep

**Knee knockers** are sheep that have learned the best way to avoid a dog is to cling to the human. These sheep gather around the person's knees and follow the person no matter what the dog does. In extreme cases, the knee knockers will follow the human whether there is a dog or not. Sheep like these are bad for dog training because the dog doesn't have to be in the correct position to impact the sheep. This teaches the dog wrong behaviors and gives you a false sense of confidence in your dog's abilities.

As bad, if not worse than knee knockers, are the **bottle babies**, sheep that were bottle-fed as babies and learned that humans are their source of food. They often run to humans and do not fear them. Many bottle lambs also jump on humans—something that's cute when they weigh 20 pounds, but not so cute when they weigh 140 pounds. Like the knee knockers, bottle babies are not good prospects for dog training because the dog does not have to be correct to bring them to you.

**Flighty sheep** may dash to the barn at the sight of the dog, crash into fences, or just run. They are fine for freshening up an experienced dog, but not good for starting young dogs. This is because the sheep will run, whether the dog is correct or not. The dog gets frustrated, as does the handler. On top of that, they can be dangerous to people, the dog and themselves.

**Ewes with their lambs** can be very protective. Sometimes even docile ewes will charge humans and dogs who come near their lambs. Moving ewes and lambs requires a handler and dog who have very good stock sense. To keep the ewes and lambs from panicking or becoming aggressive, handlers and dogs must be gentle, but firm. When training young and inexperienced dogs on sheep, avoid having sheep challenge the dog and charge at him. This can destroy a dog's confidence. Working with or moving ewes and lambs is best left to very experienced dogs and handlers. Likewise, avoid using rams, as they can be aggressive to dogs and humans and are not a good choice for dog training.

**Sour or abused sheep** have been chased or improperly worked by dogs. They might run to the fences or not move at all.

## How can I keep my sheep suitable for dog training?

We all get busy, and we often look for the fastest, most efficient way to complete chores. However, some things that we do for efficiency turn sheep into bad dog-training prospects. For instance, if you call your sheep to the barn every night and feed them in the barn, they may want to run to the barn when you're using them for dog training. Sheep that try to escape your practice field and run to the barn are difficult to use for dog training. Likewise, if you deliver hay to your sheep on a four-wheeler or another motorized vehicle, the sheep learn to come running when they hear or see it. Always fetching or gathering the sheep teaches them to run to the nearest person. Rather than always fetching, incorporate some driving or pushing the sheep away. Making sheep into pets and feeding them treats will likely turn them into knee knockers. If you have one or a few "bad sheep" that don't work well for your dog, get rid of them; they will sour the rest of the flock. Don't keep troublemaking sheep.

Keep as many sheep as you can and rotate which ones you use in training. If that's not an option, plan to buy new sheep and sell used sheep as often as practical. Most sheep will eventually sour to dog training. If the same group of five sheep is worked every day, they're going to sour on training faster than sheep that live in a flock of 100 and are rotated for training. You can keep your sheep fresh longer by making sure your dog treats them correctly. Don't allow your dog to harass or mistreat the sheep. Keeping fresh, workable sheep takes planning, effort and investment. For those not lucky enough to have a large sheep operation, having good sheep for young dogs is one of the biggest challenges of training sheepdogs.

Never let your dog or anyone else's dog abuse the sheep. Sheep that have been chased, harassed and hurt by dogs have learned there is no way to "win." They may go into fight or flight mode at the sight of the dog and will not respond properly to a dog that is treating them kindly. Training with abused sheep can ruin your dog and can be extremely dangerous, as these sheep may blindly run over a human to escape a dog. Remember that sheep respond to pressure and release by both the dog and handler.

---

### A Shepherd's Journey

When a friend came to train dogs, she commented how good the flock had become for dog training. Instead of running at the sight of a dog, they were putting their heads down and grazing, and only moving when the dog pressured them. "I sold the problem children," I said, noting that a few weeks prior to her visit, I'd sorted out six ewes that had become difficult to work. They often broke from the group or just ran toward the barn. Selling those six sheep changed the dynamics of the flock and made it better for dog training. –Beth

---

# Chapter 16
# Get Hands-On Experience with Sheep:
# Practice Without the Dog

Imagine teaching someone to speak Spanish to you when you yourself are unable to speak Spanish. That is what you are doing if you are trying to teach your dog to herd sheep, and you yourself do not know how to move sheep.

Some people who train and work with herding dogs grew up around sheep or worked on sheep farms. They have a distinct advantage when training herding dogs. Those who don't have much sheep experience can learn more about sheep by working around them. When training a herding dog, you must know where the dog should be to impact the sheep. Learning to move sheep without a dog will help you do that. The exercises in this chapter are designed to help you learn to read, move and react to sheep. You must be comfortable working around sheep before you introduce your dog to sheep.

## A few things to know before starting

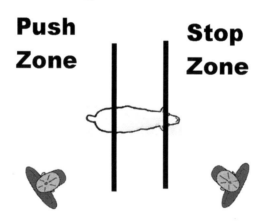

*Your body position in relation to the sheep affects the animal's movement. When behind the hip, you push the sheep forward. When in front of the eye, you block or stop movement.*

1.  **Pay attention to where you are in relation to the sheep's eyes.** If you want to block the sheep or stop their forward movement, position yourself in front of their eyes. If you're even with their eyes, that tends to hold them. If you want to push them forward, position yourself behind their eyes.

2.  **Sheep, like dogs, respond to applying and releasing pressure.** If you want sheep to move, put pressure on them or step into their space (flight zone). Quick and aggressive movement may startle them or cause them to bolt while slow and gentle movement may make them move slightly or not at all. Once the sheep move, reward them by taking the pressure away or backing away from the sheep. Keeping pressure on sheep after they have responded can sour them and teach them not to respond to humans or dogs. Moving out of their flight zone will often stop their movement.

3.  **Some groups of sheep have an obvious leader.** Others do not. Pay attention to see if one sheep moves first and the others follow.

4.  **When discussing position in these and future exercises, references are made to an analog clock face.** Imagine the face of a clock superimposed on the practice field.

## Exercise 1: The gather

A basic task every herding dog should know is how to gather sheep and bring them to you. In this exercise, you'll practice gathering the sheep into a group and moving them to the end of a small field or paddock *without a dog*. This exercise is designed to:

- Give you a feel for the sheep's flight zone;
- Give you a feel for how your body position (facing head-on or sideways) impacts the sheep; and
- Improve your observation skills around sheep.

### What this exercise should look like

The sheep will be grazing at the end of the field near the 12 o'clock position. You'll be at the other end of the pasture near the 6 o'clock position. Walking quietly and without disturbing the sheep, you'll move in an arc, either clockwise or counterclockwise, around the sheep so that you are behind the sheep. Once behind the sheep, you will gather them into a small group and move them to the 6 o'clock position.

### Equipment needed for this exercise

- A paddock or small field. The field should be a minimum of 100×50 yards (the size of a football field) and no larger than 3 acres. In a larger field, you're less likely to disturb the sheep, but you will have to walk a lot more.
- About 5 to 25 good sheep (no knee knockers, bottle babies, flighty sheep, ewes with lambs or rams). This exercise will not work if your sheep are used to running to you to get fed. If you don't have sheep, try this with ducks or turkeys. However, while fowl have flight zones and will flock, their movement is not exactly like sheep. Sheep are preferred.
- Comfortable shoes. You'll be walking a lot.
- A notebook, a pen and observational skills.
- Optional: a stock stick or shepherd's crook.

> ### How to use a stock stick
>
> A shepherd's crook or stock stick is a handy tool when moving or sorting sheep. The stick should not be used to hit or strike animals. Instead, it's used as an extension of your arm. By waving the stick, you can turn the sheep, push them forward, block them or chase them away from you—all depending on where you move the stick.

### Steps for this exercise

1. Start with the sheep on the end of the field opposite from you, near the 12 o'clock position. Ideally the sheep should be spread out and grazing. If they will not stand, try placing hay where you'd like them to stand.

2. Walk quietly in an arc either clockwise or counterclockwise. Make sure your arc is wide enough so that it does not disturb the sheep. As you are walking, watch the sheep. Are they continuing to graze? Are they looking at you or cocking an ear in your direction?

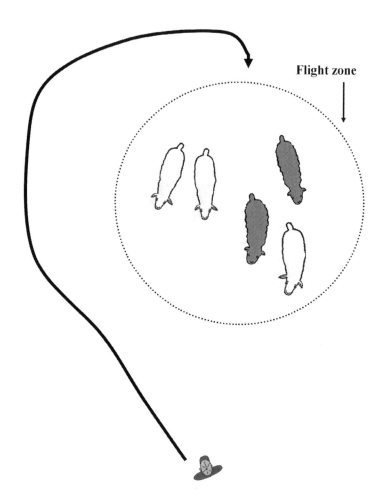

*Walk in an arc around the sheep, staying out of their flight zone.*

3. As you move behind the sheep, try gathering them into a group. This usually involves taking a few steps to the left, and then a few steps toward the right. As you do this, note your body position. Where do you have to be if you want the sheep to react? Do they react differently if you move fast or slow, or if you are closer or further away? Can you identify the leader in the group? She often has her head a little higher than the others. When the leader moves in a certain direction or stops, the other sheep do the same.

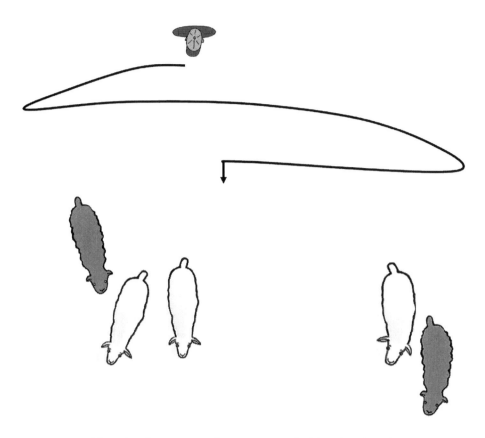

*To gather sheep, you may have to move to the left and to the right.*

4. When the sheep are flocked together, move them in a straight line toward the 6 o'clock position. Note your body position. Where do you have to be for the sheep to see or notice you? Are you always directly behind the sheep, or do you move from side to side? Do the sheep want to go straight to 6 o'clock or are they being drawn to some other spot on the field? If they are being drawn to one side of the field, where must you be to redirect them toward 6 o'clock? You may discover that you don't always have to be directly behind them to move them straight forward.

**Variations on this exercise: The flat outrun and the slice**

With these exercises, you will observe how the sheep react when you are not in the "correct" position on the gather.

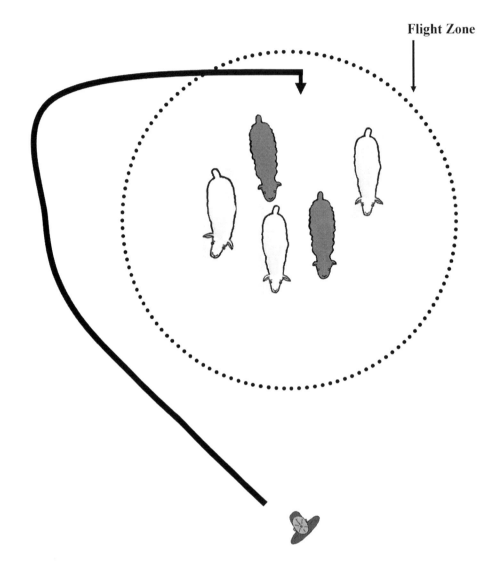

*In the flat outrun, you step into the sheep's flight zone before reaching 12 o'clock.*

**The flat outrun:** Most people and dogs have a little lazy in them. Why would you walk or run in a wide arc around the sheep when you'd get there faster by flattening the arc or going directly to the sheep? Try the previous exercise again with the sheep at 12 o'clock and you at 6 o'clock. Instead of making a wide arc, flatten the arc so that at 10 o'clock (or 2 o'clock if you go counterclockwise), you are closer to the sheep. Do they move? At what point did they feel uncomfortable and raise their heads? In what direction did the sheep go?

**The slice:** In this exercise, you will again start with the sheep at 12 o'clock and you at 6 o'clock. Make a nice wide arc until you reach 9 o'clock (or 3 o'clock if you go counterclockwise). Now, rather than continue the arc, go in a straight line toward 12 o'clock. Do the sheep react? What do they do? What direction do they go?

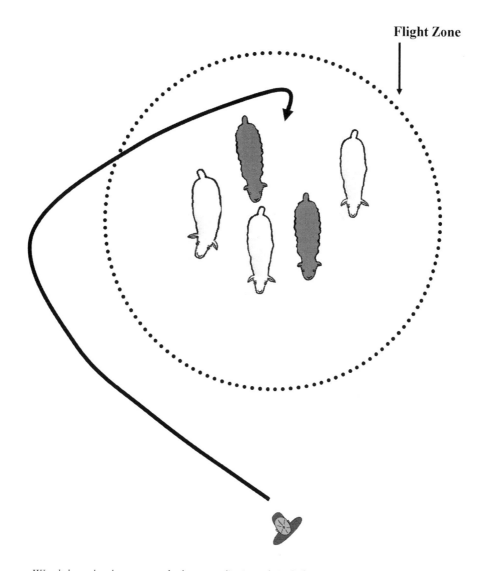

**Flight Zone**

*Watch how the sheep respond when you slice into their flight zone near the 9 o'clock position.*

### Exercise 2: Moving or driving the sheep from corner to corner

In this exercise, you'll gather the sheep and move them from corner to corner of the paddock or pasture. When done correctly, the sheep move quietly and as a group in straight lines. This exercise is designed to:

- Make you more observant of the sheep's body position and anticipate when they may veer off the line; and
- Help you understand what **draw** is and how to make adjustments for it.

> **Draw on the field**
>
> Seldom is a field neutral for the sheep. They feel a pull to certain areas of the field, such as manmade objects like barns or feeders, or natural objects such as a shade tree or a rise in the terrain. Because of this pull, or draw, you and your dog must change your position in relation to the sheep. Depending on the draw, you might have to be at 10 o'clock, 12 o'clock or 2 o'clock to keep the sheep moving forward in a straight line.

You'll use the same sheep, field and equipment that you did in the previous exercise.

**Steps for this exercise**

1. Start with the sheep on the end of the field that is opposite from you, near the 12 o'clock position.

2. Walk quietly in an arc either clockwise or counterclockwise to the 12 o'clock position and gather your sheep into a group.

3. Walking behind the sheep, move them to a corner of the field. As you move them, make the following observations:

   - Are you directly behind the group or off to one side?

   - What happens when you take a fast step toward the sheep? Do they react?

   - What happens if you flap your arms out by your side?

   - Slow down. Do the sheep react? If so, what do they do?

   - Step to the left and watch the sheep's heads. Do they change direction?

   - Can you observe where the pressure zone is on the flock (that distance from the sheep where they move away from you)?

   - If using a stock stick, what happens when you wave it off to one side? Do the sheep react differently if it is waved 1 foot above the ground or 4 feet above the ground?

4. Once the sheep are in the corner, stomp your foot at the sheep and note their reaction.

5. Turn the sheep and move them to another corner. To turn the sheep, make an arc clockwise or counterclockwise around the sheep until you are in the corner of the paddock. Walk behind them and move them to another corner. As you move them, make the following observations:

   - Where is the draw on the field (where do the sheep naturally want to go)?

   - Is it easier moving them in one direction rather than another?

   - Are you moving the sheep by blocking their heads or following their butts?

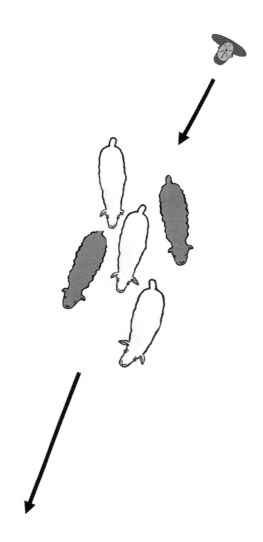

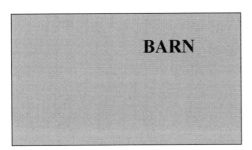

*If the sheep are drawn to the barn, then a person may just have to walk directly behind them to move them in that direction.*

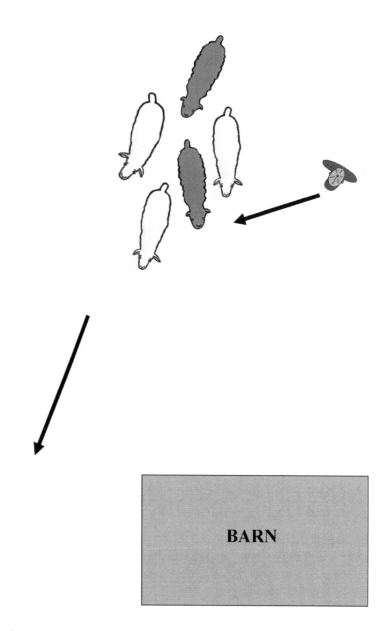

*If the sheep are drawn to the barn, and the person wants to move them to the lower left, she may be next to the sheep.*

## Exercise 3: Moving sheep quietly in a semi-packed pen

In this exercise, you'll move sheep in a smaller area, sometimes called a packed or semi-packed pen. Because one of the first exercises you'll do with your dog is in a small pen, you need to be comfortable working with sheep in it before working your dog there. This exercise is designed to:

- Help you get comfortable working with sheep in tighter spaces; and
- Learn how human body position impacts the sheep.

### Equipment for this exercise
- A fenced area no larger than 20×20 feet.

- 5 to 15 good sheep (no knee knockers, bottle babies, flighty sheep, ewes with lambs, or rams).

- Comfortable shoes.
- A notebook, a pen and observational skills.

**Steps for this exercise**
1. Walk into the pen and note how the sheep respond to you. **Note**: If the sheep launch themselves toward the fence when you enter the pen or act frantic, *stop and exit the pen*. You do not have the appropriate sheep for this exercise. They are too flighty, and you or the sheep are likely to get hurt.
2. Walk toward the sheep with a full-frontal approach. How do the sheep respond?
3. Walk toward the sheep with a sideways approach. Do the sheep respond differently?
4. Stand in front of the sheep. Turn your shoulders toward the left. How do the sheep respond?
5. Stand in front of the sheep. Turn your hips toward the left and keep your shoulders facing forward. How do the sheep respond?
6. Lean forward into the sheep and note their response. Lean back away from the sheep. How do they respond?
7. Wave your hands in front of the sheep's eyes and note their response. Move toward the rear of the sheep, wave your hand behind their eyes and note their response.
8. Choose a sheep and walk toward her head. Note how she responds.
9. Choose a sheep and walk toward her hip. Note how she responds.
10. Stomp your foot. Note how the sheep responds.
11. Back up and note the sheep's response.
12. Circle the sheep and note their response.
13. Walk parallel, past the sheep. Pay attention to how they hesitate as you approach, then speed up as you pass them.

Repeat these exercises until you can take any of the above actions and predict what the sheep will do 80 percent of the time.

## Feeling more confident around sheep?

As you work around the sheep, without a dog, you'll gain more confidence in working the sheep and become more adept at moving the sheep in the direction you'd like them to go. You'll also become more aware of your posture, positioning and pace and how that affects the sheep. As you progress in your sheepdog training, continue practicing working with different types of sheep without a dog. These skills will help you become a better shepherd and sheepdog trainer. Remember, the whole point of sheepdog training is the proper control of the sheep. The better you understand sheep, the better you will do moving them on the farm or when competing at sheepdog trials.

### A Shepherd's Journey

One of the most challenging aspects of sheepdog training and trialing is adapting to the different types of sheep. I vividly remember one of my first sheepdog trials when the very friendly sheep swarmed around me. I didn't know how to react. At another trial, the sheep weren't used to being around people, and when I stomped my foot at them, they scattered and ran away from the pen I was trying to direct them into.

It became clear that if I wanted to get better at sheepdog trialing, I'd have to learn to work with different types of sheep. Volunteering to help work in the sheep pens at clinics and trials is one way to do this. It's dirty, hard and sometimes dangerous work. But it helps you learn more about sheep and how they respond to pressure. —Beth

# Chapter 17
## A Six-Way Conversation

With sheep, a dog and a person in a field, communication is going in six directions. Earlier chapters discussed how the dog communicates with a person, how a person communicates with a dog, and how people can observe and influence sheep. Now, let's focus on the communication between the dog and the sheep.

As prey animals, sheep are very aware of predators and learn very quickly how to size up a dog. With their excellent vision, sheep may notice a dog hundreds of yards away and decide how to respond to that dog long before he's close to them. Sheep that have been worked regularly with Border Collies are experts in interpreting a dog's body language and responding accordingly. They notice when a dog is calm and confident, when a dog is nervous and excited and when a dog is reluctant and afraid. When a dog approaches sheep in a controlled and confident manner, sheep that have experience with dogs will respond by moving away quietly. A dog who approaches sheep hesitantly may cause the sheep to turn into him and approach him. A fast, excited dog may cause sheep to bolt down the field before he gets close to them. The sheep see that dog's behavior as a threat long before the dog makes contact. A dog's color may affect how sheep respond to him. Black or mostly black dogs tend to appear as more of a threat than white or mostly white dogs. Because mostly white dogs may resemble livestock guardian dogs, they may have more difficulty getting the sheep to respond to them. The degree of "eye" the dog has will also affect how sheep respond to him. Because eye is a predatory stalking behavior, a dog with strong eye may bring out a fight or flight response in some sheep.

How sheep respond to dogs varies depending on the sheep's breed, age, experience and environment. Sometimes sheep that are set out on lush pasture or grain are more interested in eating than moving away from a dog. A dog has to look confident and push hard to get these sheep going. Range ewes, with little or no exposure to herding dogs, will often face or even charge a dog, or they may bolt wildly away from the group. This is because their only exposure to dog-like animals may be coyotes trying to kill them or livestock guardian dogs who live with them. It takes a very special Border Collie to handle these semi-feral ewes. The dog must have confidence, sheep sense, speed, power and patience. Sheep that have been worked with the non-eye dog breeds, such as many of the American Kennel Club herding breeds, may not move off a Border Collie at all because they are accustomed to a dog barking and bouncing into their flight zone. Sheep that are sour or worked by dogs a lot may start walking the course when they see a dog, regardless of what the dog does. Lambs may have no idea what a dog is and walk over and sniff the dog instead of moving away. A ewe with a young lamb may aggressively charge a dog, especially if the dog appears hesitant or overly predatory.

Just as sheep become experts at evaluating dogs, dogs learn to read sheep and adjust to different types of sheep. Some of this behavior is instinctual, and some dogs are naturally better at handling sheep. However, much of this skill is developed from training and experience. A dog can learn to see when a sheep is sick and then hang back and take the pressure off that sheep. A dog can read an aggressive ram and give him space to move away but be ready to bite if charged. A dog can learn to move young lambs along by a gentle nuzzle and learn to stay 50 yards back from a wild Barbados while still controlling her.

Your dog will learn his body language communicates his intentions to the sheep. By dropping his head, leaning into the sheep, turning his head quickly, increasing his pace, or even showing his teeth, a dog is telling the sheep to respect him. A dog can turn his head or eyes away, turn sideways or lie down to calm frightened sheep. He can prevent a sheep from breaking at the pen just by shifting his weight from one paw to another.

The only way your dog can get the experience he needs to become skilled at handling all kinds of sheep is to go out and do it. This means you should keep a variety of sheep, work at other people's places and go to dog trials. It means hundreds of hours spent working different kinds of sheep in different situations. There is no short cut to teaching your dog how to deal with a variety of sheep. You simply have to make it part of your training plan.

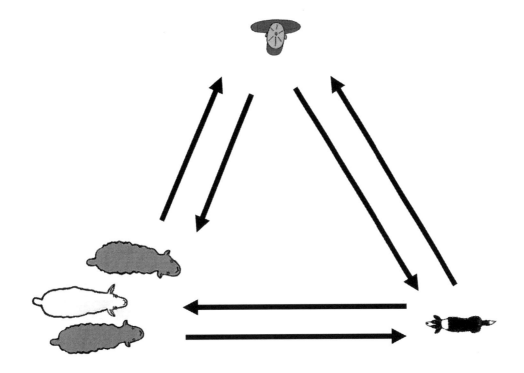

*A conversation between three different species*

## The six-way conversation on the field

Remember as you train and trial your dog, a six-way conversation is happening on the field.

First, you are using verbal cues, whistles and body language to communicate with your dog. You are also reading your dog's body language, evaluating his mindset, and adjusting your cues or body position according to what the dog is telling you.

At the same time, your dog is watching the sheep, reacting to their body language, and making decisions as to how to control the sheep. The sheep are responding to the dog's position and posture and reacting based on the dog's actions. A complex predator and prey conversation is constantly ongoing.

Finally, you must watch and interpret the sheep's behavior and respond accordingly by positioning your dog and yourself to control and influence the sheep as a team.

Many, sometimes very subtle, interactions happen simultaneously. There is a lot to watch and react to, and things can happen and change very quickly. This multi-species conversation is one of the reasons that sheep dog training is such a challenging and fascinating endeavor.

## A Shepherd's Journey

During my first trial out West on range ewes unused to being worked by herding dogs, I sent my 2-year-old dog on his outrun. When he got behind the sheep, he just stood behind them, looking at them and then looking down the field at me. He was wagging his tail and had a puzzled look on his face. He had never before worked sheep that did not just walk off when he approached them, and he did not know what to do.

I walked up the field to rescue him. The next day, I was lucky enough to be able to use him to set out the sheep. This enabled me to show him how to push into the sheep quietly but with enough forward motion and authority to make them move. He figured it out and was able to complete the course on range sheep at the next trial with no difficulty –Kay

# Part 3

# Basic Sheepdog Training Exercises

# Chapter 18
## Getting Started

---

The upcoming chapters provide lessons and steps to teach your dog the herding elements included in an open trial course. As you move through them, remember that there are many ways to teach a behavior. The specific training approaches selected for this book were chosen based on:

- They are novice-handler friendly. The training approaches selected are fairly easy to understand and apply.

- They have a high success rate for the typical Border Collie.

- They are widely used and have a history of good outcomes.

- They follow the principles of science-based approaches and rely on shaping behaviors with minimal aversives.

As you move through the training chapters, take time to go back and review what you learned in the first two parts of the book.

## General tips for your sheepdog training sessions

- Training is hard work and takes dedication, planning and effort to succeed. You can't train a dog successfully by just messing around with your dog a couple times a week.

- For a young dog and novice handler, plan on five to six training sessions per week. Any fewer and you will not make progress, yet most young dogs benefit from some time off. So, plan on one or two days off each week.

- Don't work a young dog more than once a day. After working a young dog, put him away in a quiet place. He needs time to absorb and process what you are teaching him.

- The quality of the session is more important than the quantity. Most young dogs learn best in sessions that are about 20 minutes long.

- Get in the habit of having the dog practice lie down and recall exercises on his way to the sheep. This reminds the dog to pay attention to you and that access to the sheep is predicated on calm, obedient behavior.

- Never let your dog go to sheep without your permission. If the dog leaves to work sheep before you've released him, block him from the sheep and start over.

- If you need to use your dog for chores, make sure he works correctly. If you allow him to ignore cues, slice his flanks or chase sheep in order to finish your chore, you will undo your training.

- Never let the sheep escape or run over the dog in training. The lesson plans in this book set the dog up for success with the right sheep and the right environment. One reason many novice handlers have out-of-control dogs is that the dogs have learned not to trust the handler because the handler stops the dog in the wrong place, uses the wrong sheep or lets the sheep get away from the dog.

## The four phases of learning

A dog goes through four phases when learning a new behavior: acquisition, fluency, generalization and maintenance.

**Acquisition**: The dog is just figuring out what is wanted. Make this phase as stress-free and error-free as possible.

**Fluency**: The dog becomes reliable, quick and relaxed doing this behavior. This stage makes the right behavior a habit.

**Generalization**: The dog practices the new behavior in different places and situations. This phase teaches the dog to perform the behavior regardless of distractions, difficulty or distance.

**Maintenance**: The dog continues to practice the behavior to keep it fluent. The dog's behavior is only as good as his last training session.

The lesson plans in this book focus on the first two steps of teaching a behavior, but it's important that you remember to work on the last two steps as well.

# Chapter 19
## Keeping the Goal in Mind: The Ideal Trial Run

The coming chapters give step-by-step exercises for teaching your dog to herd. Before jumping into them, you should have a clear picture of what you are working toward. Because USBCHA sheepdog trials are based on real farm work, they can provide a good picture of what your final training product should look like.

While this chapter provides a detailed description of an ideal open trial run, note that open trials vary because of the fields and the sheep. Some may require a dog to cross a creek, go up hills or go through a gate to another pasture. Some outruns may be 300 yards, while others are 800 yards. Some trials use three sheep, others four or five. To learn more about them, you can watch videos of trial runs or attend USBCHA trials. As you progress in your herding training, take time to watch top-performing dogs.

> **A note about USBCHA dog trials**
>
> Sheepdog trialing, as done by the USBCHA and the ISDS (International Sheep Dog Society), is the most difficult, complicated, and challenging of dog sports. It involves working your dog at great distances, teaching particularly challenging training concepts, and caring for and understanding a third species (sheep, goats, or cattle). To succeed in this sport, you have to be determined, self-critical and focused. It is also expensive and time-consuming. You will likely feel discouraged and disheartened at various points in your journey. You will have to deal with adversity, unfair and difficult conditions, and the luck of the draw. You will have to travel to far flung locations, run your dog in any kind of weather, work with bad sheep and tolerate the vagaries of judging. This sport is not for the faint of heart.

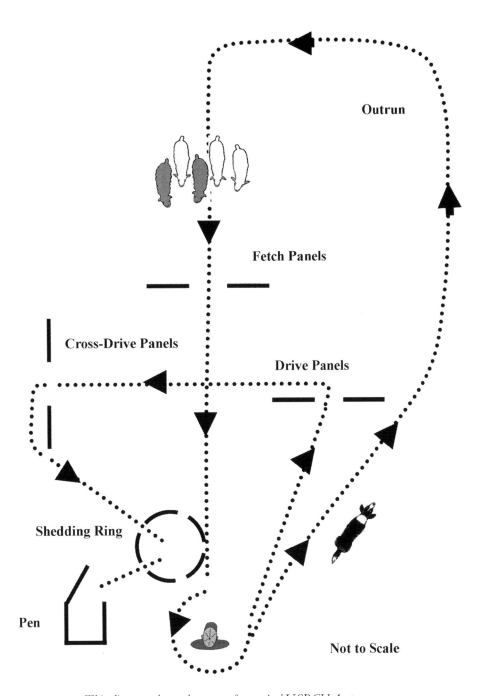

**Outrun**

**Fetch Panels**

**Cross-Drive Panels**

**Drive Panels**

**Shedding Ring**

**Pen**

**Not to Scale**

*This diagram shows the setup of a typical USBCHA open course.*

## The gather (outrun, lift and fetch)

Note: In a trial, the dog can arc to the left ("**come-bye**") or the right ("**away to me**") to gather the sheep. Depending on the field, one way may be easier than the other.

The handler and dog walk to the post and pause. Standing quietly next to the handler, the dog scans the 50-acre field, looking for the five sheep that are grazing near a tree some 500 yards away. While he may not see them, he trusts that the sheep are out there because he and his handler have practiced outruns thousands of times and in many different places.

*The handler and dog stand at the handler's post and scan the field for sheep. Photo courtesy of Carol Clawson.*

The handler says, "Come bye," and the dog sprints in an arc toward the left. The dog casts wider, turning his head periodically and looking for the sheep. When the dog runs with purpose over a hill and out of sight, the handler says nothing, just holds a whistle to her mouth, waiting for the dog to come out of the dip.

The dog comes up the hill, looks for sheep, and seeing none, continues casting to the left. In another 100 yards, the dog spots the sheep and widens his circle a bit more so that he doesn't disturb the sheep. The sheep graze, unaware of the dog arcing around them.

As the dog continues the arc to the point of balance, he sizes up the sheep. Where do they want to go? Are they being drawn into a gully on the left or do they want to run back to their sheep friends in the set out pen? The dog also notes where his handler is. Instinct and training tell him the sheep should go directly to the handler.

The lift, defined at the moment the dog makes contact with and takes control of the sheep, should be smooth, cautious and steady. He listens for a whistle from his handler and watches the sheep, noting their posture, their ears, their eyes. The sheep, too, are sizing up the dog. Is he a threat? Should they run in fear? Should they turn and fight him? Or should they just ignore him and continue grazing? The handler observes the situation and keeps her whistle in her mouth, ready to give the dog direction if needed. Over the years, the handler and dog have practiced the lift thousands of times, from various distances and with different sheep.

*The dog and sheep size each other up during the lift of a sheepdog trial. Photo courtesy of Carol Clawson.*

As the dog walks forward in a calm, confident manner, the lead ewe eyes the dog, faces him and stomps her foot. The dog continues walking toward the ewe. When he's just a few feet from her, the ewe sighs and turns toward the handler; the other four sheep follow, breaking into a trot.

The dog adjusts his pace so the sheep continue moving at a slow trot. Every few steps, he looks around the sheep, noting where the handler is, making adjustments, and listening to the handler. The handler wants to keep the sheep moving on a straight line and at a steady pace. To do this, she whistles to the dog, instructing him to go left, go right or steady.

The lead sheep balks as the sheep approach the **fetch panels**, a set of panels about halfway between the set out point and the handler. The sheep have spent their lives on the open range and are not used to going through gates or tight places. Watching the sheep, the dog lowers his head and slows his pace. He is watching and anticipating the sheep to move to the left or right. When the lead sheep trots forward through the panels, with the other sheep following, the dog again picks up his pace, continuing on his path toward his handler.

*The dog fetches, or brings the sheep, to the handler. Photo courtesy of Carol Clawson.*

As the sheep near the handler, their attention turns toward her. Is she a person to be feared? The handler sizes up the sheep too, noting the leader and the straggler. She watches how the sheep react to her. Are they people-friendly or wary of humans? This information will come in handy during the penning and shedding elements of the course.

## The drive

**Note**: The trial host or judge determines the direction of the drive and tells the handlers prior to the start of the trial.

The dog and handler work in tandem to move the sheep around the handler and up the field toward a set of panels that are about 200 yards away. The goal is to keep the sheep moving at a steady pace and in a straight line between the handler and the panels. To do this, the handler instructs the dog to make short flanks to the left or to the right. Sometimes she asks the dog to pause; sometimes she tells the dog to walk up into the sheep's flight zone. The dog holds the pressure and keeps the sheep moving at a trot.

As the sheep approach the panels, the lead ewe pauses. The handler gives a short flank whistle to the left and then to the right. From the corner of her eye, the lead ewe sees a dog behind her to her left and then to her right. Those glimpses are enough to encourage her forward, through the panels. The other four sheep stay close to the leader.

Once the sheep are through the panels, the handler whistles, "Away to me," and the dog circles to the right. This movement catches the sheep's eyes and they turn left across the field. The dog must now move the sheep across the field about 200 yards to another set of panels. As the dog moves the sheep, the handler watches the sheep, making sure they are on a path that takes them in a straight line through a second set of panels.

*The dog drives the sheep through a set of panels. Photo courtesy of Carol Clawson.*

As the sheep approach the second set of panels, the handler is ready to give a short flank whistle if the sheep balk. They don't. Once through the panels, she whistles, "Away to me," and the dog arcs to the right, turning the sheep left toward the handler.

The handler visualizes a straight line between the panels and the center of the shedding ring, a 40-yard-wide circle marked by piles of sawdust. She positions the dog so the sheep move in a straight line from the panels to the center of the shedding ring.

## The shed

**Note:** The trial host or judge determines whether the dog and handler shed (separate one or more sheep from the group) first and then pen the sheep, or pen first and then shed. Sometimes other obstacles are included in this section of the course.

As the sheep approach the shedding ring, the handler slows the dog. When the sheep enter the ring, the handler walks into the shedding ring. She eyes the ewe she'd like to separate from the group. In the shedding ring, she positions herself so the sheep are in a line between her and the dog.

*The dog and the handler work together to shed, or split, the sheep. Photo courtesy of Vernon Bewley.*

"In here," she says, motioning with her hand and turning her body. The dog darts in front of the last sheep and stops, holding the sheep in place. When he steps forward, the sheep turns from the dog and away from the other sheep, thus completing the shed. The judge yells, "Good." The handler says, "Come bye," and the dog circles around the single sheep and drives her to the other sheep.

## The pen

With the sheep gathered as a group, the handler gives her dog a "lie down" cue and walks toward a free-standing pen. As she opens the gate and holds onto the pen rope, she tells the dog to walk up and the sheep move toward the far corner of the pen. In the other hand, she holds the stock stick which she uses as an extension of her arm.

Because the sheep are wary of her, she takes a step back from the pen gate. Both she and the dog are watching the sheep's heads and ears, looking for signs of hesitation or thoughts of bolting. The lead ewe stops, eying the dog and the human and looking for escape routes. The dog takes a step forward, and the ewe looks toward the handler. The handler takes a step forward. The ewe eyes the dog who takes another step forward. The lead ewe takes a step into the pen, with the other four sheep behind her. The handler taps the stock stick on the ground and quickly closes the pen gate.

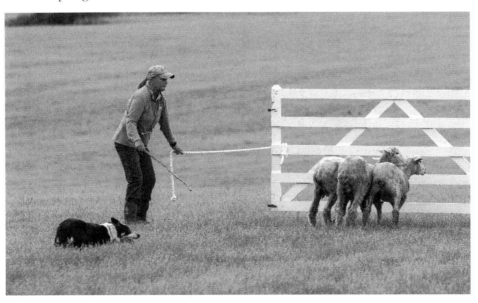

*The dog and the handler work together to move the sheep into the pen. Photo courtesy of Vernon Bewley.*

# Chapter 20
## Introducing Your Dog to Sheep in the Semi-Packed Pen

The ideal herding dog should be calm, yet keen, attentive to the handler, yet focused on the sheep, and unafraid of, yet kind to the sheep. He should be confident about walking into stock and not work frantically, dive into or bite stock. This chapter focuses on teaching the dog to relax and be calm, quiet and attentive when he's next to sheep—and even when the sheep face him. The goal is to get him into the right *emotional state* for training and working around sheep.

### What does the semi-packed pen teach a dog?

We prefer to introduce dogs to sheep in the semi-packed pen, a 10×10 ft. pen that is about 80 percent full of sheep. The dog has room to move around but remains in close proximity to the sheep. The semi-packed pen is designed to address your dog's excitement level or anxiety right away, and to teach him to be calm, quiet, attentive and unafraid when near the sheep. By carefully and correctly putting the dog in the "red zone" and teaching him to relax in the intense pressure of a small space with a sheep facing him, you are reducing his stress levels for the rest of his training program. If this training is done properly, you will hopefully prevent fear-based gripping, chase or excitement-based gripping, or a reluctance to move into the sheep when necessary. After the dog is comfortable in the semi-packed pen, you will then teach him about staying off the sheep, balance and developing a feel for sheep.

Errorless learning is the idea of teaching so that the learner doesn't make mistakes, and thus never rehearses the wrong way of behaving. By starting the dog in a semi-packed pen, on a leash, the handler greatly reduces the opportunity to chase, bite, run off contact, avoid the sheep and many other unwanted behaviors. The semi-packed pen method reduces the likelihood of the dog learning these unwanted behaviors.

> ### Why does a dog's emotional state matter?
>
> As dog trainers, it is easy to focus on what the dog is doing and forget about how the dog is feeling. Some trainers believe that if the dog does what he's told, it does not matter how the behavior was trained. How something was taught matters to the dog, and in the long run, to the trainer as well. Here's why. If the action was taught in a way that caused the dog to be anxious, fearful, frantic, or frenzied, those underlying emotions are present when the dog performs the behavior. These emotions, in turn, can result in the dog making mistakes. The point of the semi-packed pen work is to make sure the dog's initial emotional response to sheep is one of confidence, calm and control.

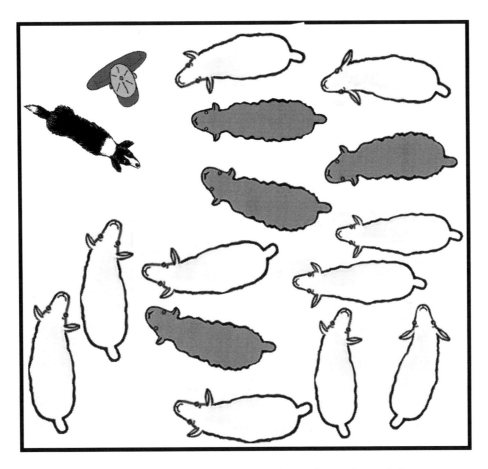

*During the semi-packed pen work, you'll teach your dog to relax in the intense pressure of a small space and even when the sheep are facing the dog.*

## Why start with the semi-packed pen?

While most of the methods in this book are widely used, the semi-packed pen is a slight deviation from how many trainers start their dogs. Most trainers start the dog in a round pen or a field that is a few acres or larger. At some point in training, though, most handlers train their dog in a semi or tightly packed pen. We like to use it as an initial step because it's more easily controlled by the handler, puts the handler in the dog's mental picture, gets the dog in the correct mental state, and, if set up properly, is relatively safe for the sheep and handler.

Starting in a semi-packed pen differs from the more traditional method of starting a dog in a large field (more than a few acres) or a round pen. Starting in a large field has its downsides, especially for inexperienced handlers, non-athletic handlers or those who do not start dogs on sheep frequently. In a large field, the dog may become excited and try to bite the sheep or chase the sheep into a fence, and an inexperienced handler may not be able to position herself to stop it correctly. Instead, the handler may swat or yell at the dog for being incorrect, which can create anxiety, fear or even excitement in the dog. The dog will remember this time of excitement and anxiety and, in times of stress, the chasing or biting behavior might resurface.

### A Shepherd's Journey

One of my mentors, Bruce Fogt, taught me the packed pen exercise early in my sheepdog training journey. I have found it extremely helpful with my dogs, as it helps them learn to be calm and get comfortable being in close proximity to the sheep. I think of the packed pen as a crutch to help those of us who don't have the hours and hours of practical sheep work to give our dogs so that they become comfortable around sheep. I have over the years modified the packed pen exercise so that it suits my needs. All of my dogs now start with the semi-packed pen lessons described in this chapter, and I have found they are more relaxed and confident around the sheep. –Kay

## Guidelines to keep in mind

To get the most use and success out of the semi-packed pen, follow these guidelines.

**The pen should be about 80 percent full.** The dog should be able to touch the sheep as well as stand in the "highest" pressure zone, about a foot from a sheep's head.

**The dog must be on a line.** This prevents the dog from rushing past the pressure of the sheep's heads and getting to their butts. With the dog on a line, the handler can gently but firmly make sure the dog goes slowly and confidently around the sheep, that the dog can and will stop in the pressure zone, and that the dog will stand in the pressure zone (in front of the sheep's face) quietly, neither turning his head nor trying to lunge in and grip the sheep. By standing next to the dog, patting the dog or helping to move the sheep's heads away, if necessary, the handler gives the dog the confidence to stand in the pressure zone and relax.

**The sheep must be the right type.** Weaned lambs are ideal. They are small enough to not hurt too much if they bump into you or the dog. They will also tend to face or even sniff the dog without charging him. This forces the dog into the pressure zone without much risk. Older, bigger ewes that will butt or charge a dog can seriously injure or scare the dog, and that is the opposite of what you are trying to achieve. Sheep that frantically bolt into the fence or at the handler are dangerous and should not be used.

**The handler must read the dog's body language correctly.** A dog who is frantically trying to grab a sheep, a dog hiding behind the handler, and a dog with his tail high or tightly tucked, are all stressed. The handler needs to relax the dog, keep the dog in the pressure zone and continue with the pen exercises. If working with a young dog, he should not be going through a fear period. If the dog is showing extreme fear and does not start to relax after some time in the semi-packed pen, stop doing the exercise. Wait a couple of months, and then try it again. For novice handlers, we recommend the dog be a minimum of 8 to 10 months old before starting this exercise.

**Know what the final product should be.** The dog should look forward to the pen exercise and stand calmly, quietly and confidently (jaw relaxed, tail down and loose, facing the sheep) in the pen even with sheep facing or sniffing him. The dog should be relaxed and able to move around sheep in the pen without gripping or being frantic. He should be able to lie down on cue even in the pressure zone.

**Be willing to stop or skip this exercise.** While this exercise has many benefits, it can be difficult or even dangerous for a novice handler who is unfamiliar with sheep or who is unable to read and react to her dog. It is also dangerous if you have flighty, aggressive or unsafe sheep and a pen that is not solid and safe. We strongly recommend that novice handlers have an experienced handler help them with this exercise. If it cannot be set up safely, then it is better to skip it.

## What are the advantages of starting in a semi-packed pen?

- **Safety**: While you, the dog or the sheep can still get hurt, the small space keeps the dog and sheep from building up speed.
- **Control**: You are close to your dog and have him on a line. The dog has to pay attention to you. He is on a line, in a small space with you and that forces him to keep you in his mental picture.

- **Sets up for success**: You are minimizing the chances of the dog biting or chasing the sheep. If he does try to bite, you are standing right there so you can properly time and deliver an appropriate correction.

- **Teaches calmness**: The dog learns to be comfortable when in close proximity to sheep.

- **Avoids confusion**: The dog learns that being around sheep doesn't mean chasing or biting them or being yelled at. He learns that it is safe and okay to be close to the sheep. Later, you will teach him to stay at the correct distance to control the sheep.

## What the semi-packed pen work does and does not do

The semi-packed pen work is designed to do the following:

- Prevent chaos and injury.

- Keep things calm and controlled.

- Teach the dog to be close to the sheep without being anxious or aggressive.

- Teach the dog to keep the handler in his mental picture.

The semi-packed pen work does not teach the dog to develop a feel for the sheep, nor does it teach him about finding balance or the proper working distance. Those skills are learned when the dog moves into a larger area.

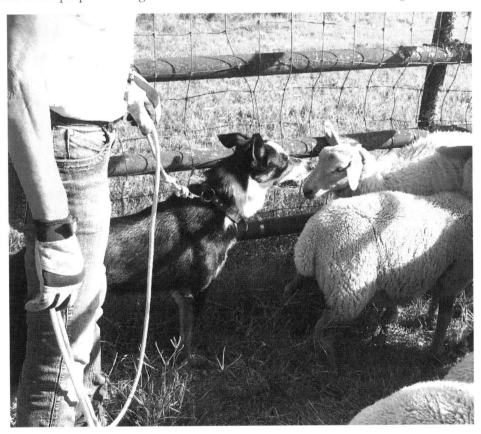

*This dog is learning to relax while being just inches from the sheep. Photo courtesy of Kay Stephens.*

## When can my dog start these exercises?

While an experienced trainer can start their dog on this exercise when he's 5 or 6 months old, a novice handler should wait until the dog is at least 8 to 10 months old and no longer in a fear period. You don't want to risk the young dog getting hurt or scared.

## What will my dog learn in the semi-packed pen exercises?

After completing these exercises, your dog will be able to do the following:

- Approach the sheep from outside the pen calmly and under control.
- Be able to lie down, come to the handler and pay attention to the handler before being allowed to enter the pen.
- Calmly enter the pen and relax around you and the sheep. He will be able to stand in the pressure zone without being frantic or afraid.
- Stand calmly next to the sheep, even if the sheep are facing him.
- Squeeze between the sheep and the fence without being afraid or fearful or biting the sheep.
- Circle around the sheep on a leash in both directions. He will later circle around the sheep off-leash.
- Change directions when you step into his path or block him.
- Lie down with sheep nearby.
- Come to you ("that'll do") with sheep nearby.

## What equipment do I need for these exercises?

**A secure 10×10 ft. pen.** The fencing or walls must be such that a foot or leg does not become caught or entangled, and the dog or sheep cannot escape. Fencing that is covered with plywood works well. Pipe fencing, if the spacing is correct, can also work. Woven wire fencing can entangle a dog or sheep leg. The ground or flooring of the pen should offer good traction. Avoid footing that is slippery, rocky or uneven. Sand is ideal.

**About 15 calm sheep.** The number of sheep can vary, depending on their size and the size of the pen. The pen should be about 80 percent full with only a small amount of open area. If possible, use weaned lambs that have been worked by dogs and do not panic when seeing a dog. Weaned lambs are more likely to be curious and face the dog. They're also less likely to seriously charge you or your dog. Avoid using sheep that will fight or butt the dog. Also avoid flighty sheep that try to escape by jumping over the pen wall or throwing themselves against the fence or the handler. The ideal sheep will flock together or stand calmly when the dog enters the pen. The best size of sheep is in the 50 to 70 pound range, or even smaller. Excessively large (150+ pound sheep) can hurt you or the dog if they run over you or crush you against the pen. You can test the sheep's reaction to a dog by taking an experienced dog into the pen. In most cases, the sheep are going to react more calmly to an experienced dog than a youngster. If the sheep run into the fences with an experienced dog, then they are probably not appropriate for a younger dog.

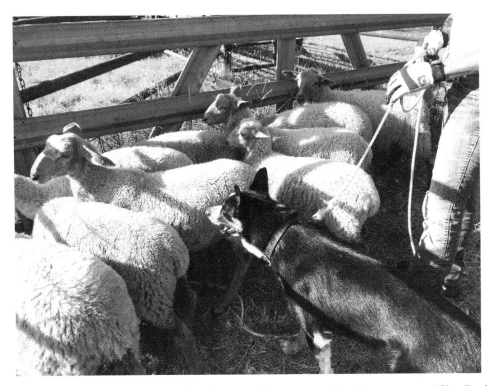

*These recently weaned lambs move away from the dog and do not charge him. Photo courtesy of Kay Stephens.*

### Having trouble finding the right sheep? Consider kid goats

For the exercises in this chapter and the next, just-weaned Boer goats or Spanish cross goats may be a good option if you don't have the right type of sheep. The key, though, is to use the Boer kid goats when they are young and only for these exercises. Goats don't flock as well as sheep, so they can be frustrating for a young or inexperienced dog to gather and drive.

**A long line and buckle collar.** For these exercises, a 10 ft. line is appropriate. Because you will be holding the line, instead of letting it drag, use a thicker line than you will use in arena or small field exercises. Keeping a dog on a line helps set up your dog for success. When training a beginning sheepdog, keep the dog on a line or leash when entering a pen, paddock or pasture. This keeps your dog from taking off and working sheep on his own. This also helps you and the dog practice success and good behaviors. Until the dog has a reliable recall when around sheep, the dog should remain on a long line for sheep work. For working in a small pen, a 10 ft. line is appropriate, but as you move to larger areas, you'll want to move up to a 25 to 30 ft. line.

The line should be lightweight, so it does not interfere with the dog's movements and made of a material that does not tangle easily. Keep in mind that the line will get wet and muddy. Biothane, because it is soft and easy to clean, is a preferred material. Nylon is more likely to cause rope burns. Nylon/cotton combinations are softer than 100 percent nylon lines, but also absorb water. Whatever type of line you choose, make sure that it can't get caught on a foot or other objects. Handles should be cut off, and the line should not have knots.

Never wrap the long line around your hand. Hold it as shown in the photos. This allows it to slide through your hand and not get tangled in your fingers.

**Gloves and sturdy shoes.** Gloves will protect your hands from rope burns. Wear shoes that will provide good traction and protect your feet from sheep hooves.

**A good attitude and time.** This exercise may try your patience and take longer than you expect.

**A ball cap or a rolled up plastic or paper feed sack** (wrap the feed sack with duct tape). These can be used to correct the dog if he tries to bite. They can also be used to make the sheep move off the dog. At some point in these beginning exercises, your dog will forget you are there or invade your space. If done correctly, slapping a ball cap or rolled feed sack against your leg is a great way to increase your personal space and to get the dog's attention.

**Recommended: An experienced handler.** Because an experienced handler is likely to have better observational skills and timing, she will be able to react to the dog and the sheep more quickly. If an experienced handler is unavailable, you can try recording your training session and watching it later.

## Exercise 1: Introducing your dog to sheep in the semi-packed pen

Upon successful completion of this exercise, you and your dog will be able to enter the small pen in a calm, confident manner. Your dog will be able to stand in the pen with the sheep and be neither afraid of nor over stimulated by the sheep. Your dog will lie down when asked and will respond to a "that'll do" cue.

### Why is this exercise so important?

Two principles of good animal training are showing the animal the correct behavior and having the animal in the right emotional frame of mind. This exercise shows your dog the proper way to behave around sheep and simultaneously teaches him not to be afraid of sheep. You are teaching him to relax and listen to you while close to the sheep. It is relatively easy to get the dog to relax and listen when the sheep are a distance away. By teaching the dog early in his training on how to relax and listen when close to the sheep, you are preventing problems later in your training. While this and the next few exercises may not seem as fun and exciting as later ones, they are building the foundation for your sheepdog training. Remember, your training is only as good as its foundation—and one of the most important parts of the foundation is the dog's attitude, which should be calm control towards the sheep and focus on you. While you may be tempted to skip these foundational steps, it will leave holes in your training and come back to haunt you. Taking the time to build a strong foundation will help you progress faster in later exercises.

**Step 1. Before getting your dog out of his kennel or crate, place the sheep in the pen and allow them to settle.** If an experienced herding dog is available, have that dog circle the sheep a few times.

> ### Should I let my dog watch me set up the sheep for the exercises?
>
> Do not allow your dog to watch you move the sheep around and then set them up for your training session. Sheep are the reward for the dog, and the reward should only be given when the dog is behaving appropriately. A dog who is watching you move sheep or that is running the fence line as you move sheep is "working." By keeping your dog in a kennel or crate and away from viewing the sheep, you are controlling the reward and saving prime learning minutes for the actual training you want to do.

**Step 2. Get your dog out of his kennel or crate and attach a long line or long leash to him.** Walk to the semi-packed pen and stand outside the pen gate. Ask for a lie down and a that'll do before going into the pen. If the dog won't do these behaviors outside the pen, he won't do it in the pen. His access to the sheep should be predicated on doing these obedience behaviors.

If, upon seeing the sheep, your dog exhibits frantic behavior such as lunging, barking or leaping, take him far enough away from the sheep so that he can focus on you instead of the sheep. Get his attention by saying his name or swatting your leg with the ball cap. Once he calms down and focuses, you can proceed. Another alternative is to take him behind a barn or other barrier so that he cannot see sheep. Then work on basic obedience, such as walking nicely on leash, sitting, lying down and coming to you. Remember that sheep are the ultimate distraction and reward for a herding dog. It is okay for the dog to be excited about seeing the sheep and even a bit rowdy, but he shouldn't be dragging his handler on leash or screaming.

If your dog is uncertain or hiding behind you as you get near the pen, stop and allow the dog to relax and look at the sheep. Showing fear as you approach the pen may be a sign that your dog is not ready to start his sheep training. Don't rush the process. If he needs to just stand outside the pen for several sessions, that is fine. If he is obviously afraid, consider postponing the start of his training for a few weeks. He should be curious about the sheep, under control and calm before you enter the pen.

**Is your dog out of control as he walks to the pen?** While a perfect obedience-type heel is not expected, the dog should not be circling around you and lunging out of control. This behavior indicates your dog doesn't have enough basic training. (See Appendix A for teaching obedience behaviors.) If this is the case, go back and work on that before introducing him to sheep. If you allow your dog to enter the pen after he drags you out of control to the sheep, you are rewarding his bad behavior. Now is the time to teach him that he will be rewarded with access to the sheep when he walks nicely to the pen.

---

## A note about obedience training

Some herding dog trainers say that no obedience training should be done before a puppy goes to sheep. The manner of obedience training matters. If the obedience training is heavy-handed, using aversive methods, physical abuse or shock collars, the dog may become afraid to work the sheep because he's afraid of being corrected. If the obedience training is done using positive reinforcement, then obedience training is a benefit to herding work. It teaches the dog to "learn how to learn" and how to focus on and respond to a human. Do not expect your dog to be able to perform obedience around the sheep at the beginning of his herding training. The sheep are a huge distraction, and the dog has to learn to generalize his obedience training to the sheep. More information about obedience training is in the appendix of this book.

---

**Step 3.** Upon entering the pen and getting closer to the sheep, the dog may hide behind the handler, eat poop or lunge at the sheep. As a handler, you must remain calm and confident. You can project confidence with both your voice and body language. Take a deep breath, drop your shoulders and relax your feet. This helps you, your dog and the sheep relax. Remind yourself that this is not a speed exercise.

If the dog is hiding behind you, give him time to settle and talk to him in a calm, confident tone. As he relaxes, take a half step to one side. Watch his body language. If he settles, take another step to the side. Your goal is to have him sitting or standing next to you in a quiet, calm manner.

Eating sheep poop when working sheep is an avoidance behavior and shows the dog is stressed. If your dog does this, redirect him by patting him or talking to him. Give him a scratch behind his ears and continue standing and watching the sheep in a calm, confident manner.

If the dog lunges at the sheep, give him a verbal correction. Keep him at your side and wait for him to settle. If he is so worked up that he can't focus, try slapping a rolled up feed sack against your leg and giving a sharper verbal correction. Remember that lunging can also be a sign of fear. If his hair is poofed up on his back, he's afraid. Stop the lunging and biting with the leash and then make the dog just stand quietly in the corner.

If your dog is curious and confident, then, still holding the line, step closer to the sheep. Allow your dog to sniff the sheep. Allow the dog to just to "hang out" and watch the sheep or sniff them as long as he is relaxed and comfortable. Your dog is not being asked to do anything but stand close to the sheep and remain calm.

113

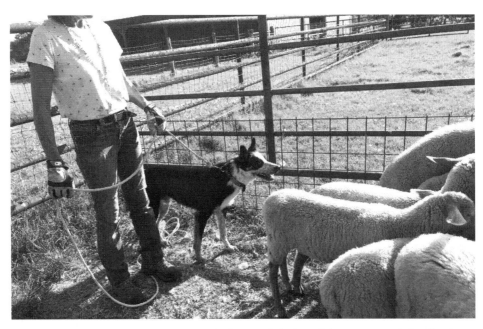

*The dog is learning to go quietly between the sheep and the fence. Photo courtesy of Kay Stephens.*

You might have to do this exercise several times. Your dog may become bored with the exercise because he is looking at, but not working, the sheep. Do not move on until you and your dog can enter the small pen in a calm, confident and controlled manner 80 percent of the time. Plan to spend at least 15 minutes in the pen each time, making sure the dog is emotionally calm, focused, and neither avoiding the sheep nor lunging at the sheep.

### What happened to my sweet dog?

Don't be surprised if your attentive, well-mannered Border Collie turns into a sheep-obsessed creature that does not recognize you during these exercises. Your goals during these exercises are to introduce your dog to sheep in a controlled setting and to take care of your sheep. Once the dog learns that calm and attentive behavior means access to sheep, his attitude will change.

## Introducing the "that'll do" cue on sheep

All sheepdogs must learn to leave the sheep and come to you when called. When a young dog is learning this exercise, keep three factors in mind:

1.  The dog must be calm, confident and focused before you can work on obedience in the pen.

2.  Set your dog up for success. Stand parallel to the dog just a few feet from him and on the same side of the sheep. Call the dog. If he comes to you, praise him. If he doesn't, step slightly into him, give a tug on the line and repeat the cue.

3.  Reward your dog for coming. A reward can be verbal praise or a scratch behind the ears. For many herding dogs, the ultimate reward is allowing them to go back to work. Mix it up. Don't always make the "that'll do" cue be the end of the training session. Give a "that'll do" cue, rub your dog's ears or shoulder, and then let him go back to interacting with the sheep.

## Introducing the "lie down" cue on sheep

The "lie down" cue is one of the most important cues in herding. Think of it as brakes on a car. You wouldn't drive a car without brakes. You shouldn't work your dog around sheep if he doesn't have brakes. When working with sheep, your dog must lie down when told. When working on this cue remember these two guidelines:

1. Set your dog up for success. It's easier for a dog to lie down when the sheep are not moving. In these early exercises, only ask for a down when the sheep are still. In the beginning, stand directly in front of the dog to cue the down. Then, try from next to the dog's shoulder. Your dog should reliably lie down on the first cue.

2. Reward your dog for lying down. This might be verbal praise or a smile. You can also reward by stepping away and letting him go back and interact with sheep.

## Exercise 2: Circling the sheep in the semi-packed pen

Upon successful completion of this exercise, you will be able to walk your dog on a line around the sheep in both directions. The dog will be moving confidently beside you—and will neither lunge at nor bite the sheep. You will also continue working on the "lie down" and "that'll do" cues. You will use the same equipment, sheep and setup as in the first exercise.

This exercise is designed to get your dog comfortable with circling the sheep. This is not balance work. That is covered in the next lesson. Instead, circling the sheep in the semi-packed pen helps your dog become comfortable moving in both directions around the sheep. Because most dogs prefer going in one direction over the other, this exercise helps you address that issue before moving to a bigger pen.

**Note**: When doing this exercise, watch both the dog and the sheep. Sheep are masters at assessing dogs. Even gentle, calm sheep may take advantage of an inexperienced dog and try to head-butt him or ram him into the fence. As a handler, you must be prepared to block (either wave your hand in front of or step in front of) the sheep to protect your dog. You must also watch the dog and make sure he doesn't dive into or bite the sheep.

**Step 1**. Enter the pen with your dog on a leash or long line. Your leash should be in your hand so it doesn't tangle and you don't trip on it. It should be slightly loose so there is no tension on the dog, but snug enough so that you can quickly stop the dog it he starts to lunge or bite. Observe your dog. If he is calm and confident, go to Step 2. If he is unsure, eating poop or lunging at the sheep, go back to the first exercise.

**Step 2**. Once inside the pen, place the lead in your left hand. Keep the line short enough so the dog can't get more than two feet in front of you. In your right hand, hold a ball cap or rolled up feed sack. Walk in a clockwise direction, with the dog next to the pen wall and you between the dog and the sheep. You should be lined up with the dog's shoulder. Use your body position to show the dog where he should be. When doing this exercise, many dogs will try and dive into or jump toward the sheep. You must be prepared to block and give a correction.

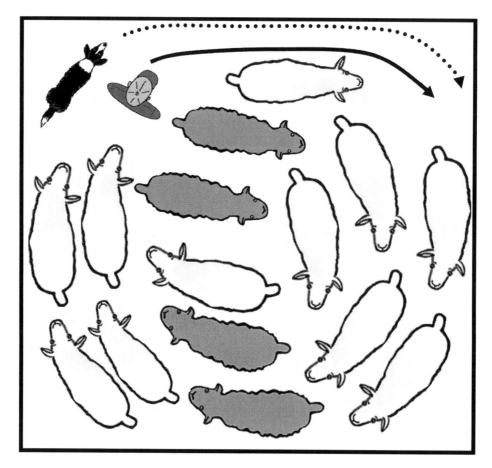

*The dog circles to the outside next to the pen wall while the handler stays at the dog's shoulder and between the dog and the sheep.*

For corrections to be effective, they must take place at the right time, in the right location and be of the correct intensity. If the dog dives into the sheep, the *correct time* is as soon as he thinks about diving into them. You can tell he's thinking about diving in when his mouth and tail position change. The *correct location* is to place yourself between the dog and the sheep. The *correct intensity* depends on the dog and the level of the transgression. For some dogs, a verbal correction may be enough. Still others may respond when you slap a feed sack against your leg. After the correction is given, *evaluate* it. Did it change the dog's behavior? A change of behavior would be the dog stopping the behavior and showing some sign of acknowledgement through his body language. This could be his ears back, his tail dropped or his head slightly turned. Remember, you want to give the mildest correction possible that changes the behavior.

**Step 3**. Once your dog can circle the sheep clockwise, while beside you, in a controlled, confident manner, change directions. When you change directions, change the lead to your right hand and the ball cap or feed sack to your left hand. It is really important to switch hands when you switch directions to avoid you or the dog getting tangled in the line. Circle the sheep in a counterclockwise direction with the dog to the outside near the pen wall and you between the dog and the sheep. As your dog becomes more comfortable with this exercise and is not diving into the sheep, you may allow him to forge a few feet in front of you as long as the dog stays on the fence line and does not move into the sheep.

Now stop and ask for a "lie down." Walk toward the corner, away from the sheep, and give a "that'll do" cue.

**Test**: Can your dog enter the pen in a calm, confident manner and, while on leash, circle the sheep to the left and circle the sheep to the right? Can he do this 80 percent of the time? Can he do this correctly at the beginning of the session? If so, then move onto Exercise 3.

## Exercise 3: Dog circles sheep without a line and changes direction

Upon successful completion of this exercise, your dog will circle the sheep in both directions in the small pen. Your dog will also turn and change directions when you block or stand in front of him. You will use the same equipment, sheep and setup as in the first two exercises. The purpose of this exercise is twofold. The dog is becoming more comfortable circling the sheep without diving in or biting them. He is also learning to respond to his handler in the presence of sheep.

**Step 1**. With your dog on a leash or a long line, enter the pen. Observe your dog's attitude. If he is calm and confident, circle the sheep as you walk beside him. If he tries biting at or diving into the sheep, go back to Exercise 2. If he is calm and confident, drop the line and follow his hip as he circles the sheep.

Observe your dog. Is he circling in a confident manner with his tail down and relaxed, not tense or tucked tightly? Or is he excited with his tail up? Is he maintaining distance from the sheep or is he jumping or diving into them? If he is jumping or diving into them, step between him and the sheep and give him a correction as suggested in the second exercise. Change directions and repeat Step 1.

**Step 2**. Once he is circling in both directions with the long line dragging, then go to Step 3.

**Step 3**. Get him to change directions by using your body to block his movement. This blocking movement will be used in future exercises, so take the time to make sure that your dog is responding to your body language. Because this exercise moves quickly and requires fairly accurate timing, it's helpful to have an experienced person helping you. If you cannot, consider taking a video and watching it so that you can evaluate your movement and timing.

Start this exercise by allowing the dog to circle the sheep. Instead of following him, turn around and go in the opposite direction. You will meet the dog as you circle one way and the dog circles the other way. When he approaches you, he should turn and go in the other direction.

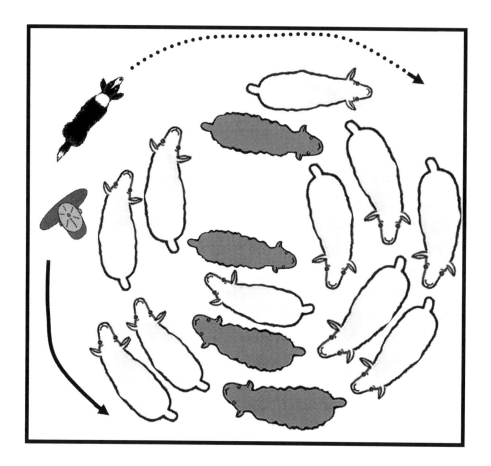

*When the dog circles clockwise, the handler goes counterclockwise and blocks the dog so the dog turns and circles counterclockwise.*

Some dogs may react to you and turn. Rather than turning, other dogs may try to go around you. Be prepared to block the dog's movement so he turns. To do this, make your stance wider, thus creating a bigger space for him to get around. You can also wave and slap a feed sack to your side. You might also consider adding a verbal correction. If a dog is really one-sided or wanting to only go in one direction, pick up the line and physically turn him to the other direction. At this point, do not get hung up on the direction change. Let him get comfortable with circling calmly and correctly in one direction, and then gradually insist on the other direction.

For the body blocking to be effective, you must give it at the right time and in the right location. If the dog doesn't respond to your presence, then you must give a correction.

**Step 4**. Once your dog is able to circle in one direction and change directions, start him in the opposite direction and make him change directions.

### Are dogs left-pawed or right-pawed?

Some dogs prefer circling counterclockwise, while others prefer clockwise. Almost all dogs will be more relaxed going one way, and tighter and stiffer going in the other direction. Most learn to work in both directions. Because it is easy to block the dog, the small pen is an ideal setting to get the dog comfortable going both ways.

**Step 5**. Now it is time to put it all together. Start circling with your dog. If the dog is staying on the fence and off of the sheep, drop the line and turn in the opposite direction to block him. Once he turns in the other direction, turn 180 degrees and block him again. Do this a few times.

**Step 6**. Test your "lie down." When you are standing between the sheep and the dog, ask him to lie down. Ask for a "that'll do."

## Evaluating your dog and determining whether to move on
Before moving onto the next lessons, you and your dog should be able to perform the following behavior goals:

- The dog can calmly approach the semi-packed pen on a loose lead and lie down and recall before entering the pen.
- The dog stands calmly and confidently in the semi-packed pen on and off leash.
- The dog calmly and confidently can circle both directions without cutting into or upsetting sheep.
- The dog will lie down and recall with you on same side of sheep.
- The dog can face sheep calmly.
- The handler can effectively block the dog from circling sheep with body position.

# Chapter 21
## Starting Balance Work in the Training Pen

In the last chapter, your dog learned to be calm and confident close to the sheep. Now, you can introduce balance, the foundation for the outrun, lift, fetch and flanks. Balance is the correct position and distance the dog must be in to control the sheep and hold them to the handler. The introduction to balance work will take place in the training pen, which is larger than the semi-packed pen.

### What should I know before starting?

Before doing these exercises, review the skills to be taught and have a clear picture of what each should look like. If you can, have an experienced handler with an experienced dog demonstrate balance work. Also, have a clear understanding and picture of the following terms.

**Balance:** Balance is the dog's ability to "read" the sheep and put himself in the best position to control the sheep and hold or bring them to the handler. Balance consists of the dog's distance from the sheep, his position in relation to the handler, and his pace. The position of the dog varies with the situation and the sheep. Sometimes the dog is in the 12 o'clock position relative to the handler. Sometimes, depending on the pressure or draw the sheep may feel, the dog is in the 10 o'clock or 2 o'clock position. Think of balance as trying to move a ball in a straight line across a sloped surface. To keep the ball from rolling down the slope, you have to push from the side instead of directly behind. Most young dogs need guidance to learn where the balance point is and to develop a feel for the sheep. To help your dog, you must understand balance. One way to learn balance is to work the sheep without a dog, as described in Chapter 16.

**Flank:** Flank is the movement of the dog around the sheep. It should be at the correct distance from the sheep, have a circular shape, and be at an appropriate speed for the situation.

### Why must my dog learn balance?

Balance work is vital to the long-term success of your herding dog. When working close to the dog, a skilled handler may be able to use obedience, such as commanding a dog stop in the correct spot, to bring the sheep straight to him. However, at greater distances the dog may be out of sight and hearing, and the handler can't direct the dog. The dog must know where he must be to influence the sheep and bring them straight to the handler. Balance work is one of the hardest lessons for novice handlers to do properly, and it's one you don't want to skip.

### What makes balance exercises so difficult?

When teaching balance work, a lot happens at once. The dog is moving, the sheep are moving and you are moving. The sheep may try to escape or run toward a fence. The dog may dive into or bite the sheep. You must be able to observe and understand what is happening, react to it and correct errors the dog makes. Good observational skills, correct timing and the athletic ability to position yourself in the right spot are needed.

One of the biggest challenges in trying to teach balance work is finding the right sheep. If the sheep have been worked by dogs a lot or are tame, they will often gather around the handler and the dog doesn't have to be correct to bring them to you.

## What strategies can I use to make balance work easier?

Mastering the semi-packed pen work in the previous chapter will help your dog be calm and exhibit self control around the sheep. When starting balance work, use a training pen, a fenced area that is about 50 ft. wide by 100 ft. long. This gives the dog enough room to practice balance and develop a feel for sheep, but also gives you some control over the situation. While experienced handlers may start balance work in a larger field, less experienced handlers usually benefit from working in a small space. For balance work, it's also crucial to have the right type of sheep. (This is discussed later in the chapter.)

**An experienced handler is very helpful at this stage of training.** With so many moving parts, it helps to have someone watching what is going on. If you're not athletic or have difficulty with balance work, an experienced handler can help by working with your dog for a few sessions.

**Consider a trainer.** Because balance work can be difficult, both in training skills needed and physical ability required, and because it requires the right type of sheep, some people send their dog to a trainer for a month or two to "start" the dog, or to teach balance work and the beginning stages of the outrun, lift and fetch.

## What equipment do I need for these exercises?

**A 50 x 100 ft. training pen.** A training pen with two rounded corners and two square corners gives you the most versatility. You'll come back to the training pen periodically during your training, so take the time to set up a proper training space. In an ideal world, the sides of the training pen would be covered or solid so the sheep are less likely to run into them. Some people make the sides appear more solid by attaching snow fence or construction fence to them. Others wire cattle panels to T-posts because the wire will break if the sheep hit the fence. (Sheep will run into fences if scared.) Because sheep are drawn to other sheep, make sure the sheep in the training pen can't see sheep outside the training pen. Before starting the exercises, check the fencing for any sharp or protruding objects and remove them. The footing should not be rocky or slippery. Solid turf or sand works well.

**About 4 to 10 calm sheep.** The sheep you use for this exercise are crucial. Avoid sheep that are suicidal or homicidal. You don't want sheep that will run into fences and harm themselves, nor do you want sheep that will attack your dog or try to run over you or your dog. At this stage of training, the dog is learning about circling the sheep and balance. Adding flighty sheep to these beginning exercises makes training so much more difficult and dangerous for you and the dog. Having too friendly sheep can be just as dangerous. You don't want sheep that follow you regardless of what the dog does. Before starting your inexperienced dog on the sheep, work the sheep with an experienced dog. If the sheep are flighty or too clingy with an experienced dog, they probably won't work for these exercises. Consider borrowing some dog-broke, calm sheep for a few months or getting just-weaned Boer goats for these exercises.

### A Shepherd's Journey

Finding the right sheep turned into a roadblock for me when starting my young dog. I sorted out some sheep I thought would work. However, when I put my calm, experienced dog in the training pen with them, the sheep lifted their heads and ran to the fence. The experienced dog and I could not get them to settle down. I knew they wouldn't work for a young, inexperienced dog.

I then borrowed a group of dog-broke sheep from a friend. When I tested them on my experienced dog, we did the balance exercises just fine. However, when my young dog stepped into the paddock, one launched herself into the fence. The others ran. They weren't the right sheep either.

Because I was new to teaching balance work, I needed calm sheep that would not run over me or the dog, or run into fences, or bolt. In the end, I opted to have an experienced trainer, who kept calm, dog-broke sheep specifically for training young dogs, to start my dog on sheep. –Beth

**A long line and buckle collar.** Because you will be working in a larger area and the dog will drag the line, use a longer, lighter line than you used in the semi-packed pen. A lightweight, biothane line that is 8–15 ft. long is ideal. Avoid longer lines because they can tangle. Also avoid parachute cord or nylon lines as they can cause serious rope burns. The line is used to help catch and stop your dog if things get out of hand. It also gives you an easy way to end a session with a keen dog who may not come when called.

**Gloves and sturdy shoes.** To protect your hands from the line and to avoid falling.

**A ball cap or rolled up feed sack wrapped in duct tape.** These may be used to get your dog's attention or to block your dog. They are not used to hit your dog. They may also be used to keep overly friendly sheep from clinging to you or trying to run you over.

**Recommended: An experienced handler.** Because an experienced handler is likely to have better observational skills and timing, she will be able to react to the dog and the sheep more quickly. If an experienced handler is unavailable, you can try recording your training session and watching it later.

## What will my dog learn from these exercises?
Once you and your dog have mastered these exercises, your dog should be able to:

1. Enter the pen calmly.
2. Keep his distance off the sheep (just outside the flight zone) when circling.
3. Go to the balance position.
4. Change directions when blocked, without cutting in.
5. Go around the sheep and next to the fence without speeding up or moving into the sheep.
6. Hold the sheep in a corner and stop the sheep if they try to break away.
7. Lie down and recall.

## What is the purpose of these exercises?
These exercises are designed to introduce your dog to the elements of flanking, the outrun, lift, fetch and balance work in a controlled setting. You are also teaching your dog the proper way to approach sheep and the proper pace to move sheep. You want your dog to be able to work in a relaxed manner and to focus on you. The number of sessions you will spend in the training pen depends on many factors such as your dog's personality, his amount of eye and tension, and your skill in being able to help the dog work correctly.

## Exercise 1: Teach your dog to circle the sheep at the correct distance
The first step in teaching balance work is teaching the dog to stay the correct distance away from the sheep. The correct distance (just outside the sheep's flight zone) varies with the dog, the sheep and the situation. In this exercise, your dog will circle around the sheep, with his line dragging and you between him and the sheep. This exercise also is the foundation of flanking exercises.

During this exercise, you'll also continue to practice "lie down" and "that'll do" a few times randomly. It is easy to fall into the habit of only stopping or recalling your dog when the training session is over. Dogs get wise to that sequence quickly, and your dog's consistency on those two cues will decrease once he connects that "lie down" and "that'll do" only happen when he is going to leave the sheep.

**Note:** Make the first three steps in this exercise part of your training routine. While they won't be listed in future exercises, they should be done for every exercise.

**Step 1.** Before getting your dog out of his kennel or crate, place the sheep in the training pen and allow them to settle. If you have an experienced herding dog available, have the dog circle the sheep a few times.

**Step 2.** Walk into the training pen with your dog on leash and stop. Evaluate your dog's attitude. Ideally, the dog should be interested in the sheep but also able, with a little help, to respond to your cues. If he is too excited to respond to your cues, it is okay to slap your hat or rolled up feed sack on your leg to get him to settle down. You can also take your dog out of the pen and approach the pen again. You may have to repeat this a few times. Once your dog is responding to you, move onto the next step.

**Step 3.** Evaluate the sheep. Ideally the sheep should notice the dog, but not run from him. If the sheep act frantic or run upon seeing the dog, they are probably not going to work for this exercise. At this stage of training, it is crucial to have the right type of sheep.

**Step 4.** Do several repetitions of lie down and that'll do before letting the dog have access to the sheep. This keeps him focused on you and reminds him that access to the sheep is dependent on responding to your cues.

**Step 5.** If this is the first time doing this exercise, walk with your dog on a long line and walk with him as he circles the sheep as you did in the semi-packed pen exercise. As in the semi-packed pen exercise, you'll be between the dog and the sheep and walking near the dog's shoulder to keep him from turning into the sheep. This gives the dog a chance to get over his initial excitement before you turn him loose. Watch for the dog to relax and drop his head and tail before you drop the line.

**Step 6.** Once your dog is calm with you as you both walk around the sheep, lie your dog down. Position yourself directly between the dog and the sheep. When facing the dog, drop the line. Encourage the dog to circle in his preferred direction. To do this, take a step toward his inside hip. If your dog tries to cut in instead of turning out as you send him, stop him and step briskly toward his head and shoulders as you send him. His first motion should be sideways, not forward. This is the introduction to flanks, and you want him to do it correctly from the very beginning. If he insists on being tight, focus on his shoulder and push him out as he circles the sheep. Continue to stay between the dog and the sheep as he circles. This keeps you in a position to block him he if tries to cut in toward the sheep.

*The handler stays between the dog and sheep as the dog circles the sheep. Photo courtesy of Kay Stephens.*

**Note:** If your dog is one-sided and only wants to circle in one direction, just focus on the direction he wants to circle. It is difficult for a beginning handler to force the dog to his more difficult side, and it can cause stress, slicing or gripping. Once the dog has mastered his preferred direction, then work on the other direction.

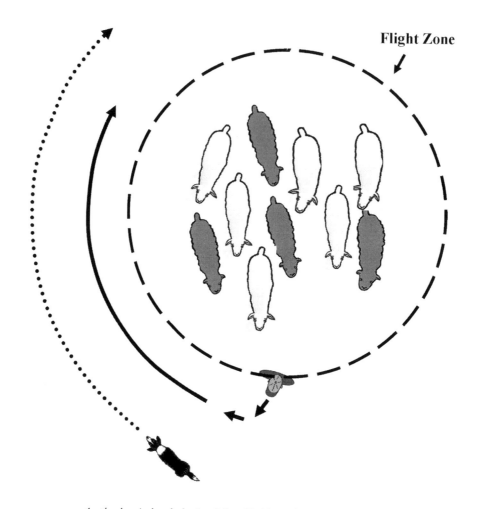

**Flight Zone**

*As the dog circles clockwise, follow his hip and circle around the sheep.*

As the dog circles, follow his hip around the sheep, making sure you are between the dog and the sheep. This encourages him to keep circling. His distance around the sheep should be the same. He should neither flare out, nor cut in. Remember, where you face the dog is where the pressure is applied. If you want him to move around the sheep, face his tail or hip. When you want him to stop or change directions, step in front of his head and face his nose. If you want to push him out or stop him, directly face his head and step toward him. If you want him closer to the sheep, face away or sideways to him.

Evaluate your dog's behavior. Is he keeping the correct distance from the stock? The correct distance is where he is influencing them, but not diving into them or causing them to scatter. If your dog is diving into the sheep, he needs a correction. Focus on the timing, location and intensity of your corrections. The *correct time* is as soon as he thinks about diving into the sheep. A dog who is thinking about diving into the sheep shows signs such as speeding up, turning his head or shoulder into the sheep, changing his ear set, showing tension in his mouth, or moving his head or tail in a more upright position. The *correct location* for a correction is to place yourself between the dog and the sheep. The *correct intensity* will depend on the dog and the level of the transgression. You want to give the mildest correction that changes the dog's behavior. After the correction is given, the dog should immediately show some sign of response with his body language. This could include moving off the sheep, relaxing his body or watching you. Remember to release the pressure on the dog when you see the dog respond to the correction by speeding him up or stepping away from him.

**How can you tell whether your dog has mastered this exercise?**
- Does your dog approach the training pen calmly and under control?
- Does your dog begin circling the sheep when you step toward his hip or tail?
- Is he circling with his body relaxed and supple in both directions?
- Is he keeping his distance constant as he circles the sheep?
- Does he stop and come to you when asked?
- Can he do the exercise reliably 80 percent of the time?
- If you can answer yes to these questions, then move onto Exercise 2. If you cannot, continue working on Exercise 1.

## Exercise 2: Teach your dog to balance the sheep to you and change directions

This exercise introduces balance, which is the position the dog must be in to bring the sheep to you. Taking the time to teach your dog to be comfortable, confident and correct in this exercise is key to success in future exercises. While it may not seem or look as exciting as some later exercises, don't be tempted to rush through it.

Once the dog is circling at the correct distance, you will then move to the opposite side of the sheep from the dog and use your body position to help him balance. When the dog is in balance and keeping his distance, you will walk backward a few steps and then have him repeat the exercise circling in the *opposite direction*. Do not start backing up until the dog is flanking cleanly around the sheep without cutting in.

The keys to this exercise are to *keep moving from side to side* and to *back up* so you are not just walking in a straight line all of the time. Many novice handlers get so involved in either watching the sheep or the dog that they forget to move. You must move so the dog has a place to take the sheep. When the dog is at the balance point, you are going to walk backward and move away from the sheep. Before trying this exercise with the dog, review the steps and illustrations carefully. For many people it's also helpful to walk through the exercises without the dog.

You will use the same equipment and setup that you did in Exercise 1. Also, you will follow the same prep steps (1–3).

**Step 1.** Once you are in the training pen with the dog and the sheep, and both the dog and sheep are settled, get between the dog and the sheep. When facing the dog, drop the line. Cue the dog to circle in his favorite direction by stepping to the side. When the dog starts to move, watch to make sure he turns cleanly to the side and does not step into the sheep as he starts to move. (This is teaching the dog how to flank, so you want to be sure he does it correctly from the very first time). As the dog circles, follow his hip around the sheep and evaluate his behavior. Is he keeping the correct distance from the stock? The correct distance is when he is moving in a smooth arc around the sheep and where he is influencing them, but not diving into them or causing them to scatter.

**Note:** As your dog gets more comfortable with this exercise, you should take just a few steps toward his hip, instead of continually following him around.

*When doing balance work, the sheep are between the dog and the handler. Photo courtesy of Beth Murray.*

**Step 2.** Now start teaching the dog to balance to you. Move to the opposite side of the sheep from the dog. As he circles clockwise, walk counterclockwise on the other side of the sheep and block him. When he changes directions and is going counterclockwise, walk clockwise on the opposite side of the sheep to block him again.

Continue this exercise until the dog is easily changing directions and keeping his distance behind the sheep. He should start anticipating your actions, and changing directions as soon as he sees you start to move.

Quickly move back and forth and make this step exciting and challenging as the dog gets better at it.

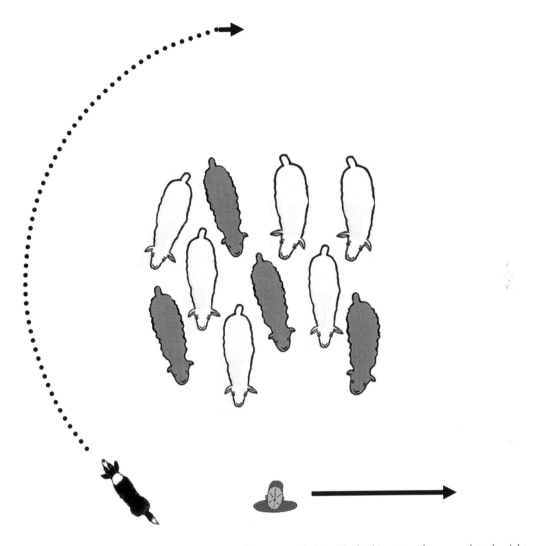

*As the dog reaches the balance point, block him to encourage him to stop circling. To do this, step sideways and to the right.*

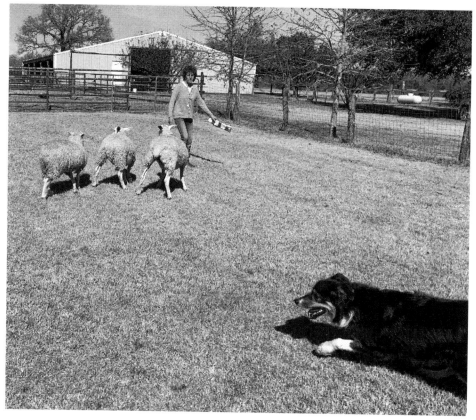

*The handler steps to the side to block the dog and help him find balance. Photo courtesy of Kay Stephens.*

**Step 3.** After the dog has mastered Step 2 and is quickly and easily moving side to side to counter your movements, you can then allow the dog to stop on balance directly across the sheep from you. For some dogs, you may use a verbal cue or "lie down" when the dog is at the balance point to help the dog find the right spot. Most well-bred Border Collies will "feel" the balance point and instinctively want to stop at that position. When the dog stops and faces the sheep on balance, reward him by stepping backward and letting him have the sheep. Walk backward a few steps. *Only back up if the dog is giving ground and not cutting into the sheep.* Be very careful to not move away from the sheep if the dog is tight as that rewards the dog and can easily teach the dog to slice or cut in on his flanks. Make sure the dog's flanks are open and clean before you start moving backwards. It is a common novice error to back up too soon and pull the dog into the sheep.

When the dog is on balance, walk backward a few steps and zigzag back and forth from side to side. When you change position, the dog should change position to mirror your position and should not get closer to the sheep. As you walk backward, pay attention to the dog's distance from the sheep. Also evaluate his attitude toward the sheep and his pace. You want him to be at a distance where he is making an impact on the sheep, but not so close to them that he is running the sheep over the top of you. As he moves the sheep toward you, he should be walking or trotting.

Always be ready to correct the dog for diving into or rushing the sheep. To correct him, you'll step directly toward the dog's head and through the sheep if needed. Body presence is enough to stop some dogs, but others need a verbal correction or a slap of the feed sack against the leg. Your correction should be strong enough to make an impact (stop the dog), but not so strong that he wants to stop working. As you block the dog and force him to change directions, pay close attention to his body. The dog should turn back over his haunches and pivot to change directions and not get closer to the sheep.

*The dog is keeping the correct distance from the sheep and not cutting in with his body. Photo courtesy of Kay Stephens.*

*When the handler blocks the dog, the dog prepares to change directions. Photo courtesy of Kay Stephens.*

*The dog turns on his haunches. Photo courtesy of Kay Stephens.*

*The dog continues his turn without stepping into the sheep. Photo courtesy of Kay Stephens.*

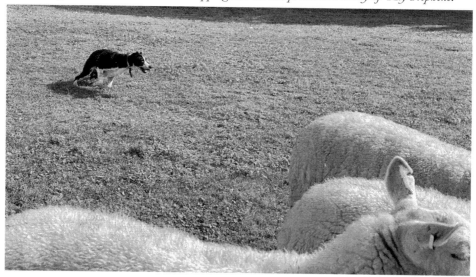

*The dog is pivoting on his rear legs. Photo courtesy of Kay Stephens.*

### Keep moving

The biggest mistake people make when doing balance work is to stop moving. When you stand still during balance work, your dog has nowhere to take the sheep. Remember, he is supposed to hold them to you. In this exercise, you are teaching the dog to balance the sheep to you, and he can't learn that if you are not moving. Because you must *keep moving* and *keep changing positions* relative to the sheep (you can't just back up), it helps to have an experienced person helping with this exercise. If you are not physically able to back up and move from side to side quickly, get someone to help you. Before trying this exercise with the dog, review the steps and illustrations carefully. Many people find it helpful to walk through the exercises without the dog. That is also a good time to make sure your working area is free of stumps, rocks or other obstacles you might trip over as you back up and move around.

**Step 4.** After the dog brings the sheep to you, immediately repeat the circling and balance work. Step to the side to encourage the dog to circle. Follow his hip for a few strides to make sure he is keeping the correct distance, then step sideways to the opposite side of the sheep and stop him at balance. Step backward a few steps so he can bring the sheep to you and zigzag, changing your position in relation to the sheep.

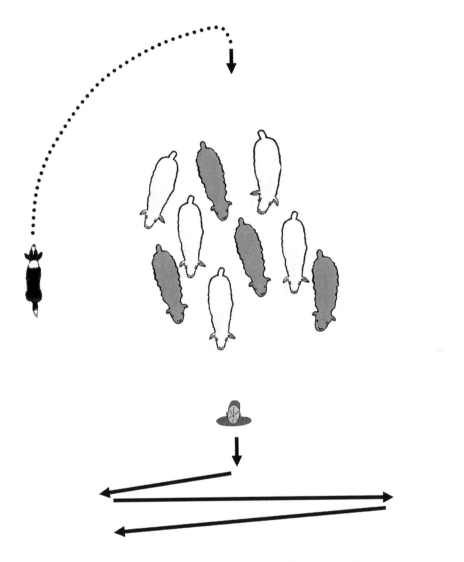

*Walk backward and zigzag. Your dog should respond by moving to balance.*

**Note**: When doing balance work, make sure that you step directly to the side of the sheep to block the dog and do not step through the sheep. The only time you want to step through the sheep is if the dog is wrong, such as diving into the sheep or bringing them to you at too fast of a pace. Otherwise, try to keep the sheep between you and the dog.

**Step 5.** After you have done a few circles and little fetches, stop moving and tell the dog to lie down. Step away from the sheep and to the same side of the sheep as the dog so you are close to the dog and ask for a "that'll do." If the dog doesn't come to you, step into the dog, pick up the line and give it a quick tug and release. Then reward your dog by doing this exercise again.

**Step 6.** Continue practicing the circling and balance work so that you can circle, balance and fetch continuously for 5 to 7 times. Mix up your directions so that you sometimes go counterclockwise a few times and then clockwise a few times.

If your dog is slow or shows hesitation or reluctance, speed him up as he circles by following him around and shushing him. If he's reluctant to walk up, turn away and give him the sheep. If he's running frantically, steady him with a verbal correction or block him.

**Step 7.** After you have done 4 to 5 circles and little fetches, tell the dog to lie down. Step away from the sheep and ask for a "that'll do." Then reward your dog by doing this exercise again.

### How can you tell whether your dog has mastered this exercise?

- The dog should circle in both directions easily and with his body relaxed and arced around the sheep. He should not be tight or stiff.
- The dog stays on the edge of the sheep's flight zone as he circles the sheep.
- You can easily block the dog and force him to change directions without the dog trying to go around you or cut in.
- The dog should turn cleanly back when you block him and not cut in toward the sheep. As he changes direction, he should pivot over his rear end.
- When the dog changes directions, he turns parallel to the sheep in his first step of the flank and keeps his distance as he circles the sheep.
- The dog moves away from you to counter your action and to balance when you step to the side. The dog does this with speed and enthusiasm.
- The dog does not dive into or grip the sheep.
- The dog comes to you and lies down when asked 80 percent of the time.

If your dog is performing this exercise correctly and reliably 80 percent of the time, then move onto Exercise 3. If you cannot, continue working on Exercise 2.

## Exercise 3: Teaching your dog to go between the sheep and a fence

Sometimes a dog must gather sheep that are near a fence. Going between the sheep and a fence and moving sheep off the fence are often stressful situations for a dog. The dog must learn to do this without losing his cool or biting the sheep. Teaching the dog in a small, controlled setting with tame, dog-broke sheep builds his confidence. During the semi-packed pen exercises, the dog was working in close proximity to sheep and the fence. Hopefully what he learned there will carry over to this exercise where the sheep are next to a fence. Your dog will circle around the sheep to the balance point, lift the sheep and bring them to you in a calm manner. As he circles and approaches the sheep, the dog will maintain his pace, without speeding up or stopping. You will use the same equipment that you did in the previous exercises.

**Step 1.** Sometimes the sheep will naturally gather near the fence, especially if they are drawn to the barn or other sheep. If they don't naturally go there, move the sheep to the fence yourself.

**Step 2.** Place your dog in a down position about 10 yards from the sheep. Position yourself between the dog and the sheep.

**Step 3.** Step toward your dog's hip and encourage him to move around behind the sheep by following his inside hip. Some dogs may not want to go between the fence and the sheep, and this will encourage him. Some dogs will try to avoid the pressure of going between the sheep and the fence and instead try to go in front of the sheep. Be prepared to block the dog if he tries to circle in front of the sheep.

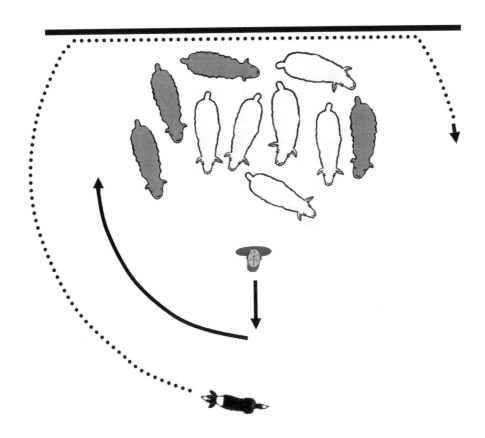

*Step toward the dog's hip and follow his hip around so that he goes between the fence and the sheep. Be ready to block the dog if he changes directions or tries to dive into the sheep.*

*Follow the dog's hip so he goes between the fence and the sheep. Photo courtesy of Kay Stephens.*

As the dog circles around behind the sheep, prepare to block him so he stops or at least hesitates between the sheep and the fence. Some dogs will try to avoid the pressure of the fence and circle behind the sheep without stopping at balance. Once the dog reaches balance, back up a few steps.

Some dogs speed up as they approach sheep standing near a fence. Before working on his pace, get him to circle and lift the sheep from the fence a few times. To slow the dog down, give a mild correction as soon as the dog starts to speed up. Take a step toward the dog and give a verbal correction or slap your hat against your leg.

How can you tell whether your dog has mastered this exercise?

- Your dog begins circling the sheep when you step toward his tail. He keeps his distance and flanks cleanly.
- Your dog keeps a consistent pace and distance when circling.
- The dog goes between the sheep and fence and lifts the sheep in a calm, confident manner.
- The dog reliably performs this exercise 80 percent of the time.

## Exercise 4: Holding the sheep to you in a corner

In this exercise, you are going to stand in the corner of the training pen and have the dog fetch and hold the sheep to you, even when you try to shoo the sheep from the corner. This exercise teaches the dog to have a better feel for the sheep and a better ability to hold the sheep together. This will help the dog when he's learning driving and penning later in his training. It's also a good opportunity to make sure the dog keeps a correct distance as he moves to head the sheep.

**Note:** Do this exercise only if you have the right type of sheep. Avoid using large sheep or sheep that clump to you or try to run over you. Older lambs are often ideal for this type of exercise. For your safety, consider placing a gate panel in the corner and standing behind it.

**Step 1.** Standing near a corner of the training pen, encourage your dog to circle toward you.

**Step 2.** Walk backward toward the corner, allowing your dog to fetch the sheep to you. Once the sheep stop, your dog should also stop. Give a lie down cue to keep him at the correct distance.

**Step 3.** Allow the dog and the sheep to stand for a few seconds. Now encourage the sheep to escape by waving your hand, stomping your foot or stepping toward them. Be ready to step out to push the dog around to the head of the sheep. You want the dog to arc out to the sheep's heads to stop them and move them back into the corner, not chase or grab them. If he's cutting in and chasing instead of heading them, go back and work on the circle and balance exercises before doing the corner work.

*Encourage the dog to arc out and stop the sheep. Photo courtesy of Kay Stephens.*

**Step 4.** Your dog should try and stop the escaping sheep and bring them back to the corner. Because this is an exciting, stressful situation, your dog may try to bite the sheep. Be prepared for this. If he tries to bite, step toward him and give a verbal correction. Keep stepping toward him until he bends away from the sheep. Watch his body language. He should remain calm and keen, not stiff or frantic. Cue him to lie down. Now walk back to the sheep and set up the situation again. During all of these exercises, you should ask for a "lie down" and "that'll do" randomly in the sessions.

If your dog allows the sheep to escape, step out and push him around to the heads and have him gather them as he would in an outrun. Remember to keep this exciting. You want your dog to like holding the sheep to you in a corner. Once a dog masters this exercise, he usually likes to fetch the sheep into a corner and hold them there.

### How can you tell whether your dog has mastered this exercise?

- Your dog arcs out in a clean flank to the head of the sheep.
- The dog calmly and confidently holds the sheep to you.
- The dog can manage the excitement of sheep breaking away without gripping or diving in.

After you've mastered all four exercises in this chapter, you are ready to move onto working in a larger field. Plan to continue practicing these exercises throughout your training journey. Good balance is an essential trait of a good working dog. Much of the later training takes the balance out of the dog by forcing him to give up balance to meet the artificial requirements of trial work. Because of this, it is important to go back and put the balance back in your dog on a regular basis. Working in different places, working fresh sheep, and working different numbers and types of sheep will all help your dog keep his balance tuned up. Balance is one of those things that if you don't use it, you will lose it.

## Gripping: When good dogs do bad things

In general, gripping (biting the sheep) is only acceptable when the sheep is facing the dog, challenging the dog or refusing to move away from the dog. An appropriate grip is generally accepted as a quick bite on the sheep's nose with an instant release. Biting the sheep on any other part of the body, or when the sheep is moving away from the dog, or not releasing the bite instantly is considered undesirable and will usually result in disqualification at trial. The one exception, depending on circumstances, could be a dog cleanly nipping the hock or lower back leg of a sheep that is stopping in spite of the dog's best efforts. You may encounter some gripping issues early on in your work in a semi-packed pen, but it is usually in the larger and more exciting situation of the training pen that gripping may show up and need to be addressed.

Gripping is usually a symptom of an underlying issue with the dog. Thus, there is no one answer for how to address inappropriate gripping. Some common reasons that a dog will grip include overexcitement, being too close to the sheep to control them properly (usually after slicing a flank), fear of the sheep, high prey drive, confusion or frustration in the training process, and having been allowed to use gripping as a method to handle sheep in his early training. Some dogs also have a short temper and will resort to biting if the sheep do not respond to the dog's presence quickly.

*Because the sheep is facing and challenging the dog, a grip is acceptable. Photo courtesy of Carol Clawson.*

*When the dog's prey drive kicks in, he may exhibit an incorrect grip as shown here. Photo courtesy of Carol Clawson.*

*This dog is too close to the sheep to control it properly and is exhibiting an incorrect grip. Photo courtesy of Carol Clawson.*

Since there are many "causes" for gripping, it is best to evaluate each dog as individual. Notice when the grip occurs. What is the dog doing before he grips and what is his body language telling you? Is he aroused, scared, or excited? What are the sheep doing when the grip happens? Are they running away, facing the dog, splitting apart or refusing to move?

Once you've identified the type of situation where the grip is happening, find a way to isolate that situation and address the underlying issue. Here are some examples:

- If the dog grips when the sheep run, and he is slicing his flank (instead of arcing out to their heads), then work on opening up his flanks. A good place to practice opening up flanks are when the sheep are held in the corner of the training pen and not moving.

- If the dog is singling off one sheep to chase and bite (often high prey drive), then get him in a small area, such as the semi-packed pen, where you can correct that behavior as it starts and remind him that you control the access to the sheep.

- If the dog is biting a sheep on the rear end because it's not moving away, teach the dog patience and teach the dog how to move sheep from a distance by a quick approach and stop method.

- If the dog is clearly showing signs of fear, go back and work in the semi-packed pen and help him gain confidence working in close proximity to the sheep.

One thing you shouldn't do is to use a shock collar to stop gripping. Again, the collar uses pain to stop a behavior and does not teach the dog the correct behavior. It can also make the dog more anxious and nervous around the sheep as he will learn proximity to the sheep is linked to being shocked. Finally, between the handler's usually slow reflexes and the slight lag time in applying the shock, the shock usually happens after the grip and does not teach the dog not to grip.

# Chapter 22
## Teaching the Outrun, Lift and Fetch

Once your dog is comfortable doing balance work in a small, controlled setting, it's time to move to a larger field to teach the outrun, lift and fetch. The exercises in this chapter are designed to teach your dog to perform an outrun while keeping the correct distance from the sheep, lift the sheep in a confident, calm manner and bring the sheep to you at the proper pace. The dog should be developing a feel for the sheep as well as listening and responding to you.

A dog who performs these exercises reliably is useful for some farm work (though some additional training is recommended). For those interested in competing in trials, the outrun, lift and fetch often make up 50 percent of the points in USBCHA trials. While a dog will not be ready for competition yet, he will have a solid foundation for future competitions.

## What will my dog learn in these exercises?
Once you and your dog have mastered these exercises, your dog will be able to do the following:

- Calmly walk onto the field and relax around you and the sheep.
- Perform balance work in a large field, while maintaining clean, open flanks.
- Complete gathers of 100 yards or more in both directions.
- Lift the sheep in a calm, confident manner.
- Fetch the sheep to you at a slow trot and in a straight line.
- Lie down on the outrun.
- Lie down on the fetch.

## What terminology should I know before starting?
**Outrun**: The dog arcs around the sheep to the balance point behind the sheep. When the dog circles the sheep, he must stay far enough away from the sheep so that he doesn't disturb them or cause them to move.

*The ideal outrun* is shaped like an upside-down pear, with the widest part being when the dog is even with and moving past the sheep. The dog's outrun should continue in an arc at the same distance behind the sheep. When performing the outrun, the dog should look in at the sheep, then cast away from the sheep as he judges the sheep's response. During a correct outrun, the dog checks the sheep and casts out all the way around. The dog should run with purpose and determination, but not frantically. He should not be lackadaisical or stop to sniff the ground.

If he's too close and disturbs the sheep, he's too tight and should be corrected. In an outrun that is too tight, the dog takes a path that is in the sheep's flight zone and will disturb the sheep. Most young dogs will run too tight and must be shown the correct distance from the sheep. When the dog runs too tight, he affects the sheep while he is outrunning instead of when he is lifting the sheep. Thus, the outrun and lift get combined into one action when they should be two separate and different actions the dog does. This results in the sheep taking off too fast and not on a line to the handler.

If he circles so far away from the sheep that he is wasting time and energy, he is too wide. Sometimes he loses contact and even sight of the sheep. A dog who runs too wide is not watching or feeling his sheep. A dog who runs the fence line instead of watching and adjusting his position according to the sheep is also considered too wide. Sometimes a dog runs too wide because he has been corrected too harshly for being too tight and sometimes it's a genetic trait. When a dog is just starting out, you can allow your dog to run a little wide. However, if he starts losing contact with the sheep, you'll need to correct him.

In an outrun that is flat on top, the dog does not complete the arc of his outrun. For instance, if the dog is circling clockwise, somewhere between the 9 and 12 o'clock position on the field, the dog cuts in and toward the sheep. Dogs often learn to be "flat on top" because they are trained on sheep that start walking to the handler as soon as they see a dog; the dog then cuts in to keep up with the sheep. Making sure that does not happen is important in helping to teach your dog to correctly finish his outrun. Correcting an outrun that is too flat is best done when just starting to teach the outrun. During the shorter outruns, you are in the best position to make a correction.

While an outrun can vary from 30 to 1,000 yards, the dog should still arc around the sheep at the correct distance from them.

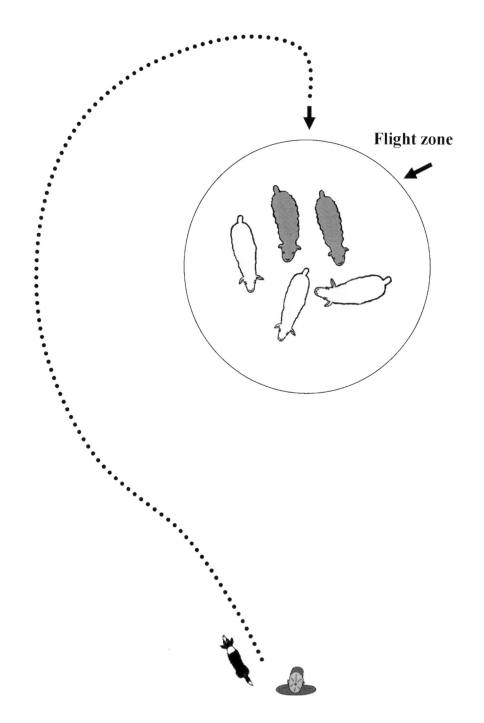

**Flight zone**

*The ideal outrun is shaped like an upside down pear.*

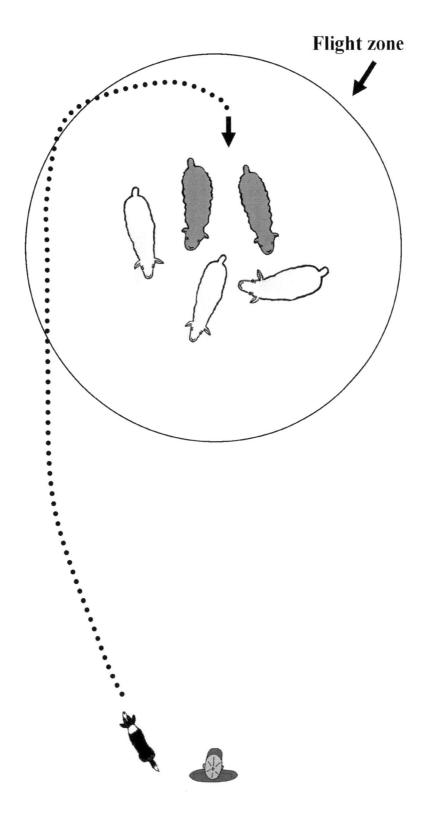

**Flight zone**

*If a dog is too close or tight on the outrun, he will disturb the sheep.*

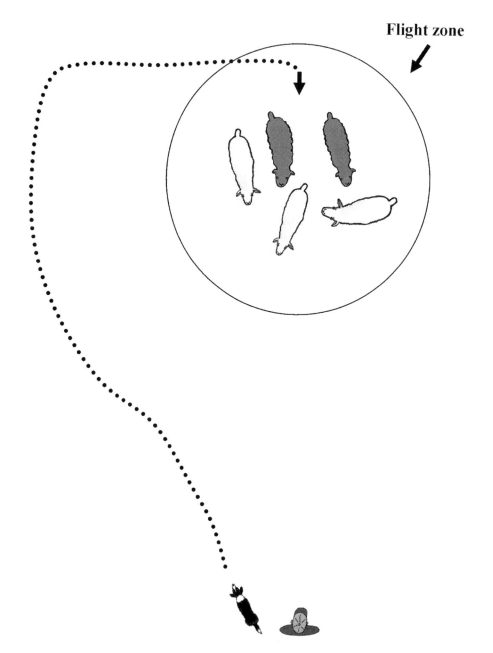

**Flight zone**

*A flat outrun. Notice the dog cuts in closer to the sheep as he goes behind them*
*instead of keeping his distance until he reaches the point of balance.*

**Lift**: The dog first makes contact with, or impacts, the sheep during the lift. During the lift the dog should approach the sheep in a slow, steady manner and be positioned to take the sheep directly toward the handler. The lift is the most important, and often the most overlooked part of training. During this introduction between the dog and the sheep, the sheep decide whether the dog should be respected, feared or ignored. In an ideal lift, the dog approaches the sheep in a calm, but purposeful manner, and the sheep look at the dog, turn and walk away from the dog and toward the handler. Although it only lasts a few seconds, the lift determines the relationship between the dog and the sheep. In a trial setting, it can determine the success or failure of the entire run. A dog who rushes in toward the sheep or hesitates may have some fear or confidence issues.

The lift and outrun are two separate actions. Teaching the lift as a separate action helps teach the dog to hesitate and slow down at the end of the outrun before he approaches the sheep. It is useful for the novice trainer to stop the dog at the end of the outrun and before the dog is allowed to approach the sheep. This helps remind the dog and the handler that the lift is a separate action from the outrun. Later, with experience, the dog will learn to rate himself on the lift and stopping will no longer be necessary.

A dog must develop a gentle, but firm, lift in order to be a successful trial or chore dog. Play close attention to your dog's body language as he turns into the sheep. It should be quiet, steady and determined. The sheep should turn off the dog quietly and calmly and move off at a walk or slow jog. If the dog approaches the sheep quickly or at a run, then you may need to run through the sheep and slow him down. If the dog is sensitive, then stop him with a "down" cue instead of running through the sheep. Once the dog learns to be relaxed and under control, then he can be allowed to finish his outrun and lift on his own, without the lie down cue.

**Fetch**: Once the sheep have lifted (started their movement toward the handler), the fetch begins. The fetch is when the dog brings the sheep to the handler. He should do this at a steady brisk walk or slow trot and in a straight line to the handler. The dog should be at the correct distance and position behind the sheep to hold the line and control the sheep. If your dog is running as he fetches the sheep, he is chasing, not fetching. Through the balance exercises, the dog learns to bring the sheep directly to his handler and at a correct pace.

**Gather**: The combination of the outrun, lift and fetch, or the dog getting the sheep and bringing them to you, is called the gather.

## What should I know about corrections before starting?

Before starting the outrun work, review the subject of corrections in Chapter 8. Timing, location and intensity are the three components of an effective correction. In this chapter, you will be increasing the distance between you and your dog, so you likely will have to stop the dog and reposition yourself between the dog and the sheep before giving a correction. This means that your dog must have a solid lie down at any distance. Also, you must ask for a lie down and reward the behavior (letting the dog go back to working sheep) often so that the lie down does not become a predictor of a correction.

Below are some common mistakes dogs make on the gather and the steps you should take to effectively change their behavior.

**Too tight or too flat.** As your dog arcs around the sheep, observe his behavior and distance from the sheep. The best time to correct a dog is when he takes the first step toward being tight or flat. When he does, give a push-out correction using the following steps:

1. Stop him with a "lie down." This prevents the bad behavior from continuing and stops the action, allowing you and the dog a moment to think.

2. Reposition your body so that you are between the dog and the sheep. By stepping in front of the sheep, you take away the dog's access to the sheep (negative punishment). When between the dog and the sheep, you make the biggest impact when you are closer to the sheep rather than the dog. See the diagram on page 48 for an example.

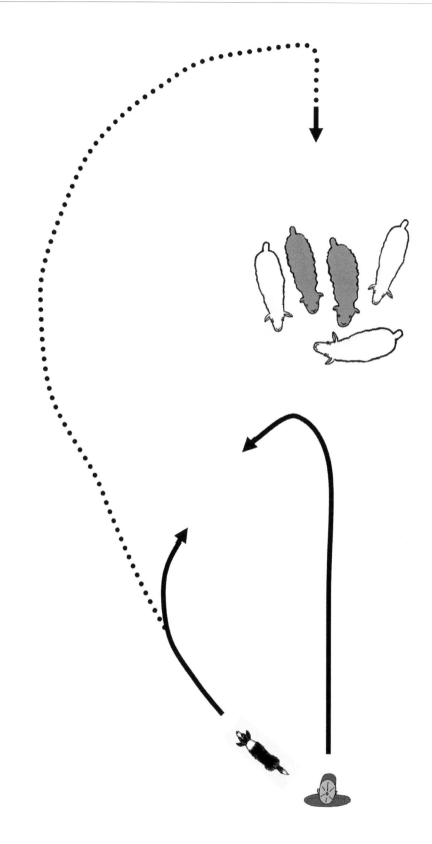

*The dotted line shows the correct path the dog should take. If he cuts in, stop him and move between the dog and the sheep.*

3. Take the following steps so that the dog gives ground or shows appeasement: Apply pressure to the dog by taking a few deliberate steps toward him. You should have direct eye contact with the dog; your shoulders should be square; you should take a full-frontal approach and step toward the dog's face. For some dogs, you'll give a growly voiced verbal correction (dogs don't speak English, so tone matters more than the actual words). For some dogs, you may slap a hat or feed sack against your leg for emphasis. The best corrections take place out of the dog's flight zone. Ideally your dog will turn his head and squint his eyes in appeasement or move a few feet farther away from you and the sheep.

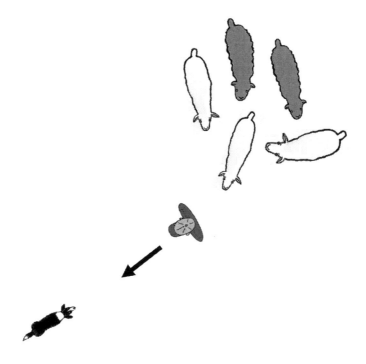

*Step toward the dog. The dog should show appeasement.*

4. Once he takes a few steps away or shows appeasement, tell him to lie down. Then move back to your original position and shush your dog to continue his outrun.

5. Observe and evaluate the correction. If it was a successful correction, the dog should take a wider path around the sheep.

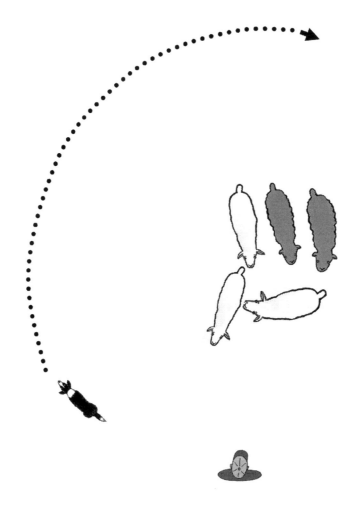

*The dog should take a wider path around the sheep after the correction.*

### A Shepherd's Journey

When I was working with my young, keen dog who was too tight or close to the sheep, I stopped her and tried correcting her. Instead of showing appeasement, she tried to evade me and get to the sheep. After evaluating the situation, I realized my body language was wrong. I wasn't squaring my shoulders, taking a full frontal approach toward her and making direct eye contact with her. Once I changed my body position, she turned her head at my approach and took a wider path around the sheep. —Beth

**Too wide**. If your dog runs too wide, try getting him to come closer by calling his name. You can also put him on a long 30 to 50 feet, lightweight line and tug and release the line when he goes too wide. Don't give a steady pull as that causes the dog to pull back against you. Again, the timing and location are critical. As soon as the dog starts getting too wide, call his name or tug and release the line. He should respond by looking at you or taking a step toward you. As soon as he responds, encourage him to move around the sheep. You can also try shushing and speeding him up to pull him in. Also, evaluate your body posture and position. Facing toward the dog could cause him to run too wide.

**Too fast on fetch.** The dog should bring the sheep to you at a steady trot, not a run. If not, follow these steps:

1. If the dog brings the sheep at a run, run through the group of sheep and toward the dog. Depending on the dog, you might also give a growly verbal correction and slap your hat against your leg. The dog should stop and may turn away from the sheep. Some dogs may try to get around you and to the sheep, so be prepared to block the dog by moving sideways and preventing him from getting to the sheep. The sheep are a reward and you control the dog's access to them. The dog earns his reward by providing the correct behavior. Any time the dog is in contact with the sheep, he is being rewarded.

*If the dog brings the sheep at a run, run through the group of sheep and toward the dog. Photo courtesy of Beth Murray.*

2. Once your dog changes his attitude (he should look thoughtful, with his head down and his mouth and tail relaxed), reposition yourself so the sheep are between you and the dog, and the dog again has access to the sheep.

3. Back up slowly and observe your dog's pace. It should be more thoughtful and at a walk or slow trot. If it's not, run through the sheep again and give a stronger correction. If the dog changes his pace, then send him on another outrun and observe his pace on the fetch. If your dog is sensitive, it's better to use the down cue to teach pace instead of a correction. Stopping the dog will create distance between the dog and the sheep and get the dog in the mindset of not rushing into the sheep. If the dog is slow or reluctant to walk up on the sheep, try backing up faster, turning your back on the dog or calling his name and shushing him a bit. You want a steady, calm and forward pace.

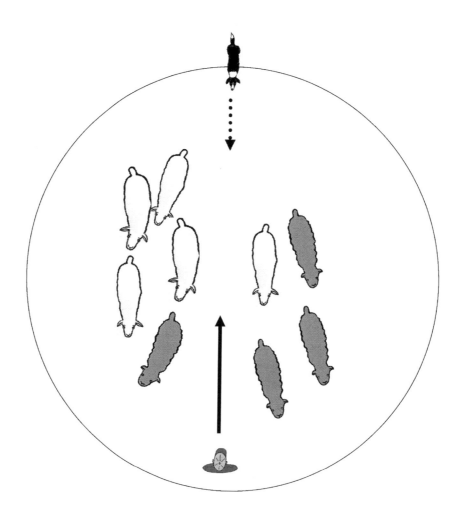

*If the dog is bringing the sheep at a run and encroaching the flight zone, run through the sheep and toward the dog.*

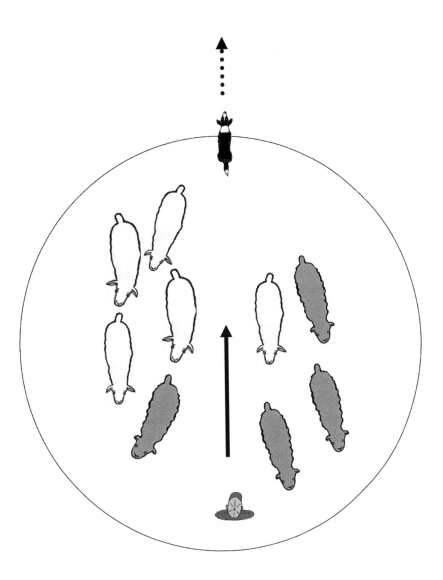

*The dog should move away from the sheep.*

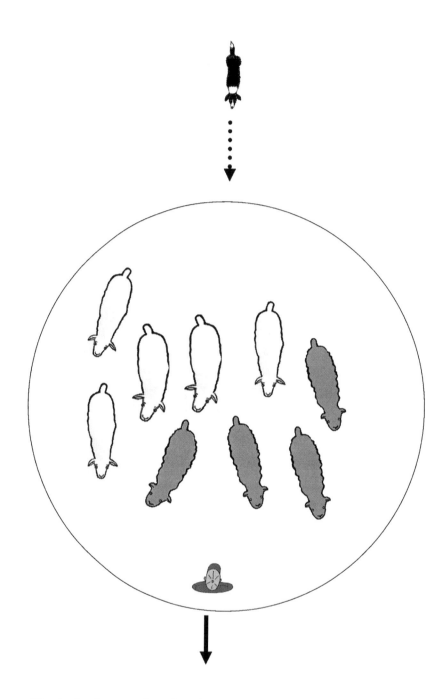

*After the dog gives ground or relaxes his attitude, then allow the dog access to the sheep. Back up and watch his pace and distance from the sheep.*

**Too slow on the fetch**: Back up faster and shush the dog.

**Off line on the fetch**: Block the dog to balance him to you.

## What equipment do I need for these exercises?

**A 5-acre field or larger**. The ideal field has minimal pressure, meaning the sheep won't be drawn to a barn or other sheep in an adjacent pasture. Avoid fields with lots of trees or objects such as farm equipment, rolls of fence, rocks or holes that the dog or sheep could fall into or hit. For these beginning training exercises, you want good visibility. Avoid fields that are so hilly that you cannot see your dog.

**About 7 to 10 calm sheep**. For these early exercises, the choice of sheep is crucial. Avoid using sheep that are aggressive to the dog or that try and run over the dog or handler. Avoid flighty or sour sheep that move before the dog completes his outrun. It is hard to teach a dog to be correct if the sheep leave before the dog hits the balance point. It is also hard to focus on the dog if you are concerned about the sheep running over you. Just-weaned Boer goats, as mentioned in earlier chapters, may be an option here.

If the sheep tend to move before the dog hits balance, try spreading hay or grain to keep the sheep in place. If the sheep feel pressure to move toward the barn, place the sheep so the pressure point (barn) is behind the dog on the lift. Another option is to have a set-out person hold, or keep, the sheep in place. If you use another person, you must first teach your dog to work around another person.

**A long line and buckle collar**. A lightweight line like you used in the previous chapter is appropriate. Depending on the dog and the handler, the dog may not require a line at this point.

**Gloves and sturdy shoes**. To protect your hands from the lines and to avoid falling.

**A ball cap or rolled up plastic or paper dog food bag wrapped in duct tape**.

**The physical ability to move around**: You will have to move a lot and react quickly in these exercises. If you cannot, consider working with an experienced handler.

## How to teach your dog to work around another person

In the following exercises, it may be necessary or helpful to have a person hold the sheep. Some dogs find working around another person very scary or upsetting. In sheepdog trials, sheep are usually held by a person at the top of the outrun. Therefore, you'll have to teach your dog to deal with this distraction and to bring the sheep away from the person setting out the sheep. Many young dogs get confused and try to take the sheep to the set-out person instead of their handler. You want to introduce your dog to the concept of a set-out person in small steps. Start with being close enough to the sheep and set-out person to help your dog.

To introduce a dog to a set-out person, you'll need the help of a friend or instructor who can play the role of the set-out person. If that person has an experienced dog who will lie quietly or sit quietly while on leash as you do these exercises, then use the dog. If the dog is rowdy, lunges at the sheep or your dog or does not stay, then don't use the dog. Return to the training pen and work your dog with the set-out person and her dog standing in the arena. The dog may be very reluctant to flank around a person and another dog, so gently push the dog to balance and keep working. You'll probably have to do this several times so the dog learns to balance to you and not the set-out person. Once the dog does this in the training pen, go to the bigger field and do balance work around the set-out person. Remind the person to stand quietly and not yell at her dog. If your dog goes to gather sheep and the set-out person is yelling at her dog, this can permanently damage a dog's ability to lift off another person.

### A Shepherd's Journey

My friend took her novice dog to a trial and sent it on an outrun. As sometimes happens at trials, it was raining. The set-out person was a large man wearing a cowboy hat and a black plastic rain suit. When the dog got to the top of the outrun, he saw what he thought was a terrifying monster, turned and ran back to his handler. It took us several weeks to retrain this dog to lift sheep with a set-out person nearby. –Kay

## Exercise 1: Perform balance work in a larger field

In this exercise, you'll perform the balance work that you did in Exercise 2 in Chapter 21, but now you will be in a larger field. Because dogs learn better when introduced to one new variable at a time, you will introduce a new variable (a large field) to the familiar (balance work).

### Why is this exercise more challenging in a bigger field?

Moving to a bigger field is a big step for both the dog and the handler. The dog is working in a new location and a situation where the sheep can escape. In the training pen, the sheep could run to a fence, but it was only a few yards away.

The handler, too, has more things to focus on, including the following:

- The sheep should be between you and your dog. Often an inexperienced handler is on the same side as the dog. This is incorrect.

- You must keep the dog from diving into or harassing the sheep. Because the sheep can escape in the larger field, the dog is more likely to be tense and dive into, split off or chase the sheep.

- You must keep an eye on the sheep and not let them run over you.

- You are constantly observing the dog and the sheep and making decisions such as whether you should move backward or to the side. You're also walking, backing up and trying to avoid falling or tripping.

### A Shepherd's Journey

When I first started working with sheepdogs, my friend and I were terrible at backing up and staying in motion so the sheep had a place to go. My friend was physically handicapped but determined to succeed in sheepdog trialing. So, she bought a treadmill and practiced walking and running backward on the treadmill so that she could be successful when she came out to work her dog on sheep. –Kay

### Performing balance work in a large field

**Step 1.** Before getting your dog out of his crate, place the sheep in the field and allow them to settle.

**Step 2.** Walk onto the field with your dog on leash and stop. Evaluate your dog's attitude. If he is attentive and under control, test his obedience by asking for a "lie down" and "that'll do." If he is excited and jumping around, wait for him to settle and then ask for a "lie down."

**Step 3.** Evaluate the sheep. Ideally they should notice the dog, but not run from the dog. If the sheep act frantic or run upon seeing the dog, they're probably not going to work for this exercise.

**Step 4.** With your dog still on the long line, give the "lie down" cue and get between the dog and the sheep. If the dog won't lie down, block him from the sheep and use a mild correction. He must attend to you and lie down before he is allowed to work sheep. Once the dog has focused on you, then face the dog and drop the line. Encourage the dog to circle in his favorite direction by stepping toward his hip. As the dog circles, follow his hip around the sheep and evaluate his behavior. Is he keeping the correct distance from the stock? The correct distance is where they notice the dog but are not moving. For this step you are between the dog and sheep, following the dog around.

**Note:** Because your dog is working in a new location, he'll probably be excited and might try diving into the sheep. Be ready to give a correction.

**Step 5.** If the dog is keeping his distance off the sheep, change your position to the opposite side of the sheep from the dog. As the dog circles, encourage him to stop and balance by blocking him. You'll do this by stepping sideways. Watch your dog and be prepared for him to try diving into the sheep.

**Step 6**. When the dog stops and faces the sheep, reward him by letting him have the sheep. Walk backward a few steps. As you walk backward, pay attention to the dog's distance from the sheep, his attitude toward the sheep and his pace. As you back up, change directions and keep the dog moving to hit balance. The dog should mirror image your movements. If you swing right, he should swing left to counterbalance you.

**Step 7**. After the dog brings the sheep to you, immediately repeat the circling and balance work (Steps 5 and 6), but in the opposite direction.

**Step 8**. Continue practicing the circling and balance work so that you can circle, balance and fetch continuously 5 to 7 times. Mix up your directions so that you sometimes go counterclockwise a few times and then clockwise a few times.

**Step 9**. After you have done 4 to 5 circles and little fetches, tell the dog to lie down. Step away from the sheep and ask for a "that'll do." Then reward your dog by doing this exercise again.

**Note**: A common mistake is to start backing up on the balance exercise before the dog has widened out enough on his flanks. The dog should be flanking in a clean arc in both directions, without coming toward the sheep, before you start backing. When you back up, you reward the dog by letting him have the sheep. If you back up when the dog is tight, you are rewarding him for being tight, and this will teach the dog to slice or cut in on his flanks, which is the opposite of what you want. Remember anytime you are backing up you are pulling the dog in towards the sheep. Only reward the dog by letting him have the sheep when he has given ground and is flanking cleanly.

## What often goes wrong with this exercise?

With a young, excited keen dog and an inexperienced handler, this exercise can quickly spiral out of control. Some find it helpful to stop the dog, recall and restart frequently rather than trying to do it 5–7 times. The downside is that this can make the dog more mechanical, rather than feeling his sheep. The upside, though, is that you will have more control and safety.

## What can you do if you are struggling with this exercise?

Try returning to the training pen and practice balance work there. If you are struggling in the training pen, spend more time there working on balance work. Wait to move onto a bigger field until you can perform balance work successfully at least 80 percent of the time in the training pen. If you're able to perform balance work in the training pen, but not the big field, evaluate what is happening in the bigger field. A video of the lesson may help you evaluate the problem.

**Is the problem the sheep?** Are the sheep moving around more in the big field than they were in the arena? Do they run from the dog? Sometimes sheep will settle and graze if they are hungry. Try penning them away from food overnight and work them in the morning when they want to graze. If that does not work and the sheep run to you or bolt from the dog, consider finding different sheep.

**Is it you?** This exercise has lots of moving parts. You have to watch the sheep and the dog and concentrate on what direction you must move next. For many handlers, the natural inclination is to stop moving and watch. *For this exercise, you must keep moving.* To get more comfortable with the exercise, try doing it without the dog. Imagine where the dog is and walk through the steps you must take. You can also try videoing the session and evaluating your movement. If you're still struggling, see whether you can find a more experienced handler to help you.

**Is it the dog?** Is the dog settling when he walks onto the field? Do you need to spend more time allowing him to settle? What is his attitude when you send him around the sheep? Is he adjusting his position to counterbalance you when you change positions? If not, you may need to push him around by stepping more aggressively to the side and slapping your hat or feed sack at him. Go back to staying with the dog as he circles the sheep to keep him off at the correct distance if necessary.

## Has your dog mastered this exercise?

- Does your dog circle the sheep in a smooth arc, with his first step to the side and not cutting into the sheep, when you step toward his hip or tail?

- Does your dog move to balance and mirror your actions when you step to the side?

- Does your dog bring the sheep toward you without diving into them and while staying on the edge of the flight zone?

- Does your dog do this in both directions?

- Does he stop and come to you when asked?

- Can he do the exercise reliably 80 percent of the time?

If you can answer yes to these questions, then move onto the next exercise. If not, continue working on the balance work in a larger field.

## Exercise 2: Teaching the 30-yard outrun in your dog's preferred direction

If your dog is reliably doing balance work in a bigger field, introduce gathers (outruns, lifts and fetches). The outrun is taught in incremental stages. First, the dog learns to perform the 30-yard outrun correctly in one direction and then the other. Then, the dog learns to perform a 40-yard outrun in both directions. Once he masters that, the outrun is lengthened another 10 yards, and so on and so on. Because the outrun behavior has been bred into Border Collies, it is tempting to skip steps and lengthen the outrun too quickly. Don't do it. You may miss small errors that creep in. The dog can start stopping a few steps short, running too tight or lifting too rashly. The next thing you know, you have big problems and bad habits.

When teaching a dog to correctly perform a 30-yard outrun, you are building the foundation for the dog to perform longer outruns at the correct distance, pace and manner. The 30-yard distance is big enough to teach the basics and small enough to easily reach and correct your dog.

In this exercise, you will introduce the elements of the outrun, lift and fetch at a distance of 30 yards. You will use the same field, sheep and other equipment that you used in Exercise 1. You will also repeat Steps 1 to 3.

---

### Should I say "come-bye" or "away to me" when practicing outruns?

At this stage of training, avoid giving directional cues such as "come-bye" or "away to me." Just send the dog with a sshh noise or by stepping to the side. If the dog is not doing his outrun correctly (slicing in or running too wide), then the dog could associate the directional cue with the incorrect movement. Wait to add the cue until the small outrun is consistently the correct shape and speed.

---

**Step 1**. With your dog on the long line, give the "lie down" cue and step halfway between the dog and the sheep. When facing the dog, drop the line. Encourage the dog to circle in his favorite direction by stepping to the side opposite of where you want him to go. **Note**: Depending on the dog, the line may be unnecessary at this point.

**Step 2**. Do not stand still and hope your dog does the outrun correctly. You must move and teach your dog to be correct. If you anticipate him stopping short on the outrun, follow his tail to make sure he finishes the outrun. If you anticipate him not going deep enough, or far enough behind the sheep, walk toward the sheep (if he's not deep enough, you can walk or run through the sheep and block his access to them). If you anticipate him overrunning, walk toward the other side to block him. If he's perfect, cue him to lie down, pause, then back up and give him access to the sheep.

As the dog outruns, evaluate his behavior. Is he keeping the correct distance from the stock? The correct distance is where he is influencing them, but not diving into them or causing them to scatter. The sheep should notice the dog by lifting their heads or cocking their ears, but they shouldn't run. If you anticipate your dog being too tight or too close to the sheep, too flat or diving into the sheep, be prepared to walk to the sheep and block him.

**Step 3**. As your dog approaches the balance point, be prepared to step sideways and block him if he circles past balance. At this stage, you are still showing him where balance is. Pay attention to your timing and body position. On his first step past balance, move to block him and give a verbal correction.

**Step 4**. Observe how your dog approaches the sheep. Plan to stop your dog at the end of the outrun (when he reaches balance point) and before he turns into the sheep. The outrun and lift should be two different exercises for your dog at this point in his training. As the dog lifts, he should be calm, confident and steady as he approaches them. If he dives into them or tries to bite them, give a correction. Focus on your timing, location and intensity of the correction.

**Step 5**. Observe the dog's pace as he begins the fetch. The sheep should be walking or trotting. If the sheep are running, your dog is likely bringing them too fast. Step through the sheep and correct the dog. If the dog is hesitant, encourage your dog by shushing or calling his name and keep backing up or turning your body away from the dog to release pressure.

**Step 6**. Once the dog brings the sheep to you, tell him to lie down. Reposition yourself so that you and the dog are on the same side of the sheep. Give a "that'll do" and practice the exercise again.

### Has your dog mastered this exercise?

- Does your dog perform the outrun without cutting in when released?
- Does your dog perform the outrun at the correct distance, neither too tight nor flat on top?
- Does he stop at balance? He should begin feeling where the balance point is.
- Does he lift the sheep slowly and steadily, with confidence, but without diving into them?
- Does he fetch the sheep at a steady trot and in a straight line to you?
- Does he stop when asked at the end of the outrun and at the end of the fetch?
- Does he come when asked?
- Can he do the exercise reliably 80 percent of the time?

If you can answer yes to these questions, move onto the next exercise: the 30-yard outrun in the other direction.

---

### Should I let my dog watch other dogs work?

Some trainers like to tie their young dogs out to watch while they work other dogs. I think it's a risky practice. Young dogs or pups may be put off by corrections being applied to the working dog. They may be very excited to watch and bark and lunge, which means the handler needs to stop and address that behavior instead of training the dog on the field. In my mind, it's a waste of the young dog's attention span. For most young dogs, and especially novice handlers, it's best to keep your dog away from the sheep until it is his turn to work. For advanced dogs, training them to lie quietly and wait their turn is a good training option, if you are prepared to handle the situation by focusing on good behavior in both dogs. Even so, it can be very tricky to correct one dog without upsetting the other dog. –Kay

---

## Exercise 3: Teaching your dog the 30-yard outrun in the other direction

In this exercise, you'll repeat Exercise 2, but in your dog's weaker direction. Your dog is likely to be tighter, flatter on top or to stop short on his weaker side, so think about what help he'll likely need before sending him. After sending him, start walking, either to push him around, push him out or block him. Be prepared to stop your dog, reposition and correct him when practicing the outrun.

Once you have mastered the 30-yard outrun in both directions try switching it up. Send your dog in one direction. After he has completed that outrun, send him in the other direction. Can he consistently perform well in both directions? Can he do this the first time you take him onto the field? You will probably discover your dog is naturally more comfortable on one side than the other. To keep him equally good in both directions, practice the 60/40 rule where you work his weaker side 60 percent of the time.

## Exercise 4: Lengthening the outrun

Once your dog can reliably perform outruns at 30 yards in both clockwise and counterclockwise directions, lengthen the outrun. Do this process in 10-yard increments. Increase the distance only when the dog can perform correctly at the new distance in the first few minutes of training and 80 percent of the time.

**The biggest mistake people make is increasing the distance of the outrun too quickly.** For instance, if the dog is performing 30-yard outruns, a handler sets up a 50-yard outrun. If the dog does that once, the handler jumps to a 100-yard outrun. Because the dog is uncomfortable doing this, he's more likely to be incorrect. As the distances increase, it's harder for the handler to correct the dog. While it's tempting to increase the distance of the outrun quickly, you'll build a better foundation if you do this in incremental steps. You have the most control when the outrun is short, so get it correct at the shorter distance first.

**Try back chaining the outrun.** Back chaining refers to teaching the last part of a behavior first. To do this, start in one location and move the dog farther away from the sheep each time instead of moving the sheep farther away from the dog. Because the dog has already learned the top of the outrun in one location, it's easier to lengthen the outrun without losing the correct behavior at the top. Later, you will move the sheep to different locations.

**As the distance between the dog and the handler increases, the control over the dog decreases.** You have to move and react. If the dog misses a cue or performs incorrectly, don't just stand there, do something! For most dogs, this means going closer to the dog and making sure the dog responds. It is easy to fall into the trap of standing still and yelling at the dog. If the dog starts to get tight or misses a "lie down," immediately get close enough to impact the dog and make sure you get the correct behavior. This often means running to get yourself in position quickly.

**Don't let the dog practice the wrong behavior.** If something isn't working, stop and evaluate. Go back to the training pen if needed. Remember, you are adding a big variable: distance. This is where most dog training falls apart. Watch any trial and you will see how the obedience improves as the dog gets closer to the handler. This is mostly due to lazy training. Instead of going out to where the dog is wrong, handlers stand and yell at the dog. Standing and yelling teaches your dog that you won't come out to him and that obedience at a distance is optional. Move every single time. Pay special attention to how deep or far the dog is behind the sheep as he finishes his outrun. Most novice dogs tend to come in too shallow and disturb the sheep. This quickly becomes a bad habit.

When you lengthen the outrun, start with the dog's preferred side. Once he's performing correctly at the longer distance on his preferred side, work on his weaker side. After your dog can perform the outrun in both directions and consistently at 40 yards, then increase the distance to 50 yards. Continue increasing the distance of the outrun by 10-yard increments.

## Exercise 5: Teaching the stop on the outrun

Useful herding dogs stop on cue, even on an outrun. For a dog who's excited to gather his sheep, this can be a challenge. As with other exercises, you'll teach this in steps. First, teach the dog to stop on the outrun when he's within 10 yards of you and you can control him with the long line. After he masters that, incrementally increase the distance and difficulty.

You will use the same equipment and setup that you used in the previous exercises. Even if you haven't had your dog on a line for the outrun exercises, you will want to attach a line for this.

## At what stage of training should I teach this?

Your dog should consistently and confidently be able to do a 100-yard outrun in both directions. If he is hesitant or unsure about doing an outrun at this distance, he's not ready for this exercise.

## Steps for teaching this exercise

**Step 1.** Set up your dog for a 100-yard outrun. With the long line dragging the ground, send your dog on an outrun. In this exercise, the sheep are at 12 o'clock and the handler is at 6 o'clock.

**Step 2.** Tell him to lie down before hitting 9 o'clock if clockwise and 3 o'clock if counterclockwise. If he lies down on the first cue, shush him and encourage him to complete the outrun. Finishing the outrun is his reward for lying down.

If he does not lie down, start by giving a verbal correction and stepping toward the dog. If he responds with a lie down, reward his correct response by shushing him on around the sheep. If he ignores the verbal correction, give the line a tug and release. Then get between him and the sheep. Repeat the cue and make him lie down. Holding the line, take him away from the sheep. Set up another outrun and repeat this exercise. If he lies down, he is rewarded by getting to finish the outrun and get access to the sheep. If he does not lie down, take away his access to the sheep. **Note:** If the dog repeatedly ignores the lie down until you verbally correct him, then skip the verbal correction, give a quick tug and release of the line and follow the same steps.

## How do I increase the difficulty of this exercise?

Once your dog can consistently lie down before hitting 9 o'clock or 3 o'clock, then increase the difficulty. Ask him to lie down him between 9 and 12 o'clock (if going clockwise) or between 3 and 12 o'clock (if going counterclockwise).

**Step 1.** With the line dragging, set your dog up for an outrun and send him. After he passes the 9 or 3 o'clock position, ask for a "lie down."

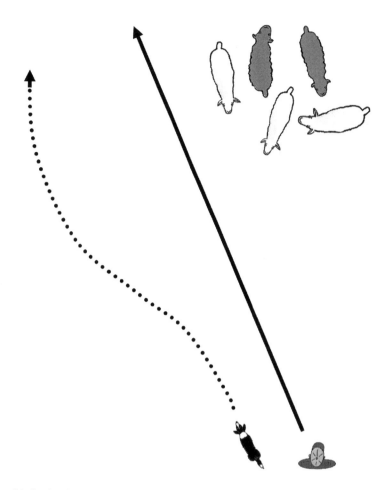

*If the dog does not lie down, then the handler must block access to the sheep.*

**Step 2**. If your dog lies down on the first cue, shush him and let him continue his outrun, lift and fetch. If your dog does not, block his access to the sheep. Pick up the line and give a "lie down" cue. Once he lies down, reward him by giving him access to the sheep. As your dog progresses in his training, have him lie down for a few seconds before shushing him on. Incrementally work up to a 5 to 10 second wait.

### How often do you do this exercise?

Don't practice this too frequently because your dog may become hesitant on his outrun. For a soft, obedient dog, you might only practice this on 1 out of 10 outruns. For a bolder dog, you might do it 50 percent of the time. For most dogs, you might ask for it about 20 percent of the time. Because you will need to stop the dog on the outrun to correct the shape of the outrun or redirect the dog, it's important to have this behavior installed early in the dog's training.

## Exercise 6: Teaching the stop on the fetch

Your dog also must learn to stop on the fetch. This exercise, like the stop on the outrun, is best taught when the outruns are still short, such as 40 yards long. As you progress, you will continue working on the stop on the fetch at greater distances.

Before doing this exercise, your dog should consistently and confidently be able to do a 40-yard outrun in both directions and bring the sheep to you in a confident manner. If he is hesitant or unsure of bringing the sheep to you, he is not ready for this exercise. Use the same setup that you've been using to teach outruns. Your dog will be on a long line.

**Step 1**. Set your dog up for a 40-yard outrun and send him.

**Step 2**. After he lifts the sheep and takes a few steps on the fetch, ask for a "lie down."

**Step 3**. If the dog lies down, shush him to get up and step backward a few steps so that he immediately has access to the sheep. If the dog does not lie down but looks at you and appears to be paying attention, repeat the cue. If he takes it, shush him to get up and step backward so that he immediately has access to the sheep. If the dog does not lie down and does not appear to be listening to you, walk through the sheep and closer to the dog so you are between him and the sheep. Slap your hat or bag against your leg and repeat the "lie down" cue. If he takes it, step to the other side of the sheep and allow him access to the sheep.

**Step 4**. Practice the stop at various spots on the fetch. For fast or keen dogs, practice stops more frequently. For softer dogs, practice stops less frequently.

## Exercise 7: Practicing the outrun in a new location

The best herding dogs are able to adapt to new locations and different sheep. They learn this by going to many new locations and working a variety of sheep. Before taking your dog to a new location, make sure you have a strong foundation on him. Your dog should be able to do the following:

- Perform a 100-yard outrun where the dog goes to balance and hesitates or stops on cue before turning in to gently lift the sheep.
- Stop on the outrun when asked at least 80 percent of the time.
- Stop on the fetch when asked at least 80 percent of the time.
- Come when called 100 percent of the time.

When going to a new location, your dog is likely to be excited and to forget some of his behaviors. Dogs do not generalize very well. As soon as you send the dog on an outrun, start walking toward the sheep at the top of the field. If the dog starts to be tight or wrong, you will be in a better position to stop him or protect the sheep.

When practicing outruns at a new place you're changing the environmental variable, so decrease the distance of your outrun by about half. If your dog is performing 100-yard outruns at his home training field, practice 50-yard outruns at the new place. Then, if he's correct, gradually work up to the distance he does at home.

Also, remember to practice the recall at various times and places during the training session. Your dog should come to you regardless of the position to the sheep. If you do lots of recalls off the sheep and then send your dog back to sheep, he learns that recalling means he gets to work sheep more, instead of predicting the end of the training session.

---

### A Shepherd's Journey

I always start walking when I send my dogs on an outrun. I want them to think I will meet them at the top. I rarely if ever stand and just watch the outrun. I am always walking toward the top. I can always back up if my dog is right, but if he is wrong, I can meet him and be in position to correct him. –Kay

---

You'll continue working on your dog's outrun during the working life of your dog. As your dog becomes reliable doing 100-yard outruns, you can incrementally increase the distance. You can also try outruns in hilly fields where the dog might lose sight of the sheep. When practicing these, remember to keep walking and to make sure the dog is correct.

# Chapter 23
## Putting Flank Directions on Cues

Your dog already knows how to flank or move clockwise and counterclockwise around the sheep. In this chapter, you will learn how to formalize the circling behavior by adding verbal and whistle cues for each direction.

## What will my dog learn from these exercises?

Once you and your dog have successfully completed these exercises, your dog will be able to:

- Perform balanced, off-balance and inside flanks that are the correct shape and distance from the sheep.
- Respond to a verbal cue for balanced, off-balance and inside flanks in both directions.
- Flank while driving and fetching.
- Respond to whistle cues for flanks.

## What is the purpose of these exercises?

Up until now, you have used your body position to indicate the direction you want the dog to go. But on the farm and in competition, you need a dog who responds to verbal or whistle cues. Because dogs are much more sensitive and responsive to body cues, rather than verbal or whistle cues, this takes time for the dog to learn. The exercises in this chapter build on each other, first teaching the dog to respond to a verbal flank cue that moves toward balance, then to one that is off-balance, and finally to respond to a verbal cue when the handler is behind him.

## What terminology should I know before starting?

Below are some common terms you'll hear to describe flanks:

**Flank:** A flank is composed of a **direction** (clockwise or counterclockwise), a **shape** (circle), a **distance** (from the sheep) and a **speed**. A correct flank should be in a circle around the sheep, neither getting wider nor tighter as the dog travels around the sheep.

**Balanced flank**: A balanced flank is the easiest for the dog to perform. The dog circles around the sheep toward balance in relation to the handler's position.

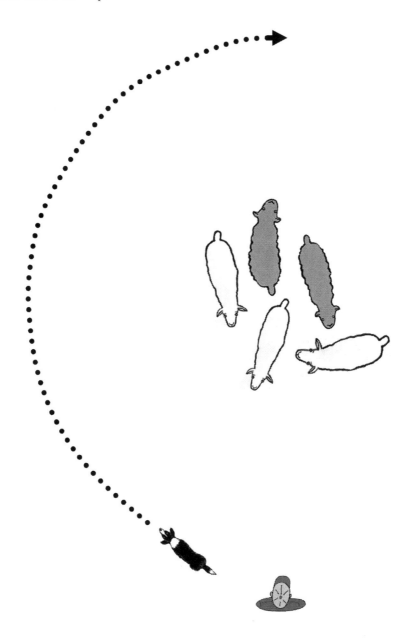

*A dog performs a balanced flank with the correct path around the sheep.*

**Off-balance flank**: The dog flanks away from the balance point. Because you've been teaching your dog to balance up until now, this is a more difficult behavior for the dog to perform.

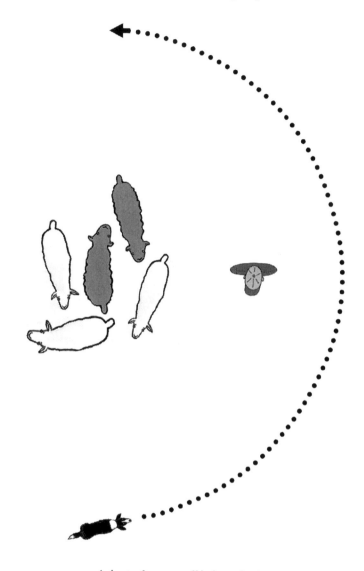

*A dog performs an off-balance flank.*

**Inside flank**: The dog circles between the handler and the sheep. This is difficult for the dog because the dog cannot see the handler—and some dogs are uncomfortable moving between the handler and the sheep. For most dogs, inside flanks are harder to learn to perform properly than balanced and off-balance flanks.

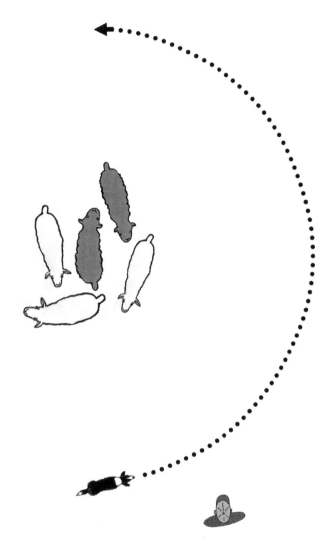

*A dog performs an inside flank.*

**Sliced flank**: Flanks should be in a circle around the sheep. The circle should neither get smaller or larger. When the dog moves in toward the sheep, it's called slicing. When a dog slices a flank, he often disturbs the sheep or causes them to move.

**Square flank**: Technically, a square flank happens when a dog turns 90 degrees, in the shape of a square, rather than a circle. However, when someone is working on "squaring up a dog's flanks," it often means making them wide enough so they do not disturb the sheep.

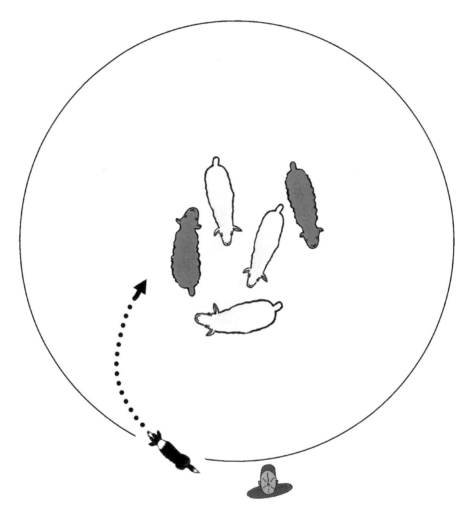

*A dog slices his flank.*

When the dog is too tight or slicing, these actions are happening:

- The dog, instead of arcing around the sheep, steps toward the sheep. This could be his first step or anywhere along the arc.
- The distance around the sheep decreases.
- The dog may turn his head or shoulders into the sheep.
- The dog gets into the sheep's flight zone before the flank is complete.
- The dog causes the sheep to move before the dog is in the correct position (unless the sheep are heavy or dog sour).

**Off-contact flank**: If, while circling the sheep, the dog's circle becomes wider, or he moves further away from the sheep, he's said to be off-contact or too wide. Often at the pen or when shedding, the dog needs to turn 90 degrees, or flank square away, from the sheep. However, most of the other times, the flank should be a circle, not a square.

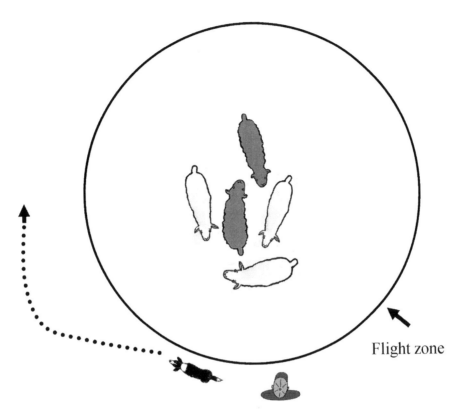

Flight zone

*A dog performs an off-contact flank.*

When the dog is too wide or off contact, these actions are happening:

- The distance around the sheep increases.
- The dog's first step may be away from the sheep.
- The dog may turn his head or shoulders away from the sheep.
- The sheep may move away as the dog loses the ability to control the sheep.

### Can I teach my dog directions without the sheep?

Some people teach their dogs to run clockwise or counterclockwise without the sheep. They may teach the dog to run in a circle around them, similar to lunging a horse, or may teach the dog to chase a toy in a particular direction. We think this is a mistake because, as you can see from our definitions, flanks are always relative to the sheep and the handler.

### What equipment do I need?
**A 50 x 100 ft. training pen**. In these exercises, you want the sheep to stand still and not bolt toward the barn or fences. In the training pen, you and your dog can focus on flanks, rather than retrieving sheep. If your sheep will stand still, you can do these exercises in a larger field.

**About 4 or more calm sheep.** Because sheep are more likely to settle when in large groups, you may want more sheep. The ideal sheep will flock together and stand quietly. Allowing them to graze or eat hay may help them settle.

**A shepherd's whistle.** Sheepdog whistles, usually triangular in shape, vary in their material and cost. For those just learning to whistle, the plastic whistles are a great choice because they are inexpensive.

*A few common sheepdog whistles are shown here. Photo courtesy of Beth Murray.*

## Exercise 1: Check the shape of the dog's flanks

Before adding a cue (verbal "come-bye" or "away to me") to a behavior (circle clockwise or circle counterclockwise), make sure the behavior (flank) is correctly shaped. If the dog is slicing his flanks or off-contact on his flanks, and then you add a cue, the dog will link the cue to sliced or off-contact flanks.

It's important that you have the flank shape correct before you start teaching the cues. You can't fix two things at once. If your dog is slicing his flanks and you are correcting for that and he is missing his cue, the dog won't know which mistake he is being corrected for doing, the direction of the flank or the shape of the flank.

Since the very first time with your dog in the training pen, you have been teaching the dog the flank's shape. In the balance and outrun exercises, you were making sure the path around the sheep was correct. Before adding a cue, check the shape of the flank and its distance from the sheep. When doing this exercise, it is helpful to have an experienced handler observing your dog's flanks. It is easy for a novice handler to miss the dog turning in on his flanks.

**Step 1.** With the sheep settled in the training pen and your dog at your side, shush him to circle around the sheep in a clockwise direction. Observe your dog. He should be maintaining the same distance around the sheep. His body should be arced around the sheep to keep the circle shape.

**If the dog is slicing, or the circle becomes smaller, take the following actions:**

1. Tell your dog to lie down.

2. Walk so that you are between the dog and the sheep (closer to the sheep).

3. Take a step toward the dog. Depending on the dog, you may verbally scold him or slap your hat against your leg (positive punishment).

4. When the dog takes a step away from you, release the pressure (negative reinforcement) and tell him to lie down. Release the pressure as soon as the dog "gives."

5. Return to your original position.

6. Shush the dog around and observe whether he is flanking correctly. If he did not change his behavior, evaluate your correction.

**If the dog is running off contact, or the circle becomes larger, take the following actions:**

1. As soon as your dog takes a step toward widening the circle, tell him to lie down.

2. Step closer to the sheep and call him toward you, then ask for a "lie down."

3. Step back to your original position and shush him around the sheep.

As he becomes more responsive to you calling him toward you, you may be able to say, "Here-here" to pull him in, rather than stopping and repositioning.

**If the dog is turning his head out, away from the sheep**, softly say his name. Since you just want him to look toward the sheep, don't be overly harsh.

**Step 2**. Repeat Step 1, but in a counterclockwise direction.

#### How do I know whether my dog has mastered this exercise?

1. Does your dog flank correctly the first time he is asked? Is his first motion to the side and not toward the sheep and does he cleanly turn back over his haunches as he turns?

2. Is his flank a circle with his body comfortably arced in both directions? If your dog is really struggling with a proper flank shape on one side, consider evaluating him for physical issues that might interfere with his ability to flex his body and push off his inside leg. Dogs, like horses, gallop on "leads." A dog flanking correctly should be on his inside lead, meaning the front leg closer to the sheep is leading as he moves.

3. Does your dog flank correctly 80 percent of the time?

If the answer to all of these are yes, proceed to the next section.

## An overview of teaching balanced, off-balance and inside flanks

Handlers often get frustrated teaching the flanks cues. Remember that you are teaching your dog to discriminate between two directional cues and this takes time. Before adding the cues, the shape and speed of the dog's flanks should be correct. Once they are, the exercises in this chapter provide an incremental approach to teaching the flanks. The steps are as follows:

1. Teach the "come-bye" flank using the steps described in the next section.

2. Get to the point where your dog reliably takes the verbal cue without relying on your body position.

3. Vary your body position around the sheep and in relation to the dog, so the dog is flanking to balance and off balance.

4. Once your dog is performing his "come-bye" cue 80 percent of the time, repeat Steps 1 to 3, but for the "away-to-me" flank.

5.    After your dog is performing both directional cues correctly 80 percent of the time, mix the cues together.

6.    After the dog is reliable on both cues regardless of your position, flanking to balance and off balance, teach inside flanks.

## Exercise 2: Balanced and off-balance flanks with a verbal cue

By now, your dog should understand how to flank correctly when you direct him with your body position. Now, you'll add a verbal cue to that action. You will start by teaching a balanced flank in one direction (clockwise or counterclockwise). Then you will teach off-balanced flanks in the same direction. Once your dog is responding to verbal cues for balanced and off-balanced flanks in one direction, you will teach the other direction.

### "Come bye?" "away to me?" "left?" "right?"

The word you put to the action is up to you. The most common verbal cue for circling clockwise, or the dog going left, is "come bye." Some people, though, say "go-by" or "left," especially if the dog was taught in obedience training that "come" means come to you. For circling counterclockwise, or the dog going right, the most common verbal cue is "away to me." Others say "right." Whatever words you choose, use them consistently.

**Step 1: Move first, then give cue.** Once the sheep are settled in the training pen, position yourself between the sheep and the dog and face the dog. Set yourself up in a neutral position so that you are in front of the dog and neither to his left or right. Take one step to your left (away from the direction you want the dog to go). Give the "come-bye" cue. Count to two. If your dog moves in the correct direction, shush him around the sheep and to balance and do a few seconds of balance work. That is his reward for making the correct choice. If the dog does not move, step further to the left to encourage him to move clockwise. Remember that where you are facing is where you are putting pressure on the dog. Facing the dog's hip encourages him to move. After you give the cue, move your body away from where you want the dog to go, thus taking pressure away from the direction you want and putting pressure on the direction you don't want.

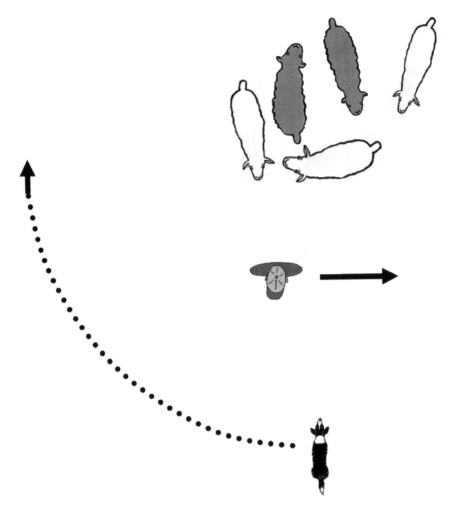

*Take one step to your left and give the "come-bye" cue.*

**Note**: Dogs are much more aware of body language than they are of verbal cues. When teaching the verbal cue, give the verbal cue, pause and then give the physical cue. If you give them at the same time, the dog will pay attention to the physical cue, rather than the verbal one. Also, don't correct your dog if he starts to anticipate the cue and flank early. At this point, your focus is on the dog understanding that you want him to flank. Later on, once he is fluent with directions, you can add a correction for flanking before the cue is given.

**Step 2: Give the cue, pause, then move**. Your dog should start to anticipate that the word means you are about to step and make him flank. He will begin to associate the verbal cue with the correct flank. This may take several lessons. Be patient. If after a few training sessions the dog is not moving on the verbal cue, but instead waiting for you to move, try increasing the speed and intensity of your movement. The dog should move on the verbal, not wait for the motion. Over time, make the motion faster and more dramatic in its intensity (almost like a correction) so that the dog would like to avoid it. You might even slap your hat or a feed bag on your leg for emphasis.

**Step 3: Cue, pause, and only move if the dog needs help**. Repeat Steps 1 and 2, but now the handler should stay in a neutral position between the sheep and the dog and face the dog. Stand directly in front of the dog and neither to his left nor right. Holding your body, hands and arms still, say, "Come-bye." Count to two. If your dog moves in the correct direction, shush him around the sheep and let him go to balance, or step back and let him have the sheep. If the dog does not move, then step quickly to your left to push the dog clockwise.

**Step 4: Get the behavior fluent**. Repeat Step 3 multiple times. Your dog should flank after your verbal cue, and you should no longer have to step and make him flank.

**Step 5: Generalize the flank cue as you change positions**. Once your dog is consistently taking the "come-bye" neutral flank, you are going to teach the off-balance flanks. This also generalizes the behavior to different situations. The dog is learning to take the directional cue regardless of where the handler is standing. To do this, have your dog lie down. Position yourself so that you are between the dog and the sheep. Take a few steps to the right. Say, "Come-bye." Pause. If the dog is correct, reward him by giving him access to the sheep. If he is not, stop him, reposition yourself and ask for it again. After the cue, if the dog hesitates, prompt the flank by doing a quick step away from the desired direction.

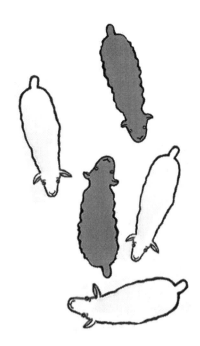

*To teach the verbal cue for a balanced flank, stand in a neutral position between the dog and the sheep.*
*Be careful not to move your hands or change your body position before you give the cue.*

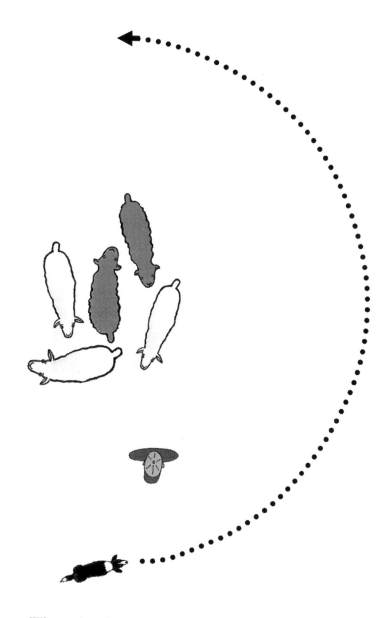

*When teaching the verbal cue for the off-balanced flank, position yourself between the dog and sheep, but a few steps to the right of neutral position.*

**Note**: If your dog goes in the wrong direction, give a mild "that's wrong" signal, such as "ah-ah," followed by a "lie down." This verbal "ah-ah" is to interrupt the dog's behavior and give him a clue that he has made an incorrect decision. It is almost a "no reward marker." It lets the dog know he will not be allowed access to the sheep and we are going to try again. Do not give a severe correction because your dog has not been taught the cue. Also, do not let your dog complete the flank if he goes the wrong way. Always stop him and start over if he takes the wrong flank. Allowing the dog to finish the flank and have his sheep is a reward, and you do not want to reward an incorrect response to cues.

**Step 6: Continue to proof the cue..** As your dog becomes more consistent at responding to the off-balance flank cue, then increase the difficulty and position yourself parallel relative to the sheep. Give the cue and pause. If he takes it correctly, he gets access to the sheep. If he doesn't, reposition and ask again. See diagram, page 163.

**Step 7: Increase the difficulty.** Move your position off to the side and behind the sheep. Give the cue and pause. Allow access to the sheep if he is correct. If he's not correct, give a verbal "ah-ah," stop him, reposition and try again.

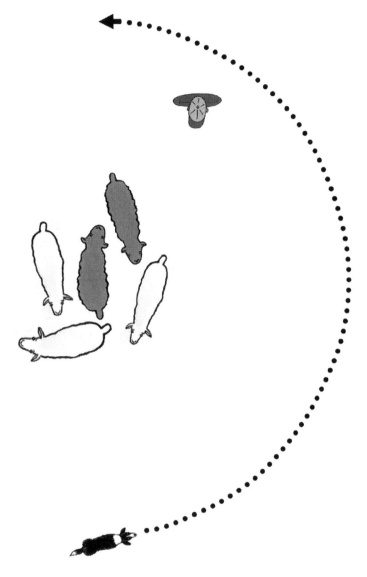

*Move to the side and behind the sheep. Then ask for the off-balance flank.*

**Step 8: Continue to monitor the shape of the dog's flanks.** Continue to monitor the shape of the dog's flanks. As you step away from the dog, he may pull in. If that happens, stop the dog, position yourself between dog and sheep and correct the shape of the flanks as described earlier. Constantly monitor the dog's body position to make sure he pivots sideways as he changes directions.

### What if my dog is consistently flanking in the wrong direction?

If your dog is consistently flanking in the wrong direction, evaluate these possible causes:

- Is he overexcited or confused?
- Are the sheep leaving, causing the dog to want to move? Once the dog is trained, he will have to flank regardless of the sheep's behavior, but in the beginning, help the dog by having sheep that will more or less stay in place.

- Is your cue clear and consistent (same word, same tone, same loudness)? If the cue is different, then it is a different cue to the dog. For instance, the dog interprets "away to me" and "away" as different cues. While first teaching cues, they should be as consistent as possible. Later, you can vary the tone or length of the cue to affect the speed or length of the dog's flanks.

- Are you stopping your dog every time he is wrong? Allowing the dog to have the sheep is a reward, so don't let him have the sheep for incorrect behavior.

- Is your verbal cue coming a few seconds before your physical cue? Many people unconsciously move their hands or arms to help the dog, and the dog relies on those physical cues instead of the verbal cue.

- Are you rewarding the dog when he is correct by stepping back, releasing pressure and allowing him to have the sheep?

- Are you having to correct sliced flanks while doing this exercise? If so, that will confuse the dog. Fix the flank shape before you add directional cues.

> ### A Shepherd's Journey
>
> A herding friend always moved her hands when giving a cue, even when she tried to hold her body still. As a result, her dogs were watching instead of listening to her, and this made teaching verbal cues almost impossible. I finally gave her a different behavior to think about. "Keep your hands in your pockets" was her cue to stop moving her hands. It worked. People, just like dogs, learn from being shown the right thing instead of being criticized, or punished, for doing wrong. –Kay

### How will I know whether my dog has mastered the "come-bye" flank cue?

Plan to spend at least a week (five or more sessions) teaching the "come-bye" flank cue. Some dogs may take a lot longer, so be patient. Evaluate your dog about once a week. Does he respond to the verbal cue 80 percent of the time when you are in various positions on the field? If he does, then move on to teaching the "away-to-me" or counterclockwise cue.

### Teaching the "away-to-me" flank cue

You will use the same steps for teaching the "away-to-me" cue that you did for the "come-bye" cue. When teaching this cue, though, refrain from using the "come-bye" cue. You want to teach them separately and make sure your dog performs them correctly 80 percent of the time before mixing them up.

### Testing the cues

After your dog has learned his "away-to-me" cue, then you can start using both cues. The key to doing this is to be random. If you give the "away-to-me" cue and then give the "come-bye" cue, and keep alternating, the dog will learn the pattern. So, one time, you might give three "away-to-me" cues, one "come-bye" cue, then two "away-to-me" cues and four "come-bye" cues. It is easy to fall into the habit of alternating the two cues back and forth, and your dog will anticipate that pattern. Also, be careful that you practice flanking the dog regardless of the sheep's direction. Handlers tend to flank the dog to where the sheep are looking or walking, and the dog learns to anticipate that. So, it's important to practice flanking the dog in the unexpected direction.

### How do I know whether my dog has mastered this exercise?

- Does your dog respond correctly to clockwise and counterclockwise cues for balanced and off-balanced flanks 80 percent of the time? This should be regardless of your position relative to the dog and the sheep. Make sure you have varied your position relative to the dog and sheep and make sure that you truly randomize the cues.

- Is your dog taking the flank at the correct distance from the sheep?

Only after your dog can do these should you move on to inside flanks.

## Exercise 3: Teaching inside flanks

Up until now, the dog has been able to see you when flanking. However, there will be times when the dog must do an inside flank, or circle between you and the sheep. When teaching the inside flank, many handlers find out whether their dogs actually know their verbal flank cues. Here's why. While the previous exercises weaned your dog off relying on body position as a prompt, many dogs continue to rely on subtle body language for hints. As you move out of his line of sight, the dog has to transition to verbal-only cues. This is when some dogs start making mistakes because they have been picking up visual hints all along. Don't get upset with your dog if this happens. It just means that he's not to the point of verbal-only cues.

### Inside flanks are harder to teach for the following reasons:

- The handler is not in a position to easily influence the dog.

- The dog may not be able to see the handler.

- The dog feels pressure from the handler's position behind him. Up until now, the sheep were between the handler and the dog. Now, the dog is asked to come between the sheep and handler.

All these can cause the dog to have tighter flanks. In this exercise, you'll teach the flanks incrementally. You will start off next to the dog and gradually change your position so you're behind the dog and the dog is between you and the sheep. If you have sheep that will stand and not bolt to the barn or fences, practice this in a larger field.

---

### A Shepherd's Journey

I've tried several different ways to teach flanks over the years. Faansie Basson, who is a brilliant trainer and communicator, really changed my thinking about teaching flanks, and especially the inside flanks. His method is more incremental than other methods I had learned, so it's easier for the dog and involves much less use of corrections. Although the steps we use here are not the same as his, they are based on the same concept of moving the handler's presence and pressure away from where you want the dog to go. Faansie has his own methods which you can see at elfadogs-training.learnworlds.com. I highly recommend his videos and clinics. –Kay

---

**Step 1**. Start teaching this while you are standing in front of a fence. This keeps your dog from trying to run behind you. With the sheep in front of you and your dog at your left side, tell him to lie down. Give your verbal "come-bye" cue. Wait for a count of two. Give a hand wave and shush him around the sheep if he doesn't flank immediately on the verbal cue. If the dog slices, move between the dog and the sheep for a correction. **Note:** This is not an inside flank.

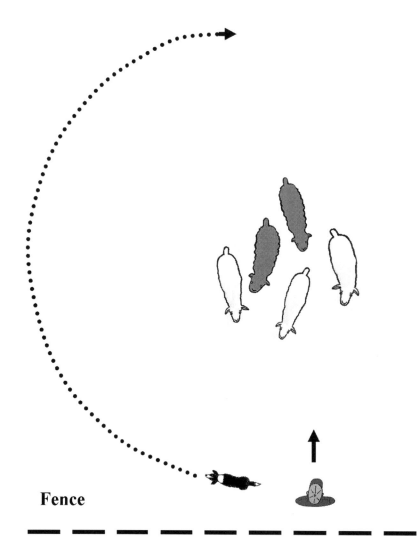

**Fence**

*Steps 1 and 2. Start with the dog at your side and be prepared to step forward and block him if he cuts in as he flanks.*

**Step 2**. Continue practicing Step 1 until your dog takes the flank 80 percent of the time. Your dog should learn to respond to the verbal cue and not wait for your physical prompt.

**Step 3**. With the sheep in front of you and your dog at your left side, tell him to lie down. Take two steps back from your dog, so you are slightly behind him and to his side. The dog should be able to see you, and you should be facing the sheep. Without moving, give your verbal "come-bye" cue. If your dog doesn't respond, shush at him. This is still not an inside flank. Repeat this step until your dog is comfortable and consistently doing it.

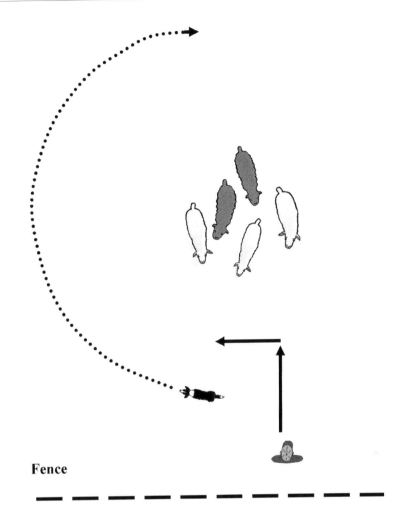

**Fence**

*Step 3. Step a few feet back and to the dog's side so he can still see you. If the dog slices the flank, be prepared to step between him and the sheep to push him out.*

**Step 4**. Stand about 10 feet directly behind the dog. Give your verbal "come-bye" cue and count to two. Shush him if needed. Be prepared to block him if he goes in the wrong direction. This is technically an inside flank, but the real challenge is the next step. Practice this until your dog is comfortable and consistent with it.

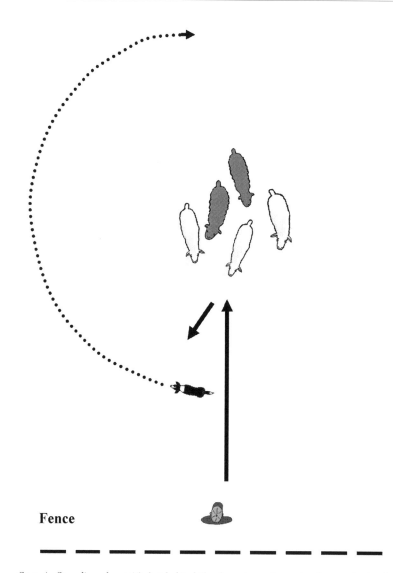

**Fence**

*Step 4. Standing about 10 feet behind the dog, give a "come-bye" cue. Again, be prepared to move between the dog and sheep if the dog slices his flank.*

**Step 5**. Stand about 10 feet behind and about 3 feet to the left of the dog. Now the dog must flank in front of you. Give the cue and observe whether your dog is taking the flank correctly. Is he maintaining his distance from the sheep, or is he cutting in toward the sheep? If he is cutting in toward the sheep, stop him with a "lie down." Now, walk so that you are between the dog and the sheep. Step toward him, telling him to get out of that and slapping your hat against your leg. When he turns away, tell him to lie down. Walk back to your position behind him and give your verbal flank cue again. *Don't correct the dog from behind him as this may cause him to turn around and look at you.* While correcting the dog from behind can be a very useful tool later in your training, don't use it as this stage as many dogs will fall into the habit of looking behind them. This is not only a fault on the trial field but causes the dog to lose control of the sheep. Before you give a correction, you always want to get between the sheep and the dog.

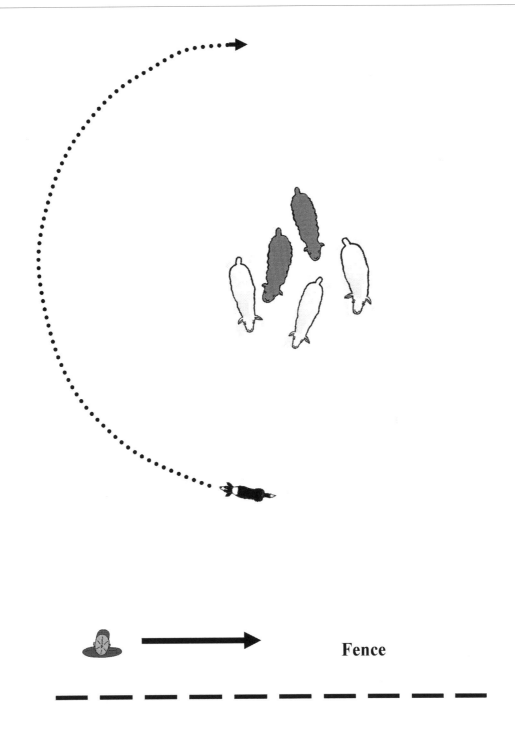

**Fence**

*Step 5. Move behind and to the left of the dog and then give a verbal cue. This is a true inside flank.*
*Be prepared to move away from the direction you are sending the dog if he hesitates.*

**Step 6**. Continue practicing Step 5 until your dog takes the flank 80 percent of the time. Your dog should learn to respond to the verbal cue and not wait for your physical prompt.

**Step 7**. When your dog has mastered the inside flank for the clockwise direction, repeat Steps 1 to 6, but for the "away-to-me" flank.

**How do I know whether my dog has mastered this exercise?**

- Does your dog respond correctly to "come-bye" and "away-to-me" cues and flank in front of you when you stand several feet behind him? (Your body presence can put a lot of pressure on the dog. Because many dogs don't want to flank closely in front of their handler, stand several feet back for novice dogs.)

- Is your dog taking the flank at the correct distance, without cutting in or moving closer to the sheep?

If you answer yes to these questions, then you are ready to teach whistle cues.

## Exercise 4: Teaching flank whistle cues

To teach the whistle cues, you will repeat the same process that you did when teaching verbal cues. Instead of giving verbal cues, you will give whistle cues. After giving the cue, you can either use verbal cues or body positioning after waiting two seconds *after* the whistle cue. Because the whistle is a more unique, salient sound than the human voice, most dogs learn the whistle faster than the verbal cue.

**What whistle sounds should I use?**

The two most important things when starting to whistle are to select sounds you can make easily and consistently and to use whistle sounds that start differently. Because the first note the dog hears starts the action, make sure the whistle cue is clear, obviously different from your other cues and easy to use. Later on, you can learn more complicated whistles. The most common whistle combinations are a long note for "down," a short note for "steady," high-low for "away to me," low-high for "come bye," and a higher pitched series of notes for "walk up." Make sure you can consistently make the whistle sounds before trying to use them with your dog.

> ### A Shepherd's Journey
>
> I got my first whistle from Francis Raley, one of the founders of USBCHA, at the State Fair of Texas Sheep Dog Trial in 1990. On the four-hour drive home, I worked on learning to blow that whistle. I arrived home with my face cramped and only able to make a sound like a dying duck. I practiced every day driving to work in my car for several weeks before I could successfully play a tune and was ready to use it on my dogs. Before using a whistle with your dog, it is really important to become fluent at whistling. –Kay

## A few more thoughts on flanks

A dog who responds to flank cues is useful on the farm and in competitions. The very top competitors, though, fine-tune their flanks, teaching them long and short flanks as well as slow and fast flanks.

Many people control how far the dog goes around the sheep—such as a few steps, a quarter circle or a half circle—by telling the dog to circle until they give a stop cue. An advanced maneuver is to teach the dog a different cue for a short flank and a long flank. Some handlers also teach a wider flank for use at the pen.

Another advanced move is to control the flank speed. Some dogs naturally flank full speed while others flank slowly. You can teach the dog to do both and do both on a cue. A naturally slow dog is taught to speed up, and a naturally fast dog is taught to slow down when asked. You will use the same step-by-step process: teaching the dog to perform off body position and then adding a verbal cue.

# Chapter 24
## Teaching Your Dog to Drive

This chapter introduces your dog to the concept of driving or pushing the sheep in a direction other than toward the handler. It is an artificial situation for the dog and takes a while for most dogs to understand it. Because of this, it's best to teach driving in incremental steps, keep the lessons short and reward the dog by letting him do something he already understands, like balance work and fetching. When you have successfully completed the exercises in this chapter, your dog should understand the concept of pushing the sheep in a calm, confident manner and holding a line, or driving in a particular direction (rather than trying to circle around to their heads).

A dog who understands how to drive is very useful on the farm. He's able to push the sheep to another pasture, hold sheep away from you while feeding and push one group of sheep away from another. For those interested in competing in trials, driving is a major component of most sheepdog trials. In USBCHA trials, the drive makes up about 30 percent of the score. While your dog won't be ready for competition after this chapter, he will be getting closer.

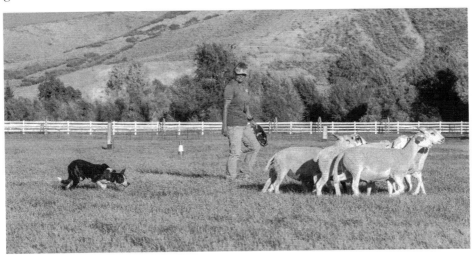

*Teaching your dog to drive is done in incremental steps. Photo courtesy of Carol Clawson.*

### What will my dog learn in these exercises?
Once you and your dog have completed these exercises, your dog will be able to do the following:

- Be comfortable when you and your dog are on the same side of the sheep.
- Walk toward a group of sheep and push them when you are in front of him and beside him.
- Have a more formalized "walk up" cue.
- Walk toward a group of sheep and push them when you are walking behind him, but still where he can see you.
- Push the sheep, stop, change the direction of the line and push in a new direction.

## What terminology should you know before starting?

In herding, **driving** is pushing the stock away from the handler or parallel to the handler, instead of bringing the sheep towards the handler. Up until this point, your dog has been fetching, or bringing the sheep to you. For the most part, the sheep have been between you and the dog. When driving, the dog is often between the handler and the sheep. Sometimes people will use the term **drive away** to indicate the dog pushing the sheep away from the handler and **cross drive** to indicate pushing the sheep parallel to and in front of the handler. Both involve the dog *pushing* the sheep rather than fetching them to the handler.

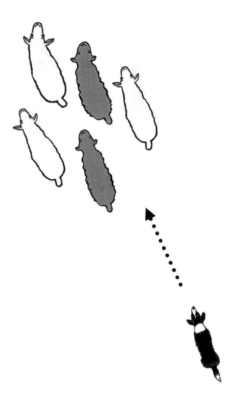

*In the drive away, the dog pushes the sheep away from the handler.*

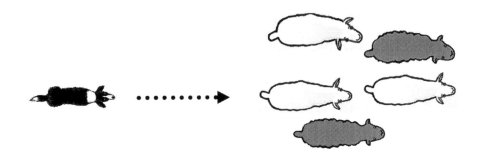

*In the cross drive, the dog pushes the sheep in front of the handler.*

## What makes driving difficult?

Most Border Collies have an instinct to fetch the sheep to their handler. This goes back to the hunting instinct to head off and bring the prey back to the rest of the pack. In most of your training up to this point, you've corrected the dog for being off balance; now you *want* him to go off balance. It is reasonable for the dog to be confused. The concept of driving, rather than fetching, the sheep, takes some dogs a long time to learn. Also adding to the difficulty is that with most of the training you have done so far, the dog is able to see you most of the time and you have been in a position to easily influence the dog. When driving, you will eventually be behind the dog and possibly out of his sight. This makes some dogs as well as novice handlers very uncomfortable. Also adding to the difficulty is the sheep; often they have gotten used to coming to the handler and will keep trying to come to the handler, and this makes it harder for the dog to drive. If you focus on relaxing, taking your time and not worrying too much about mistakes, then the process of teaching your dog to drive will be a little easier.

## What are keys to helping my dog learn to drive?

Because learning how to drive is often stressful for the dog, do the following:

- Keep the sessions short.
- Have the right sheep. The ideal sheep will move easily away from the dog, but not run away from the dog. They will also flock together easily.
- Set up the sheep in a position where the draw is minimal. Avoid setting up the sheep where they try to run to the barn or another group of sheep. Ideally, the sheep are set up with a mild draw slightly behind the dog.

- Plan your driving lessons at the beginning of your training session when you and your dog are fresh.

- Reward your dog for driving by allowing him to do balance work or outruns. Your dog will soon learn that he receives a big payoff for driving.

- Do not worry about straight lines at first. Just focus on teaching your dog to push.

- Plan to spend lots of time and miles walking with your dog. When teaching driving, you and your dog are in motion.

## Does my dog need to know his flanks before driving?

When watching sheepdog trials, you will often hear handlers give their dogs directional cues ("come-bye" and "away to me") while the dog is driving. While your dog has been introduced to flanks, don't rely on those to teach driving. Focus on the concept of pushing. A dog who is good at driving learns to hold a line on his own. This is accomplished through miles of walking with the dog and helping him when he does not hold the line. Once he understands the concept of pushing and is driving reliably, then use directional cues.

## What cues must my dog know before driving?

Your dog must have a reliable "lie down" or "stop" as well as a "that'll do" cue. Your dog should also have a "here" or "come here" cue. If he does not, work on that before moving onto the driving exercises. As you teach driving, you'll formalize the walk-up cue.

## Teaching the "here" or "come here"

When teaching driving, your dog will likely want to balance and stop the sheep. You can stop him from heading the sheep by asking him to lie down, by flanking him back into the drive position behind the sheep, by using a line or with a verbal correction. Because you want to maintain forward momentum, the "here" method is preferable because it does not take away that momentum as the other methods can. "Here" means the dog should maintain contact with the sheep but come toward you and stay behind the sheep.

Unlike the "that'll do" cue, the dog does not leave the sheep to come to you. To ease the stress of learning a new cue while learning about driving, introduce your dog to the "here" cue before you begin the driving exercises. Below are the steps.

**Step 1**. Put about 4 to 6 calm sheep in the training pen and put your dog on a long line.

**Step 2**. Holding the line, walk with your dog toward the sheep. The dog should be about 10 feet from your side. Both you and the dog should be facing the sheep.

**Step 3**. Cue the dog with his name or slap your leg to get his attention. Give a quick tug and release of the leash. Make sure the dog comes straight toward you, not bending into the sheep. If he does not come to you, step closer to the dog and try again.

**Step 4**. As soon as the dog takes a couple of steps toward you, reward him with praise or a smile, pause and then walk toward the sheep again.

**Step 5**. Repeat this exercise until your dog reliably steps directly toward you with a light tug on the leash.

**Step 6**. Once your dog is coming toward you, add the cue. Walk toward the sheep, then stop. Cue the dog with a "here-here." Once the dog comes toward you and stops, then start walking again.

**Step 7**. Practice this until your dog consistently comes toward you when cued. The dog should come toward you crisply, consistently and straight.

## What should a sample lesson plan for driving look like?

Because driving can be a hard concept for dogs, go slow and mix plenty of rewarding activities with the driving. Below is a sample training session:

1. Start with balance work.

2. Transition to a few minutes of driving.

3. Reward the driving work with a couple of outruns.

4. Do some more balance work. Work on flank cues and shape. Flanks start to tighten when you work on driving.

5. Do a few more minutes of driving.

6. Finish with an outrun.

### What equipment do I need?

**A 50×100ft. training pen**. Use the same training pen that you did for your beginning lessons.

**A 5-acre field or larger**. After the first exercise, you'll move to a larger field. The ideal field has minimal pressure, meaning the sheep will not be drawn to a barn or other sheep in an adjacent pasture. The field should also offer good visibility.

**About 4 to 12 calm sheep**. The type of sheep is crucial for teaching these driving exercises. *The ideal sheep will flock together.* If the sheep do not stay together in a group, you spend your time trying to keep them together rather than teaching the dog to push. If one sheep in your training flock does not want to stay with the group, sort it out of the flock and don't use it. Because most goats do not flock as well as sheep, they are not recommended for driving exercises. *Avoid sheep that are knee knockers.* It's harder for the dog to learn to push the sheep away from the handler if the sheep want to stay with the person. *Also avoid sheep that want to bolt or run away.* In the driving exercises, you are teaching your dog to stay behind the sheep, rather than trying to gather them. If the sheep are running or bolting, your dog's natural instinct is to fetch, or try to gather them and bring them to you. If your dog has a strong instinct to go to their heads, driving is often easier with more sheep rather than just four or five.

**A long line and buckle collar**. A lightweight line that is at least 30 feet long is ideal.

## Exercise 1: Introduce the concept of walking in an unbalanced position

In this exercise, you will introduce your dog to the concept of walking up on the sheep with you at his side. Up until this point, your dog has been fetching the sheep and bringing the sheep to balance. When your dog is behind the sheep with you at his side, he's not in balance. This makes the dog uncomfortable and is a difficult concept to grasp. By introducing this in the training pen, you have more control over the dog and the sheep.

**Note**: Because driving is counterintuitive for most dogs, learning to drive is stressful. This concept often confuses the dog, and confusion creates tension. A dog may exhibit tension by diving into the sheep or being too tight. Be patient with your dog and keep your driving sessions short.

**Step 1**. Place the sheep in the training pen and allow them to settle. With your dog on a line, walk toward the sheep and encourage your dog to walk beside you and toward the sheep. Pat your leg and turn sideways to the dog. You should face the sheep and the dog should be next to you or even slightly behind you. Don't face the dog, as this pressures him to stay back, and you want him to move forward. Watch your body position.

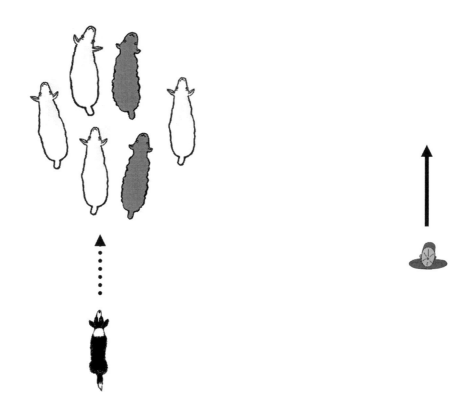

*Encourage your dog to walk forward, into the sheep.*

**Step 2**. Briskly walk several steps toward the sheep. You want the sheep to move away from you, and your dog to think he moved them. Walking with purpose helps move the sheep. If the sheep do not respond, scuff your feet a bit so the sheep move off of you and go forward. Try to stay to the side of the sheep and walk parallel to the sheep with the dog beside or slightly behind you.

**Step 3**. Your dog may want to circle and go to balance. If he starts to go to balance, give a "lie down" followed by a "here-here" and lightly pull on the line. Make sure the dog turns cleanly toward you and stops before walking forward again. Briskly walk a few steps toward the sheep. After the sheep and dog have moved forward for several steps, ask for a "lie down."

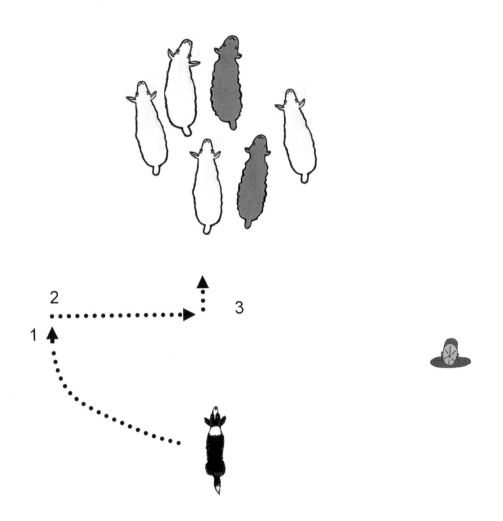

*If your dog starts to circle around the sheep, (1) say "lie down," (2) lightly tug the line*
*and say "here-here" and (3) once back in the correct position, walk forward.*

**Step 4**. Give a "that'll do" and walk away from the sheep. Send your dog to fetch the sheep and do a little balance work.

**Note**: Make sure that you make a distinction between driving and fetching. Make sure your body position is consistent. When fetching, you're often facing the dog. When driving, you are facing the sheep or the direction you want the sheep to go. When your dog is learning to drive, make sure he lies down and comes to you before moving onto fetching exercises. This helps keep both you and the dog clear on whether you are working on driving or fetching. This is really important when your dog is just learning. Once you and your dog are fluent in both these skills, keeping it separate won't be as important.

**Step 5**. Repeat this "walk up" exercise 3 to 5 times per session until your dog is comfortable with it. You and your dog should walk forward with purpose and confidence. The sheep should move away before you stop your dog. You want the dog to get the feel of moving sheep while he is at your side and without panicking about them getting away from him.

**Step 6**. Practice driving on both the left and right side of the dog.

**Step 7**. Once your dog is confidently moving forward with you, add a verbal cue for walking forward into the sheep. Most people use "walk up" as the verbal cue. To teach this, use the verbal cue just before you start walking.

### How do I know whether my dog has mastered this exercise?

- Does your dog confidently walk up on the sheep with you at his side 80 percent of the time?
- When given a "here-here" does he reliably come toward you?
- Can your dog perform this exercise without diving into or biting the sheep?
- Does he lie down and come to you when asked?

If you answered yes to these questions, move on to the next exercise.

---

### A Shepherd's Journey

When I was at a Bruce Fogt clinic and someone was working on driving, he told her to act like a general taking the troops into battle. The message was that if we wanted our dogs to have confidence driving, we had to walk and talk with confidence. As I am walking with a young dog learning to drive (there is lots of walking), I try to walk with an upright posture and confidence. —Beth

---

## Exercise 2: Introducing driving in the big field

In this exercise, you will move back to the big field and introduce driving. By the time you have mastered this exercise, your dog will walk behind the sheep for about 20 to 50 yards.

**Reminder**: Do these driving exercises at the beginning of the training session and keep them short. Then move onto herding activities the dog really likes to do, like balance work. If the dog is working well, you might try doing a few more minutes of driving after the balance work.

### What's the biggest mistake people make with this exercise?

The tendency when starting driving work is to worry about having the sheep walk in a straight line. Don't worry about keeping a straight line. It's okay for the driving to start in no particular direction or even in a semi-circle. The main focus is to keep the dog behind the sheep and to keep the dog moving. As a handler, you must keep moving. If you hesitate, your dog will hesitate. Also, stay out of the path of the dog and the sheep. It's easy to end up between the dog and the sheep if you don't pay attention. Pay attention to your position and try to stay off to the side of the dog and the sheep.

### How far away from the sheep should the dog be?

Recall the bubbles or zones around the sheep. The flight zone is where the sheep want to run from the dog while the fight zone is where the sheep will turn and fight the dog. The zones vary depending on the sheep, the dog and other variables. When driving, the dog needs to be on or just outside the flight zone bubble.

**Step 1**. Before getting your dog out of his kennel or crate, place the sheep in the field and allow them to settle.

**Step 2**. Walk onto the field with your dog on a line and stop. Evaluate your dog's attitude. Ask for a "lie down." Now send your dog on an outrun and allow him to bring the sheep to you. Even though your focus is on driving, pay attention to the outrun, lift and fetch and make sure that your dog is doing each one correctly.

**Step 3**. When the dog and sheep are near you, ask for a "lie down" and pick up the long line. Position yourself *so that you and the dog are on the same side of the sheep.*

**Step 4**. Holding the line, pat your leg, step toward the sheep and encourage your dog to walk up toward the sheep. Keep the sheep moving. If they are reluctant to move, help your dog by walking with him and shuffling your feet to encourage the sheep to move. To encourage your dog, you can cluck or slap your leg. If your dog starts to circle around the sheep, say, "Here-here." If he does not respond, give the line a brisk tug and release to get him into position. Do not give the line a steady pull.

Pay attention to your body language. Make sure you are facing the sheep and walking forward with confidence and speed. Stay even with the dog's head or slightly in front of the dog. The dog feeds off of your body language. If you are slow and uncertain, he will be as well. Remember to ask the dog to "walk up" in a calm and confident manner.

**Note**: Watch your corrections here. Avoid using a body block with a correction as it can take away the dog's forward momentum. Instead of blocking, use a "lie down." If you don't have a reliable stop, work on that before doing these driving exercises.

**Step 5**. If your dog is happily walking with you behind the sheep, continue going until something goes wrong, such as the dog trying to head the sheep or the sheep no longer flocking. Then give your dog a "lie down" cue. Call him off the sheep with a "that'll do." Repeat Steps 2 to 5.

During a training session, plan to do this driving exercise 3 to 4 times and then move onto activities the dog likes, such as balance work.

If your dog is really struggling or if the sheep separate, lie your dog down. Give a "that'll do." Then brainstorm how you can make it easier for your dog. Are your sheep sour and heavy and not wanting to move? Would working along a fence help get the driving started? Are you helping your dog by confidently pushing the sheep?

## What do I do if my sheep are flighty?

One challenge handlers have with teaching driving is the sheep. Some want to scatter or run. If the sheep are making the training difficult, practice these exercises along a fence line. When doing this, the sheep will be near the fence line and you and your dog will be behind the sheep. Position yourself so that you are off to the side, between the dog and the sheep, but closer to the sheep. The fence blocks one avenue of escape for the sheep, and it also blocks the dog, thus making it easier to keep the flow going. Follow the same steps as if you were in the open field.

*If the sheep are flighty, practice driving alongside a fence. Photo courtesy of Kay Stephens.*

**Fence**

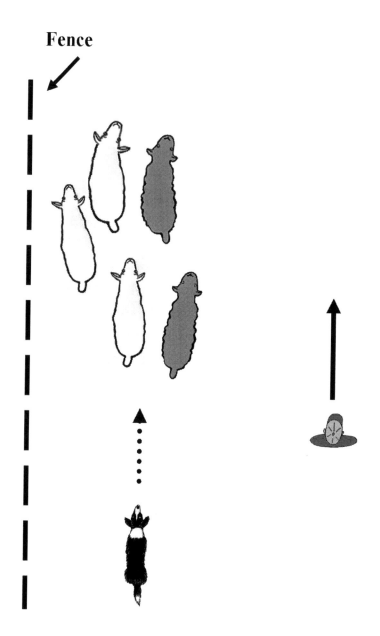

*If the sheep are flighty, practice driving along a fence line.*

**How can I tell whether my dog has mastered this exercise?**

- Does your dog walk up on the sheep with you at his side 80 percent of the time?

- Pay attention to the dog's body language. Is he confident and relaxed as he follows the sheep, or is he slow and worried, or tense? The dog should be confident and relaxed.

- When given a "here-here" cue when he starts to head, does he come back behind the sheep?

- Can he move behind the sheep for 20 to 30 yards consistently?

- Does he lie down and come to you when asked?

If you answered yes to these questions, move onto the next exercise.

## Exercise 3: Increasing the length of the drive

Once your dog is moving the sheep 20 to 30 yards consistently, increase the length of the drive. You'll continue doing the steps in Exercise 2, gradually increasing the distance, until you can reliably drive at least 100 yards. Remember to practice driving on both the right and left side of the dog.

## Exercise 4: Increasing your distance from the dog

Once your dog is able to walk up on the sheep and push them forward with you at his side for 100 yards, your next step is to drop back so that your dog is driving and you are a few feet behind him. You will still walk with your dog and in his field of vision, but you may be slightly behind him. When doing this exercise, keep these things in mind:

- You will be doing a lot of walking with your dog.
- You must keep moving in a forward, confident manner.
- Driving is a skill that takes time and practice to learn.
- At this point, focus on your dog pushing the sheep, rather than straight lines.
- Practice driving on either side of the dog. Do not get into a rut of walking on just one side. Even though you are dropping back, stay where the dog can watch you out of the corner of his eye.

**Step 1**. Send your dog on an outrun and allow him to bring the sheep to you.

**Step 2**. When the dog and sheep are near you, ask for a "lie down" and position yourself so that you and the dog are behind the sheep.

**Step 3**. Pat your leg, step toward the sheep and encourage your dog to walk up toward the sheep. Continue moving further to the side, away from the dog and parallel to, but further away from the sheep. Once your dog is comfortable with this (it may take several sessions), proceed to Steps 4 to 6.

**Step 4**. Position yourself so that you and the dog are behind the sheep. As he starts moving the sheep, continue walking but take smaller steps so that you are a few feet behind the dog but still in his vision. If he hesitates, walk forward and encourage him to "walk up." If he becomes uncomfortable, walk by his side for a few steps and then try taking smaller steps so you are just one step behind him. Stay close enough to give the dog confidence to keep moving and to help him keep momentum of moving the sheep. You also want to be in a position where you can easily control the dog. Do not get behind the dog too quickly, as that may cause you to lose control. It's okay to spend many weeks and walk many miles parallel to the dog and the sheep. Do not be in a hurry to drop back. Get the behavior solid first and keep control of the dog. Any time the dog runs around to head the sheep without your cue to do so, stop the dog, call him off and reset the training scene. Do not let the dog get rewarded for going to balance unless you send him there.

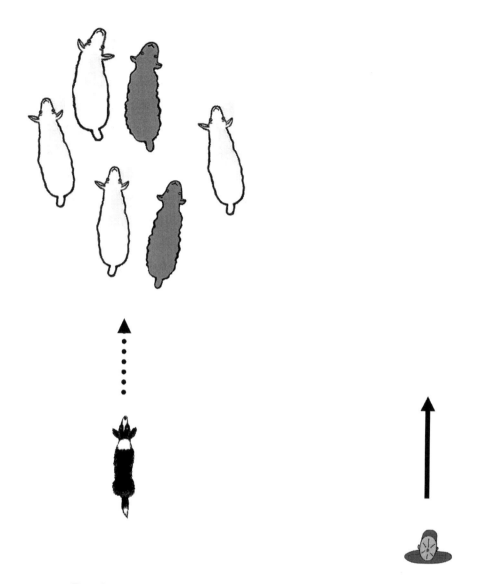

*Drop back a few steps but stay close enough to have control of the dog.*

**Step 5**. If your dog is happily walking behind the sheep and with you slightly behind him and off to the side, continue going until the moment things start to fall apart. Give your dog a "lie down" cue. Call him off the sheep with a "that'll do." When doing this exercise, pay attention and make sure that you are off to the side and out of the way of the dog and the sheep. The most common mistakes here are being not far enough off to the side of the dog and being too cautious about walking forward. Repeat Steps 4 to 5.

**Step 6**. As your dog becomes comfortable with you walking 1 to 2 steps behind him, increase the distance to 2 to 3 steps and then 3 to 4 steps until you can consistently walk off to the side and behind while driving. Because you don't want the dog to turn around and look at you, avoid getting directly behind the dog or out of his field of vision while he's driving. Stay where he can see you in his peripheral vision.

**Remember**: During a training session, plan to do this driving exercise 3 to 4 times and then move on to activities the dog likes to do.

**How will I know whether my dog has mastered this?**
- When you drop a step behind, does your dog keep moving forward?

- Does he do this 80 percent of the time?

- When given a "here-here" cue, does he come back behind the sheep?

- Can he move behind the sheep, with you a few steps behind, for 30-40 yards consistently?

- Does he lie down and come to you when asked?

If you answered yes to these questions, move on to the next exercise.

## Exercise 5: Driving the box

In this exercise, you will increase the complexity of the drive. While the dog will still have the handler in his vision for the most part, however he will change directions. The handler will also increase the distance between herself and the dog. This exercise is designed to get the dog more confident about driving and introduce him to elements of the cross drive.

**How it works**

In the big field visualize a small 30 yard square inside a bigger square. The dog moves the sheep along the perimeter of the larger square. The handler walks parallel to the dog on the perimeter of the smaller square. This exercise is performed in the big field with 4 to 6 calm sheep. As with other driving exercises, keep this lesson short and reward your dog by doing balance work or fetching afterwards.

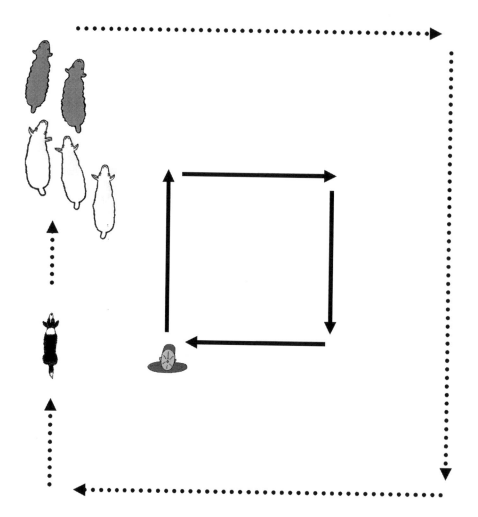

*In the box exercise, the handler walks in the smaller inside square while the dog drives a larger square. Not to scale.*

**Step 1**. Send your dog on an outrun and allow him to bring the sheep to you.

**Step 2**. When the dog and sheep are near you, ask for a "lie down" and position yourself so that you and the dog are both behind the sheep in the drive position. You are going to practice this exercise first in a clockwise direction.

**Step 3**. Pat your leg, step toward the sheep and encourage your dog to walk up toward the sheep. Slowly distance yourself from the dog and sheep, so that you are walking parallel with the sheep but about 10 yards away.

**Step 4**. When the sheep and dog are about 10 yards past you, lie your dog down. Now, you will start to use flanks to control the direction of the drive. It's a good idea to check the shape of the dog's flanks and his response to them before starting this exercise. Cue the come-bye flank and step to the side to help the dog flank correctly. (Remember to watch the shape of the flank and correct the dog if the flank is sliced.) Because you want the sheep to turn 90 degrees, you'll want to stop your dog as the sheep are turning. You can also practice using the inside flank (away to me in this instance) to help straighten the sheep. Now, ask him to walk up into the sheep. At this point, don't worry about a straight line and perfect square. Your main objective is to turn the sheep, set a new drive line and drive.

**Step 5**. Repeat Step 4 for 3 to 4 times. Then reward your dog with some balance work or an outrun.

**Step 6**. Repeat Steps 1 to 4, but go in a counterclockwise position. Now the dog will be parallel to your right side. Flanks to turn the sheep will be away-to-me flanks, and inside flanks will be come-bye flanks. Again, you are focusing on pushing the sheep (the drive), starting to hold a line and adding flanks (inside and outside) to the drive. Be ready to stop and reset if any of these three parts start to fall apart. If you are struggling, you might need to just practice driving or just practice flanking.

**Step 7**. As the dog masters the box exercise, gradually increase the size of the box and your distance from the dog. You will want to progress to where you can stand in the center of the box, and the dog drives around you.

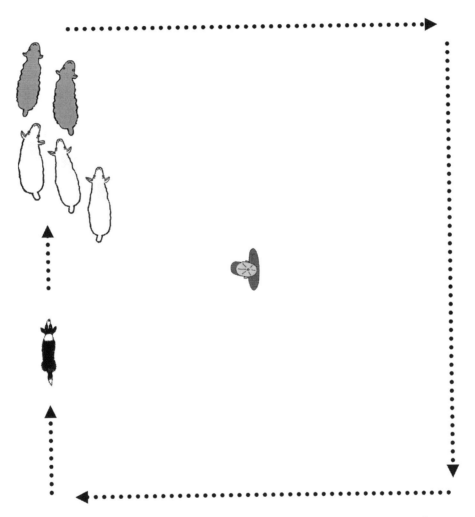

*Stand in the center and direct the dog to drive a square around you. Not to scale.*

### How will I know whether my dog has mastered this?

- Does your dog walk up readily and confidently on the sheep with you walking parallel to the dog 80 percent of the time?
- Does he stop, circle and stop (for the directional change) while keeping his flanks a correct circle and taking the direction correctly 80 percent of the time?
- Is he comfortable driving the box in both directions? Most dogs will find one direction easier than the other.

## Increase the difficulty

Now, you'll raise the difficulty of driving. To do this, take your dog to different fields, lengthen the distance of the drive or increase the distance you are from him while he is driving. Also vary the number and type of sheep you use. You can also start driving in situations where there is more pull or draw on the sheep. The dog (and you) will have to work harder to hold the line and keep the sheep moving in the correct direction. Remember that if you increase the difficulty of one element, decrease the difficulty of the others. For instance, if your dog is comfortable driving for 100 yards at home and you take him to a new field, then drop back and practice shorter drives. Always be prepared to move back closer to the dog and the sheep to help the dog in new situations.

## Don't neglect your other skills

Driving tends to take away your dog's balance and shorten or tighten his flanks. As you teach driving, keep touching on those two skills.

# Chapter 25
## Penning

Penning, or putting sheep into a pen, is an audience favorite at sheepdog trials and a useful skill on the farm. In an ideal pen, the dog and handler work as a team, applying and releasing pressure. The dog applies pressure and keeps the sheep from escaping on one side of the pen, and the handler applies and releases pressure on the other side of the pen. Their movements convince the sheep that the only place to escape to is into the pen.

At this point in his training, your dog should have the flanking and walk-up skills needed to put the sheep into a pen. As a handler, you should know where and how to pressure the sheep as well as when to release pressure on the sheep so that they move in the direction you would like. You will now use those skills to successfully put the sheep into a pen.

*The handler and sheep work together to move the sheep into the pen. With wild range sheep, the handler must stay back until the dog gets them in the mouth of the pen.*

### What will the dog and handler learn in these exercises?
The penning exercises will help you develop a strategy for penning and a feel for how your body presence and your dog's presence can work together to put the sheep in the pen. After successfully completing these exercises:

- Your dog will be able to flank back and forth to hold the sheep without cutting in, even when there is a lot of pressure from the sheep.
- You will be comfortable with applying and releasing pressure on the sheep to put the sheep into the pen.
- Your dog will be desensitized to you facing him while putting pressure on the sheep.
- Your dog will, if not already, become comfortable with your use of a stock stick or crook to control the sheep.
- You will have some strategies for getting the sheep into the pen.

## What skills should the dog and handler have before starting?

To successfully pen, the dog should have:

- The ability to control the sheep.
- The ability to flank cleanly (not slicing or going off contact) and to perform balanced and off-balance flanks.
- The ability to walk up and stop on cue.

Penning also requires the handler to know how to:

- Put pressure on the sheep to make them move.
- Take pressure off the sheep to make them slow, relax or stop.
- Read the sheep and know from their ear movement and body posture whether they are feeling pressure and the release of pressure, and which way they want to go.

## What equipment do I need?

**A 10×10 ft. or smaller pen**. Because the size and shape of the pen varies at competitions, some trainers practice with smaller pens at home. At the USBCHA National Finals, the pen is 9×8 feet. When building a training pen, it is helpful to have a gate that is on a wheel because it is easier to open and close. The gate should have a 6 foot rope attached to it. Almost no pens at trials have solid panels because sheep are wary of going into enclosed spaces. Because the dog needs ample room to flank around the pen, the pen should be placed in the larger practice field rather than in your training pen.

**About 3 to 5 sheep**. Finding the right sheep to practice penning can be a challenge. Some sheep learn they can avoid the dog by going into the pen. Because the sheep go into the pen even when the dog or person is in the incorrect position, the dog and handler do not learn to position themselves correctly. Sheep that learn to run around to the side of the pen and avoid the pen also make training difficult.

**A stock stick or shepherd's crook**. A stock stick is used as an extension of the arm. Waving it can help block or stop the sheep. Practice penning both with and without the stick or crook. Sometimes, you may not have a stock stick handy, so it's helpful to know how to pen without one. Also, because some dogs may be worried or fearful of the stock stick, you may have to work with your dog so he becomes accustomed to it. Get into the habit of carrying the stick or crook around with you to desensitize your dog to it. Finally, you'll need to practice with it and learn how it influences the sheep.

---

### A Shepherd's Journey

I once bought a dog who was so terrified from having a stick thrown at him that he turned and ran to his kennel if he saw one. For that dog, I had to train without a stick—and that can be a disadvantage at the pen. A crook or stick is a tool used to control sheep, not a dog training device. To avoid negative associations with the stick or crook, avoid using it to correct your dog or to teach him flanks. –Kay

---

## Exercise 1: Penning and flanking against a fence

To successfully pen, your dog should have correct flanks, a reliable cue to walk up toward the sheep and a stop cue. In this exercise, you will practice these skills against a fence. This allows you to observe your dog's skills and make corrections if necessary. It also keeps you from getting so focused on the task of penning that you don't observe whether your dog is correct.

**Step 1**. Stand against the fence with your back to the fence, facing the dog, and with the sheep between you and your dog. If you haven't been carrying a crook in your training, now is a good time to start doing so. Don't use it to correct the dog; only use it to block sheep if needed. Flank the dog all the way to the fence line in both directions. Watch to make sure the dog flanks all the way to the fence without cutting in. If the dog cuts in, make a correction. Again, timing is critical. As soon as the dog starts to cut in by turning his head or shoulders in toward the sheep, tell him to lie down and step between the dog and the sheep. Slap your hat against your leg and give a verbal correction. Watch to see that the dog responds to the correction by turning his head or body outwards. Tell the dog to lie down. Then go back to your original position. Do not stay in the blocking position, as you want the dog to flank correctly without blocking him.

**Step 2**. Once your dog is reliably flanking to the fence in both directions, ask for stops at different locations along the arc. He should stop immediately and not take extra steps toward the sheep. The dog should stay on the line or arc of the flank and not cut in toward the sheep when asked to stop. If the dog takes extra steps, make a correction. As soon as the dog goes to take an extra step, give a verbal correction and step between the dog and the sheep.

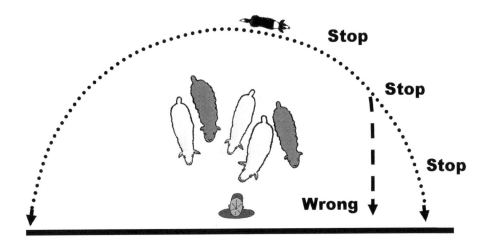

*Flank the dog in both directions, making sure he goes to the fence and doesn't cut in or slice the flank.*

**Step 3**. Once he is flanking and stopping correctly in both directions, change your position. Move to where the fence is still behind you, but you are to the side of the sheep. Repeat Steps 1 and 2.

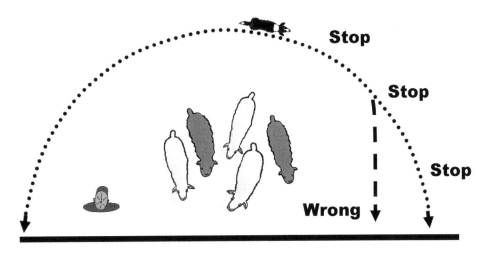

*Change your position so you are to the side of the sheep.*

**Step 4**. When your dog is successfully performing Step 3, change your position again. Move away from the fence. Repeat Steps 1 and 2.

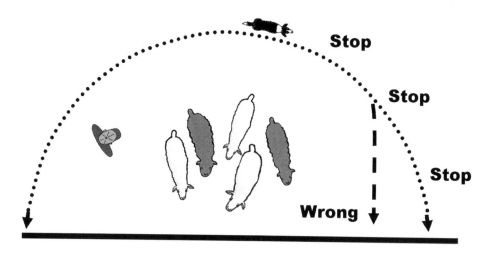

*Move away from the fence and next to the sheep.*

**Step 5**. Now, test your dog's ability to move the sheep past you. Position yourself a few feet from the fence with the sheep between you and the dog. Give your dog a "walk-up" so that he pushes the sheep against the fence. This exercise helps the dog get used to moving the sheep past you even when you are facing him.

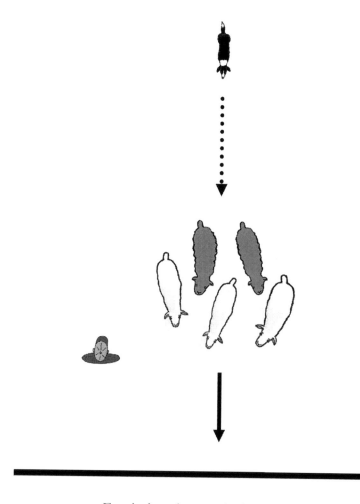

*Face the dog as he moves the sheep toward the fence.*

*The dog drives the sheep past the handler and to the fence line. Photo by Beth Kerber*

**Step 6**. Once the dog is comfortable with Step 5, step away from the fence and practice flanking the dog and having the dog push the sheep between you and the fence.

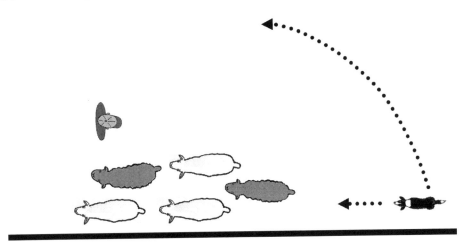

*The dog moves the sheep between the handler and the fence. The dog may have to flank out towards the handler to keep the sheep moving on the fence line.*

*The dog drives the sheep past the handler. Photo by Beth Kerber*

## Exercise 2: Practicing your sheep handling skills

In this exercise, done without your dog, you'll refresh your skills on moving the sheep and pay attention to how the sheep react to your pressure. It is a good way to practice using a crook or stock stick.

**Step 1**. With the sheep between you and a fence, move the sheep toward the fence. When they are near the fence, take a step forward and note how they behave.

**Step 2**. Select one sheep in the group and put pressure toward her hip. To do this, take a half step toward her. How much pressure do you need to move the sheep? Does she walk forward or backward? Turn toward you or away from you? Can you make a sheep move by just leaning toward it? Changing the direction of your hips?

**Step 3**. Select a sheep and wave your arms toward it. How does it respond?

**Step** 4. Lean toward a sheep, and then lean back away from the sheep. Watch how she responds to your pressure.

**Step 5**. With your crook or stock stick, practice placing it in front of the sheep's head and noting where it needs to be to turn her. Practice tapping it on the ground to see how that affects the sheep. Pay attention to how high or low you have to hold it for the sheep to notice it and respond to it.

**Step 6**. Select one sheep in the group and put pressure toward her shoulder. To do this, take a half step toward her. How much pressure do you need to move the sheep? Does she walk forward or backward? Turn toward you or away from you?

**Step 7**. Practice turning the head of each sheep in the group individually. Can you turn each sheep in either direction without disturbing the entire group? Often in penning, if you can control the lead sheep, the rest will follow. Identifying and controlling the lead sheep makes penning easier.

## Exercise 3: Introducing the pen

In this exercise, you will practice penning the sheep. Keep these things in mind:

**Let go of the rope!** In a competition, you must hold onto the rope on the gate. When practicing at home, you can drop the rope. If your dog slices a flank or doesn't stop on cue, drop the rope and change your position so that you can apply a correction. Also, as you practice changing your body position to influence the sheep, you may need to drop the rope to move away from the pen. If you need to drop the rope to do this, drop the rope.

**Be ready to correct your dog.** If your dog slices his flanks, does not stop on cue or turns into the sheep, correct him. *When training, focus on you and the dog performing correctly instead of actually penning the sheep.* Quite often, when training, you'll have to make a correction that causes the sheep to scatter.

**Penning involves pressure and release from the dog and handler.** The sheep need to feel enough pressure that they want to escape into the pen yet feel safe enough to turn their back to the dog and move into a closed space. When you practice penning, observe what happens when you take a step forward or take a step back. Let your dog take a step toward the sheep, stop him and see how the sheep respond. With the dog stopped, take a step toward the sheep and see how the sheep respond. To release pressure, take a step away from the sheep.

**Take a big breath, relax your shoulders and take your time.** By keeping yourself relaxed, you'll help the sheep and dog relax. Many problems at the pen happen when the handler and dog rush the process.

With the above tips in mind, move on to the following steps:

**Step 1.** When preparing to pen the sheep, open the gate so that it's in line with the pen. This creates a long side. The dog can then move the sheep toward that long side.

**Step 2.** Drive the sheep to the long side of the pen and aim where the gate and pen side intersect.

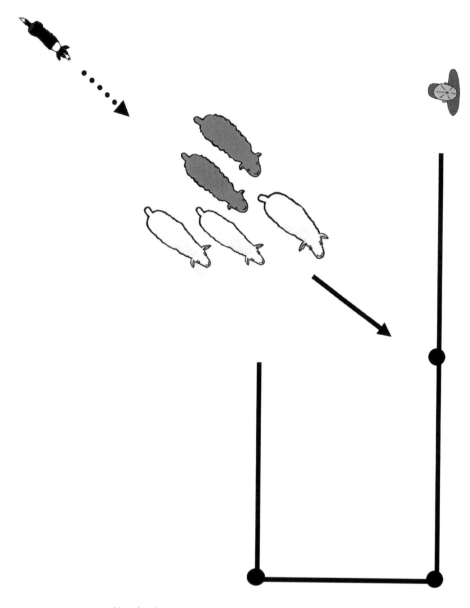

*Aim the sheep where the gate and pen side intersect.*

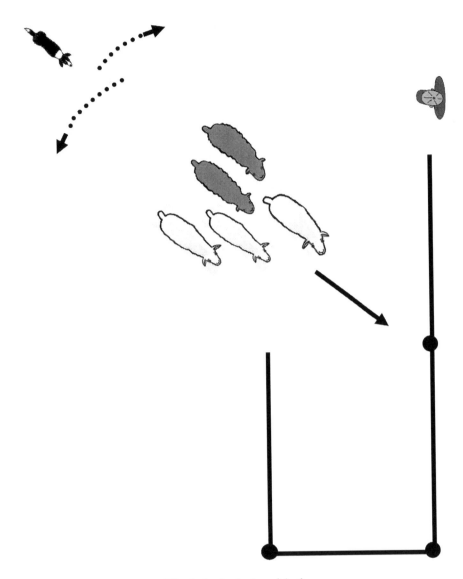

*Flank the dog back and forth.*

**Step 3**. Watch the sheep's heads and ears and determine whether you or the dog need to apply or release pressure.

**Step 4**. Test the sheep's response to your crook. Where do you need to move it to get their attention or affect their motion? Pay attention to your dog as well. If he is getting worried about you holding the sheep or waving the crook, stop, call him over to you and reassure him. Because you may stomp or move more aggressively toward the sheep, the dog may think you are correcting him and become reluctant to hold his side. Make sure to encourage the dog and help him if he becomes worried.

### What do you do if the sheep go easily into the pen?
Sometimes sheep learn to walk into the pen. This makes it difficult to train your dog. To make the sheep more reluctant to go into the pen, place a tarp in front of the pen gate or on the floor of the pen. You can also try making the gate opening smaller.

### A Shepherd's Journey

When practicing penning, I tend to get so caught up in the task of getting the sheep into the pen that I fail to notice that my dog is slicing a flank or that I am pressuring the sheep so much that they won't go into the pen. I have found that if I practice with a three-sided pen, one with no gate and no rope, my observational skills increase. While it's harder to pen the sheep with a three-sided pen, it's easier to notice how the sheep are reacting to me and the dog, and whether the dog is slicing his flanks. I also remember to move around and use my body position more. –Beth

## What are some additional strategies to use in training?

1. Practice reading your sheep. If the sheep are not afraid of people, stand in line with the pen gate. If the sheep are people shy, then take pressure off the sheep by standing farther away from the pen gate.

2. As the dog moves the sheep toward the pen, try flanking him to the left and to the right. Doing this often gives the sheep the impression that the dog is on both sides of them, and often makes them less likely to try darting around to one side or the other of the pen.

3. Practice letting your dog perform two-thirds of the work. Often handlers get excited and step in too quickly and push the sheep over the dog or out of the pen. Practice standing back and letting the dog do the work. In training at home, focus on having the dog do almost all the work so he gets in the habit of covering and holding the sheep.

4. Either take a video of your training or have an experienced handler observe you. Because penning involves pressure and release for both the dog and handler, it is difficult to observe all the moving parts and try to pen. Penning is one place where you may want the dog to flank "square" or wider than normal. You may also need the dog to turn off or away from the sheep if he is too close. These are more advanced maneuvers that you can ask an experienced handler to help you with after you and your dog are proficient at basic penning.

# Chapter 26
## Shedding

As you and your dog become better at working sheep, you will want to try shedding, the act of separating one or more sheep from the group. Shedding requires teamwork; both dog and handler must have sheep sense; and shedding tests the dog's temperament, balance, and courage.

*During the shed, the dog stops the movement on the back two sheep. Photo courtesy of Carol Clawson.*

In sheepdog competitions, shedding is an advanced skill that is only required at the top, or open, level of the USBCHA competitions. A farm dog who can shed sheep is very useful, as it can save time on the farm and reduce stress to livestock. For instance, if you want to sort out a sick sheep or a few sheep from the group, a dog who sheds can perform this task in the pasture, rather than taking the flock to sorting equipment.

Because shedding happens quickly, it is important to have a clear picture of what should happen before you start the exercise. When shedding, the dog and handler are letting some sheep escape, while stopping the escape of others. Teaching a dog to shed is challenging because the dog's instinct is to gather the sheep together rather than letting some escape. For handlers, it is challenging because they must have an understanding of how sheep behave and react to pressure. But dogs who learn to shed properly often enjoy it. Some even anticipate it and can do it with minimal help from the handler.

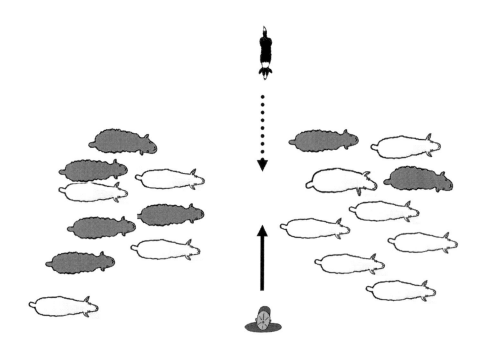

*The dog and handler apply pressure to stop the escape of the back group of sheep.*

## What will my dog learn in these exercises?

Using a step-by-step approach, you'll teach your dog to shed in a relaxed, confident manner. Shedding involves lots of moving parts and requires dogs to do something that initially makes them uncomfortable (going through the flock of sheep). This can cause tension in a dog, and that can lead to the dog biting the sheep. The shedding training is broken into several exercises so your dog will be more confident and less likely to bite at the sheep. Once you and your dog have completed these exercises, your dog will be able to:

- Come through a group of sheep and to you.
- Flank between two groups of sheep.
- Stop on cue between the two groups of sheep and keep the sheep from rejoining the flock.
- Drive the shed-off sheep away from the group.

### What equipment do I need?
**A 50×100 ft. training pen.** Some exercises take place in the training pen you have used for other work.

**A 5-acre field or larger**. After the first few exercises, you'll move into a larger field. The ideal field has minimal pressure, meaning the sheep will not be drawn to a barn or other sheep in an adjacent pasture.

**About 20 calm sheep**. When learning to shed, use sheep that do not clump tightly into groups or run at the sight of the dog. Sheep that have been worked a lot by young dogs may clump together so tightly that they are nearly impossible to shed. Ideally, the sheep will stand or graze. If you have sheep that want to move around a lot, try practicing first thing in the morning, when sheep are the hungriest and most likely to put their heads down and graze. You can also try scattering hay or corn on the ground.

## Exercise 1: Working the sheep without the dog

In order to help your dog, you should gain an understanding of how to stop sheep, let sheep escape and split groups of sheep. Practice these exercises without your dog.

**Step 1**. Practice stopping the sheep. To do this, set the sheep up against a fence line. Ideally you should be between the sheep and a natural draw, such as a barn or other sheep. You can also have a friend help move the sheep along the fence line, toward you. As the sheep approach, step in front of the lead ewe's head to stop the flock. Pay attention to where you need to be relative to the sheep's eyes to stop the forward movement of the sheep. Also note your body position that stops the sheep's motion. Are you facing the sheep head on or sideways? **Note**: If the sheep are extremely people friendly, you may need a crook or stick to help stop them. If they are so people sour that they might run over you or hurt you, get different sheep.

*The handler uses her body position to stop the forward momentum of the sheep. Photo by Beth Kerber*

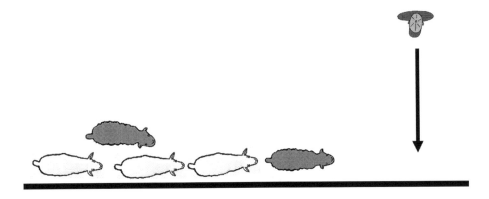

*Handler steps into sheep's path to stop them.*

**Step 2.** Practice letting the sheep escape. With the sheep along a fence and you positioned in front of them and farther away from the fence, step toward them, then step back away from the sheep and allow them to "escape" past you.

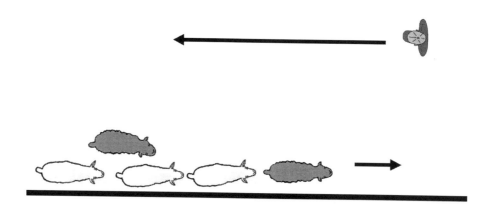

*Allow the sheep to escape past you.*

*The handler releases pressure and allows the sheep to walk past her. Photo by Beth Kerber*

**Step 3.** Practice splitting the sheep into two groups. To do this place a group of sheep near the fence line. As the group is passing in front of you, choose a sheep to stop and step in front of her eye.

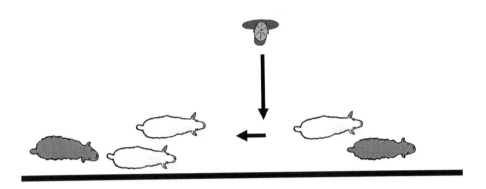

*Split the group in two by selecting a sheep to stop and stepping in front of its eye.*

**Step 4**. Practice releasing pressure and letting the sheep go. After splitting the group of sheep, step out of their path, or release the pressure, so that the sheep that you stopped can rejoin the flock. Practice this until you can reliably stop and let sheep go without the dog. Once comfortable with this, you're ready to add the dog to the exercise.

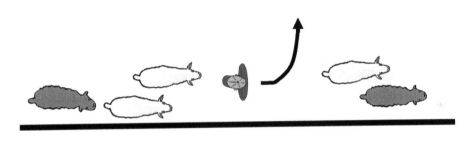

*Step away from the sheep so the stopped group can rejoin the flock.*

## Exercise 2: Teaching the dog to come between the sheep

In this exercise, you'll teach your dog to come between two groups of sheep and straight to you. Herding dogs naturally want to gather sheep into a group. To shed, the dog must be comfortable coming straight to you and going between two groups of sheep. Introducing these concepts to the dog in a controlled environment and with calm sheep helps your dog understand them and get used to it.

Your dog may be confused, stressed or worried about coming between two groups of sheep. This is quite understandable. Up until this point in his training, you have encouraged him to keep the sheep together, and even prevented him from or corrected him for splitting the group of sheep.

If you have successfully completed the semi-packed pen work and your dog promptly comes to you when called off sheep, then he should mentally be more comfortable with the shedding work. The semi-packed pen work helps dogs get comfortable working very closely with the sheep. By calling your dog to you when you are near the sheep, the dog learns to come to you with a big distraction (the sheep) nearby.

**Step 1.** Before getting your dog, place about 20 very calm sheep in the training pen. Practice breaking the flock into two groups without a dog. Make sure you can split the sheep without a lot of stomping of your feet or flapping of your arms. Up until this point in your dog's training, your motion into the sheep has been a sign that the dog is too close to the sheep. You do not want to confuse the dog by making him think you are chasing him away from the sheep. After stepping quietly into the flock, observe whether the sheep are happy staying apart. If they are not, try scattering some hay or grain on the ground to keep them quiet and to give you and the dog a chance to practice without the sheep trying to break around the dog or you.

**Step 2**. Bring your dog into the training pen and have him lie down. While the dog is lying down, separate the sheep into two groups yourself, leaving a good-sized (20 feet or more) space between the two groups of sheep. While standing between the two groups, call your dog to you and have him lie down between the two groups of sheep. At this point, don't worry about what the sheep are doing. You just want the dog to be comfortable coming to you between the two groups of sheep and then lying down between them.

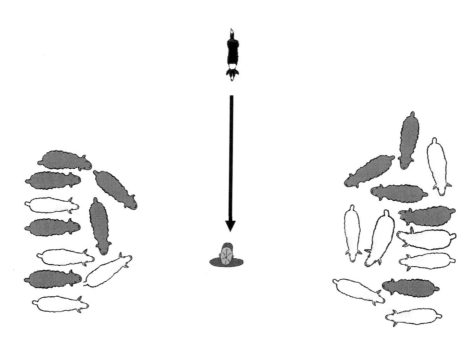

*Call your dog between the sheep and then ask for a "lie down."*

**Step 3**. Leave your dog in a down position between the two groups of sheep. Back up and call him away from the sheep and to you. Watch to make sure your dog is coming straight to you without turning into the sheep. Leave him and walk between the two groups to the other side of the sheep and repeat the exercise. He should learn to do this quickly, without tension and without turning toward the sheep. A dog who has his tail up, head up or is frantic is showing signs of tension. Repeat this exercise many times so your dog gets comfortable doing it. If your dog is hesitant doing this, try putting him on a line, calling him to you and then quickly tugging, then releasing the line.

Before moving onto the next exercise, your dog should reliably come through the sheep and straight to you. His head should point toward you, not at the sheep.

## Exercise 3: Flanking your dog between two groups of sheep
This exercise is designed to get the dog comfortable working between two groups of sheep. It also introduces him to the concept of holding one group of sheep apart from another. This exercise takes place in the training pen. Your dog will flank between two groups of sheep while focusing on one group.

**Step 1**. Place about 20 very calm sheep in the training pen. Bring your dog into the training pen and have him lie down. Without using the dog, break the sheep into two groups, leaving a big area between the groups. Make sure at least five sheep are in each group. If only a few sheep are in one group, those sheep feel more pressure to join the other group. While standing between the two groups, call your dog to you and have him lie down.

**Step 2**. With your dog in a down position between the two groups of sheep, step in front of the dog so that you are between the dog and one group of sheep. While facing the shed off sheep, flank the dog back and forth behind you. Repeat the process. Ideally, the other group of sheep should be stationary or grazing behind the dog, and the dog should be focused on the sheep that he is flanking.

When doing this, keep things as quiet and calm as possible. The dog may get excited and even dive into or bite the sheep. He might also be worried about the sheep behind him. Keep him focused on the sheep in front of him and use your body position to flank him correctly and without slicing into the sheep. Both you and your dog will find it easier to control the sheep when you keep your distance than when you are too close.

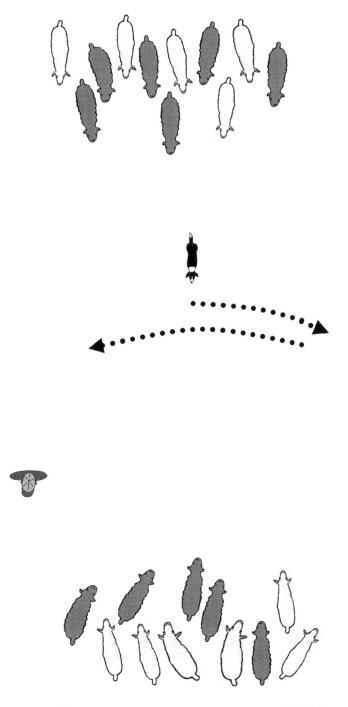

*While facing the shed off sheep, flank the dog back and forth behind you.*

THINK LIKE A SHEEPDOG TRAINER

**Note**: Observe the shape of your dog's flanks. He should neither be cutting in on the group that you are holding, nor trying to cut back to the group behind you. It is very common for the dog's flank to be too tight. If that happens, correct it. At this point, a firm verbal correction should be enough to open his flank. If he's worried about the sheep behind him, keep drawing his focus to the sheep in front of him and excite him with some fast flanks and shushing him.

---

### A Shepherd's Journey

When I taught my first dog to shed, I did not understand the importance of having her come in straight when she came between the sheep. She enjoyed driving the shed-off sheep away so much she'd turn into the shed-off sheep as she came in to start the drive away before she had really split the sheep. This worked okay when we shed our tame sheep at home, but when we went to a trial and the sheep tried to break past her, she was too close to the shed-off sheep to control them and ended up losing the sheep when they broke past her. It took me a long time to realize that keeping the dog further away from the shed-off sheep actually gave the dog more control over them, and that coming in straight between the two groups gives the dog that extra distance to control the sheep. –Kay

---

**Step 3**. If there is room in the training pen, lie your dog down between the sheep. Walk to the other side of the sheep he is focusing on. Let the dog balance the group of sheep to you while holding them away from the group behind him.

### How will I know whether my dog has mastered these exercises?
- Is your dog comfortable coming between two groups of sheep?
- Does your dog come straight to you when called?
- Can he lie down on the line between the two groups of sheep in a calm, confident manner?
- Can he flank between the two groups of sheep without slicing his flanks or kicking back to the other group of sheep?
- Can he reliably perform these tasks without tension?

If you answer yes to these questions, move onto the next group of exercises.

## Exercise 4: Teaching the dog to help divide the sheep
Up until now, you have divided the sheep into two groups yourself. In this exercise, you will teach your dog to help you.

**Step 1**. Place about 20 calm sheep in the training pen and then bring your dog into the training pen. Have him flank to the left and stop instantly on cue. Have him flank to the right and stop instantly on cue. To be effective at shedding, the dog must flank correctly and stop instantly on cue. Instantly means the dog takes no extra steps. Even one or two extra steps makes shedding very difficult. Also watch the shape of his flanks. He should be flanking almost parallel to the sheep. If he's doing this, move on to Step 2.

**Step 2**. Position yourself on the opposite side of the sheep as your dog. Pick a sheep you want to stop. Because you want your dog to be successful, select an easy sheep. Avoid selecting ones with their heads up or ones that will be difficult to stop. Ask for a flank and stop your dog in front of the eye of the sheep you want to stop. You should be on the other side of the sheep in front of the eye of the sheep you want to stop. Immediately ask your dog for a "walk up." Use your body to help your dog stop the sheep. Both you and the dog must be slightly ahead of the sheep's head to reliably stop the sheep.

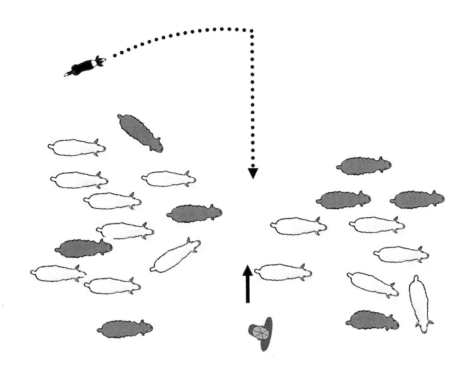

*The handler and dog should be positioned slightly in front of the sheep the handler wants to stop.*

**Step 3**. When the sheep stops or hesitates, call your dog toward you. When he is between the sheep and in front of you, help your dog block the sheep if needed. Ask for a "lie down." Flank the dog in front of the sheep. Practice flanking the dog back and forth as you did in Exercise 3. The dog should move freely and cover the sheep.

**Step 4**. If the dog is lying down and flanking well, then let the dog drive the shed group of sheep away from the other.

**Note**: Make sure your dog is coming straight toward you, lying down and flanking well between the groups of sheep before moving on to the drive away. Dogs generally like driving the sheep away, and many start to anticipate this. When they do, they may start to turn into the sheep early. This puts them in the incorrect position and makes them more likely to slice a flank, grip or lose their sheep. If your dog starts anticipating, coming in and driving away before asked, go back to stopping and flanking the dog between the two groups.

As your dog becomes fluent in shedding, he may enjoy it so much he comes in on the shed before you ask him to. In this case, practice making gaps between the sheep while telling the dog to lie down and not letting him come in. He must wait for your cue to come into the sheep.

### What if I have trouble stopping and splitting the sheep?
Stopping and splitting the sheep requires correct timing, knowing where the dog and person must be positioned and having sheep that will split into smaller groups fairly easily. Some sheep may be sour to dog work and clump together, making shedding extremely difficult, even for experienced dogs and handlers. If you're having difficulty, try the following.

**Step 1**. Put the dog away. Move the sheep up against the fence so that the sheep are between you and the fence. Practice stepping into the group of sheep and stopping the one you want. Pay attention to where you are relative to the sheep's eye. Also try stopping and letting one sheep go at a time. To do this, step in and block all but that one sheep. Then step back and release the pressure before doing it again. Watch where you must be relative to the sheep. Stepping in front of the eye will usually stop them and stepping toward their butts will let them go.

**Step 2**. Try this same exercise, but with a crook or stock stick. With the sheep positioned between you and the fence, try stopping the sheep you want with a stock stick. Think of a stock stick as an extension of your arm. Do not hit the animal with it. Instead, wave it in front of the sheep's head or tap it on the ground.

**Step 3**. With your dog, try the shedding exercise next to a fence. Position yourself so that you are between the sheep and a fence, with the fence behind you. This helps you hold your side so you can focus more on stopping the sheep instead of holding your side. Try working with your dog to stop a sheep's forward momentum. Both you and your dog should be able to move into the eye of the sheep you want to stop, and both should work together to stop the sheep's forward momentum.

**Note**: As your dog advances, he'll do more and more of the shedding work. The handler, though, still has to hold her side and show the dog which sheep to take.

*Shedding requires a dog that is quick and agile. Photo courtesy of Carol Clawson.*

## Exercise 5: Advanced shedding work

If you and your dog can easily stop the back half of a group of 10 sheep consistently, then you are ready for more advanced shedding work. In competitions, you will often have to shed one sheep from a group of three or four, or possibly two sheep from four or five sheep. The smaller number of sheep makes the individual sheep more nervous and less likely to want to leave the group and this amplifies small errors that you or your dog may make.

To prepare for trial situations, practice shedding with fewer sheep. Try shedding two sheep from a group of five sheep or, for even more difficulty, try shedding one sheep from a group of three.

Also, practice shedding in a specific area. In competition, you may have a 40-yard diameter area that is marked with sawdust, flags or rocks. To prepare for this, get used to watching for a perimeter while shedding. Set up a shedding ring and practice shedding in that specific area.

*Red Oliver and his dog perform an international shed, in which 5 ribboned sheep must be separated from a group of 20 and then penned. Photo courtesy of Carol Clawson.*

**Note**: When you practice shedding, always have the dog "win" on the shed. If the dog tries but comes in on the wrong sheep or is not successful at stopping the sheep, don't get angry with him. Getting angry with the dog may make him hesitant about shedding, and that's hard to fix. You want your dog to be happy and eager to come in on the shed. Faansie Basson always says, "Never abandon a bad shed."

If the dog is consistently coming in on the wrong sheep or not stopping the sheep, take a video of your practice or have an experienced handler observe. This may help you determine whether the problem is a timing or body position issue, and whether it is a handler or dog issue.

**Keep in mind that trial shedding can be very difficult**. You often only have a minute to complete it, and because it follows the gather and drive, you and the dog will likely be mentally and physically tired. Plus, it must be done in the ring. To prepare for that, do a lot of larger group shedding, and limit the trial practice shedding. Doing large group shedding keeps you and your dog confident, relaxed and happy.

# Chapter 27
# Final Thoughts

*A Border Collie moves a flock of range sheep. Photo courtesy of Carol Clawson.*

As you progress in your sheepdog training journey, here are some thoughts to keep in mind.

**If you don't use it, you'll lose it**. All training must be maintained by practice or the training will be forgotten. Mistakes and incorrect behaviors tend to creep into training due to the natural inclinations of the dog, the handler or the environment. If your dog's performance starts to fall apart, it's usually because you're making a small technical error that changes the dog's response, not that the dog has suddenly decided not to respond. Having someone to help you or watch you for training/handling errors is valuable no matter your level of expertise.

**Generalization of your training is important**. You and your dog must be able to correctly perform in a variety of situations and environments. To teach this, you must take your training "on the road" and work in different places, with different sheep and on different terrain. Practice the 100 rule: the dog and handler must perform 80 percent correctly for 10 repetitions and in 10 different places or settings before a behavior can be considered generalized. However, extreme stress, fear or excitement will decrease your and your dog's performance, even if a behavior is generalized. Expect that your performance on the trial field will be less than what you can do at home. If you are struggling with a training element at home, it is likely to be worse at a trial.

**Some things we train are in direct conflict with other things we train**. For example, we work to perfect and maintain the dog's sense of balance, yet we also teach the dog to respond instantly to any cue, asking him to give up or come off of balance. It requires careful attention to keep opposing actions crisp and correct. It is like working on strength and flexibility: you constantly have to do both.

**Training is never finished**. You'll continue to work on different aspects of the dog's training for the rest of his career. Every dog and every handler has their own particular strengths and weaknesses. Once you know what those are, you should address those on a regular basis. Plan to have maintenance exercises for your dog. These exercises address your dog's particular needs. If your dog naturally flanks tight, touch on opening up his flanks. If he's a little sticky or slow to walk up, remind him how to push briskly forward. Your education as a trainer and handler also is never finished. Your timing and observational skills require continued practice and polish.

**Remember to keep it fun and fresh for your dog**. Some ways to do this include releasing the pressure with balance work, working faster and freer, giving the dog a few days off, working fresh undogged sheep, or working on new things. Don't fall into the habit of drilling your dog and nagging on his mistakes. All the artificial work you ask the dog to do at trials can take the pleasure out of working stock. Pay attention to your dog's attitude. He should be keen, crisp, focused and fresh. If you notice your dog starting to slow down, seem flat or lacking in enthusiasm, first check to see whether you've been overtraining, over correcting, or failing to release the pressure and let your dog have the sheep. Make sure to break up training with balance work and with skills your dog has already mastered and enjoys doing. If your dog still seems flat or off, check for physical issues. Pain can often present as a lack of enthusiasm. Tick-borne diseases are common in working dogs and often present as a vague illness. Ear infections or damaged teeth are other common sources of decreased performance. On the other hand, if your dog's attitude is becoming wild or non-responsive, you may have stopped requiring good behavior to have access to the sheep.

**You'll find new ways to teach your dog and different methods to use on training problems, and you may want to change the order of training from what is presented in this book**. The exact details of how you train can vary quite a bit, but the overall principles of setting the dog up for success, rewarding correct behavior and preventing/stopping/correcting incorrect behavior should remain the same. Remember that the most important part of a correction is the release of the pressure. It's easy for a handler to get so caught up in correcting bad things that she forgets to release and reward the dog when he does well.

**As you get ready for trials, focus on performing well at the trial, not on winning**. Keep your focus on performing each training skill correctly, not on trying to win the trial. If you and your dog learn to perform well at trials, you will eventually start to win. If you worry about winning without thinking about your performance, you will struggle to progress. Think of trials as a place to learn what you need to work on, not a way to feed your ego.

**Keep going back to the basic fundamentals of training**. As you progress, it is easy to get excited about challenging outruns, shedding and other fun stuff. Top trainers focus on the foundations: a good stop, clean flanks, balance and response to cues. If your foundation is allowed to become weak, the rest of the training will suffer. Keep practicing and strengthening the basics on a daily basis.

**Keep learning and enjoy the journey**. You will learn something new with every dog you train, with every trial that you compete in, with every book you read and with every lesson or clinic you participate in. But as you progress, take moments to really enjoy that magical partnership that you have with your dog.

---

### A Shepherd's Journey

When Faansie Basson was standing at my side while we were watching my dog perform an outrun during a clinic, he asked what I was thinking. I knew the correct answer was that I was watching my dog, whistle at the ready, and paying attention to the dog's arc and whether the dog was checking in on the sheep. What I was thinking, though, was what an amazing and talented dog he was, to be able to judge his distance from the sheep, to read the sheep and to approach them with both confidence and kindness. I was thinking how magical it was to have a dog who worked in harmony with me, and how much I enjoyed working with the dog to move the sheep and do farm chores.

As I travel on my sheepdog training journey, I've become better at observing and reacting to what is happening on the field, but I haven't lost that sense of awe and wonder for the dogs and the partnership I have with them. That's what keeps me training and trying to improve and learn more.
—Beth

# Glossary of Terms

**Away to me**: A directional cue for the dog to circle in a counterclockwise direction in relation to the sheep.

**Balance**: The position the dog must be in to hold the sheep to the handler.

**Balance work**: This often describes the exercise done with the handler, dog and sheep where the handler moves and the dog must move to the position where he can hold the sheep to the handler.

**Balanced flank**: The dog circles around the sheep toward balance, or the position the dog must be to hold the stock to the handler. For most dogs, it's the easiest flank to perform.

**Behavior**: An observable action by the dog, such as sit, jump or run.

**Biddable**: A dog that responsive and tuned in to the handler.

**Bottle babies**: Sheep there are being or were fed bottles as lambs. They are usually overly friendly with humans and don't make good sheep for dog training.

**Come-bye**: A directional cue for the dog to circle in a clockwise direction in relation to the sheep.

**Command**: An authoritative order.

**Correction**: The minimal effective action to change a dog's behavior.

**Cue**: A verbal signal, physical prompt or whistle signal to the dog to perform a specific action.

**Cross drive**: The dog pushing the sheep parallel to and in front of the handler.

**Draw**: The pull that sheep feel to go in a certain direction. For example, they may feel a draw toward the barn, shade trees or other sheep.

**Drive**: Pushing stock away from or parallel to the handler's position.

**Ewe**: A female sheep.

**Eye (or dog with eye)**: In herding, a Border Collies use their intense stare to control stock. A dog with a "strong eye" often will not want to move around the sheep. A dog with a "loose eye" may not hold the sheep together. Different jobs and different handlers prefer different amounts of "eye."

**Fetch**: The dog brings the sheep to the handler. In USBCHA trials, the fetch is the point from where the dog lifts the sheep to the handler; it's worth 20 points of the score.

**Fetch panels**: In sheepdog competitions, the set of panels between the set-out point and the handler that the sheep must go through during the fetch.

**Flank**: The circular turn the dog makes in relation to the sheep. A flank is composed of a direction, shape, speed and distance from the sheep.

**Flighty sheep**: Very reactive sheep that may run at the sight or sudden movement of a dog or handler. They are challenging to use for training and often inappropriate for novice handlers and dogs.

**Flight zone**: The area around the sheep that, when encroached by a dog or human, causes them to move. It varies with the sheep and the behavior of the handler and dog.

**Fully trained open dog**: A dog that is training in all of the elements for USBCHA open competition and competing at the open level.

**Gather**: The dog leaving the handler's side, arcing around the sheep until he is behind them, and then bringing the sheep to the handler. In a USBCHA sheepdog trial, the gather is composed of the outrun, lift and fetch and worth 50 points.

**Gripping**: Biting the sheep.

**Hair sheep**: Sheep that have hair fibers and shed naturally. They are raised primarily for meat and include breeds such as Katahdins, Dorpers, St. Croix and Barbados.

**Herding**: The controlled movement of a group of stock.

**Herding instinct**: An innate desire to interact with, control or group animals into a flock and move them as a group.

**Knee knockers**: Sheep that have learned the best way to avoid a dog is to cling to the human, regardless of the dog's actions or position. Because they want to cling to the human, they are difficult to use for sheepdog training.

**Lamb**: A male or female sheep younger than a year old.

**Lift**: The point after the outrun when the dog makes his first contact with the sheep. It consists of speed, direction and smoothness and is often described as the introduction between the dog and the sheep. It often determines the relationship between the dog and the sheep. In a USBCHA sheepdog trial, it is worth 10 points.

**Negative punishment**: A training method where the trainer subtracts or removes something desirable from the dog's environment to decrease or weaken a behavior.

**Negative reinforcement**: A training method where the trainer subtracts or removes something unpleasant from the dog's environment to increase or strengthen a behavior.

**Off-contact flank**: If the circular turn the dog takes becomes wider, or he moves far enough away from the sheep that he no longer affects the sheep's behavior, he's said to be off contact or too square.

**Off-balance flank**: The dog turns in the direction that's going away from the balance point. For the dog, this is often more difficult than a balanced flank because it goes against his instincts and his early training.

**Outrun**: The dog leaves from the handler's side, arcs out and around the sheep and stops or slows down behind the sheep at the balance point. An ideal outrun is shaped like half of an upside down pear. In USBCHA trials, the outrun is worth 20 points.

**Pace**: The speed the dog is bringing the sheep. In most cases, a brisk walk or slow trot is ideal.

**Penning**: The action of putting sheep into a free-standing pen. In a USBCHA sheepdog trial, it is worth 10 points.

**Positive punishment**: A training method where the trainer adds something unpleasant to the dog's environment to decrease or weaken a dog's behavior or action.

**Positive reinforcement:** A training method where the trainer adds something desirable to the dog's environment to increase or strengthen a behavior.

**Power:** A dog's ability to move sheep with authority.

**Prey drive:** The desire to chase, capture and kill prey like birds, rabbits, mice and sheep.

**Ram:** An intact male sheep.

**Shed:** The act of separating one or more sheep from the group. An international shed is where five collared sheep are sorted off from a group of 20 sheep.

**Slicing a flank:** Instead of taking a circular turn around the sheep, the dog steps into the circle toward the sheep, thus getting closer to the sheep and disturbing them.

**Started dog:** A herding dog that has some herding training, but is not competing in USBCHA open courses. Most people will consider a dog "started" when he has good gathers, is learning his flank directions and has started learning to drive.

**Steady (also called "take time"):** The dog slows his pace.

**That'll do:** The dog stops working the sheep and comes to the handler.

**United States Border Collie Handlers' Association (USBCHA):** An organization governing and sanctioning sheepdog trials in the United States. USBCHA are considered the largest, most-challenging herding dog trials in the United States.

**Walk up:** The dog should walk directly toward the sheep.

**Wether:** A castrated male sheep.

**Wool sheep:** Sheep that grow wool fibers and must be shorn.

# Appendix A:
# Basic Obedience Behaviors for the Herding Dog

Three basic obedience behaviors are very useful to teach your sheepdog before you start training on livestock: name response/attention, come/recall and lie down/stop. All three can be taught using food and a clicker. While you can use other methods to teach these actions, they will be less precise and take longer. When teaching these behaviors, use a food lure to start the behavior. While you could use shaping and capturing, novice trainers usually find luring with a treat is faster and easier.

**Note:** We don't recommend teaching stock-related behaviors, such as flanks, gathers, walk-ups and driving, away from sheep. These behaviors are all in relation to the stock and depend on the stock's reaction to the dog. If these behaviors are taught strictly as obedience commands, they do not relate to the sheep's response to the dog. For example, if you give your dog a directional cue such as "away to me," the shape and speed of his flank will depend on his location relative to the stock, the number of sheep, the behavior/actions of the sheep, and his distance from the sheep.

## Training with a Clicker

Also known as operant conditioning, this training method has become extremely successful and popular in training all animal species from fish to elephants. Clicker training has revolutionized animal training and management in homes, zoos, animal parks and aquariums. It's transformed dog sports such as agility, obedience, protection training and scent work. It's also has positive impacts in human learning through use of TAG (Targeted Acoustical Guidance) in sports including golf and tennis, special needs learning and even in training surgeons.

### The reasons for this method's success include:
1. The click can be given at the exact moment that the desired behavior happens.
2. The click gives very clear information to the learner because it happens at the precise moment of the behavior, not afterwards.
3. The click is emotionally neutral so it is pure information to the learner and doesn't have any emotional baggage associated with it.
4. The method relies almost exclusively on using positive reinforcement so the learner has a very positive emotional association with the training and the trainer.
5. A skilled trainer can teach amazingly quickly and precisely using this method.

The theory is simple. The dog/learner is taught to associate the sound of the clicker (or any short, clear, unique sound) with a reward. In dogs, we simply pair the sound of the click with the presentation of a tasty food treat multiple times. The dog quickly associates the sound of the click as predicting the arrival of a food treat. It's important that the "click" occurs before the presentation of the treat. The click is not a command. It's simply information to the dog that whatever he was doing when he heard the click will result in a treat.

Once that association is made, the trainer now clicks only when she sees the dog perform a particular action she has chosen to train. For example, the trainer may click when the dog glances up at her, then deliver the food treat. Very quickly, the dog learns that looking at the trainer produces the click noise and is followed by the treat. If the dog is motivated by the treat, then the dog will begin offering the behavior of looking at the trainer more often. The trainer continues to click to mark the "looking" behavior and then deliver a treat to strengthen that behavior. If the behavior doesn't happen, the trainer simply does not click and does not treat. The absence of the click tells the learner to try again.

Now the trainer can start to manipulate or shape the behavior of the dog looking at her. She may start by clicking only when the dog looks at her for a longer time, say 3 seconds. Or she may click only when the dog looks directly at her eyes. Or she may decide to add a cue and only click when the dog looks at her after hearing "watch me." Shaping is a challenging skill for the trainer, requiring timing, focus, and a clear plan. Books on clicker training are included in the recommended reading section.

> ### Can you use clicker training for herding behaviors?
>
> The short answer is yes—if you are fluent using a clicker, understand the method, and have conditioned your dog to understand what the clicker means. In stock work, I use the clicker to mark a correct response to cues such as lie down, that'll do and flank directions. I also use it to shape behaviors such as a properly turned out flank or change of pace (speed up or slow down) behind the sheep. In these cases, the reward is not food but being allowed to continue to work the stock. The click simply tells the dog what he did correctly.

## Name response/attention

For name response, start by teaching the dog to look at you in response to his name. While there are several ways to teach this, the one below is easy and pretty foolproof.

**Note**: When training on sheep, don't insist that he look at you. You want him to stay focused on the sheep. However, you want him to acknowledge he heard you with an ear flick, head turn or hesitation in his movements.

**Step 1. Set up the environment**. Have the dog in a quiet, distraction-free area. Have a treat bag full of chopped chicken or hotdogs and your clicker. Plan for each training session to last about 10 minutes, and plan on two or three training sessions per day.

**Step 2. Lure the behavior**. Hide the treat in your fist, allow the dog to smell your fist, then slowly move your hand in a line from the dog's nose to your face. When the dog's nose is pointing toward your face, click/praise to mark the behavior and give the treat. Repeat this 10 times with your right hand and 10 times with your left hand. Repeat this training session three times.

**Step 3. Generalize the behavior**. Vary your position relative to the dog as you practice. Sit on the floor next to the dog, stand in front of the dog, and stand beside the dog. Continue to lure the behavior, click/praise and treat. The dog may (most do) start offering the behavior (looking toward your face) before you move your hands. If he does, click/praise when the dog offers the behavior, then treat. Plan on 10 repetitions/session. Repeat this session 3 times

**Step 4. Fade the lure**. Keep your hands in your pockets or behind your back. Watch the dog for any sign of looking up. If he does, click/praise and treat. If he is struggling, make a noise, (lip smack or air noise) and click/praise when the dog looks up toward your face. Plan on getting 20 click/treats per session and repeat this session 3 times.

**Step 5. Add the cue**. Only now do you add a cue. Say the dog's name once in a normal tone of voice, if he looks up, click /praise and treat. If he hesitates, then move your hand to your face (treat still hidden in fist just as you did at the beginning). Click/praise when the dog's nose points up and give the treat. Pause after saying the dog's name and give him a chance to offer the behavior before luring or prompting him with a small noise. Plan on 20 repetitions per session and three sessions.

**Step 6. Generalize the cue.** Use the cue (dog's name) to get the behavior (looking toward you) while varying your position to the dog. Work in front of the dog, behind the dog and beside the dog. Continue to click/praise and treat for his nose pointing toward your face. Be careful not to repeat the cue, but to lure or prompt the dog if necessary. Plan on 20 repetitions and three training sessions.

**Step 7. Take it on the road.** Now you have a behavior (looking at you) on cue (dog's name). The next steps are to generalize the behavior starting with new locations and mild distractions. So if you start in the laundry room, repeat Steps 5 and 6 in the living room, kitchen, etc. Then move outside and gradually add more challenging distractions. Keep the sessions short and keep the dog's success rate around 8 out of 10. Continue to give the treats for each successful repetition. Keep the dog on a long line so that he cannot get rewarded for ignoring you. Any time the dog fails to respond to the cue, reset the situation with you closer to the dog.

**Step 8. Adding a mild correction.** As you continue adding distractions and new situations, continue rewarding the dog with either a treat or by letting him have a break or do some sniffing and playing. Keep the dog on a long line. If the dog clearly hears his name, but is distracted, try the "crazy owner routine." This involves taking off suddenly and with no warning at a brisk pace in the opposite direction of the dog. Because the dog is attached to you by a line, he will suddenly find himself following you. Then you can repeat the cue and likely get a good response and then reward the dog. He will learn he had better pay attention to you as you are unpredictable and may take off unexpectedly!

**Step 9: Proof the exercise.** This last exercise is a great way to help the dog understand that paying attention to you pays off. Start this exercise in a low-distraction environment. Hold a first full of extremely tasty treats in your hand, right in front of the dog's nose. Keep your fist tight so the dog doesn't get any treats. He will likely paw, lick or mouth your hand. Keep your hand still and don't do anything. Watch the dog very closely. Because of your earlier attention training, at some point he will get frustrated, pull his nose off your hand and look up at you to see why he can't have the treat. At that moment, click or praise, open your hand and give him the treat. Repeat the exercise until the dog quickly ignores any treat and looks up at you as soon as he sees a treat in your hand. You are building the idea that for anything the dog wants, he must first pay attention to you. This will pay off when you take him to sheep.

## Stop/lie down

**Step 1. Lure the behavior.** Start in a quiet, low distraction environment such as the laundry room. Have the dog on a rug or mat so that he is not on a hard or slippery floor. Have a treat hidden in your fist. Put your fist on the dog's nose and then put your fist on the ground. It doesn't matter if the dog is sitting or standing. When the dog's nose is touching your hand while your hand is on the ground, click/praise and treat. Repeat 10 times for your right hand and 10 times for your left hand, clicking for the nose touching your hand while your hand is on the ground. It doesn't matter if the dog is standing or sitting, just that his nose touches the ground.

**Step 2. Lure the full behavior.** With a treat hidden in your fist, put your hand on the ground directly between the dog's front legs and under the chest. Click/praise and treat for his nose touching your hand, or if the dog lies down. At this point most dogs will start to bend their elbows and you can click and treat when you see that action as well. The goal is for the dog to fold up into the down position by bending his elbows and leaning backwards into the down position. This is because later, on sheep, the down cue is to stop all forward motion. It's important the dog fold back into the down position from the start. Repeat 10 times for each hand and also vary the dog's position on the mat or rug. Repeat this training session three times.

**Step 3. Get the lured behavior fluent.** Treat in hand, put your hand on the ground and click/praise if the dog lies down. Wait for a few seconds and see if the dog will lie down. Do not click for just the nose touch to your hand; wait for the full behavior. If it doesn't happen, help the dog by repeating the exercise with your hand under your knee. Sit on the ground next to the dog, with your leg closest to the dog bent so he can easily get his head under it. Put your hand with the treat under your knee and click/praise and treat when the dog touches your hand and his head is under your knee. Most dogs will lie down. If he does, click and treat. If so, repeat for about 20 responses per training session, three sessions.

**Step 4. Add the cue**. Just before putting your hand on the ground, give your "lie down" cue. The sequence is verbal cue, drop hand to ground, dog lies down, click and treat. Repeat 20 times with both the right and left hand. Click and treat if the dog lies down before the physical prompt occurs. Again, as you do this, watch how the dog lowers into the down position. Shape for the dog leaning backwards into the down position by bending his elbows, shifting his weight backwards and then lowering his back. Plan on 3 sessions of 20 repetitions per session.

**Step 5. Generalize the action**. Generalize the down relative to your position. Once the dog can do the behavior on a verbal cue, repeat the training sequence with the dog: (1) beside you on both right and left side; (2) in front of you; and (3) behind you.

**Step 6. Add a moving down**. Start with the dog on the leash in front of you. Walking backwards, give the down cue and then stop moving or step forward into the dog to stop his forward motion. Watch for the down being an almost backwards motion as the dog stops and lies down. Repeat this daily for several sessions. Next, add walking beside you and getting a down. Cue the down, then pivot in front of the dog and step into the dog to get the quick backwards down action. Continue to click and treat for the "down" action.

**Step 7. Add the three D's: duration, difficulty and distance**. Because being able to stop your dog is absolutely vital to teaching the dog to work stock, add the three D's before going to stock.

**Duration**. Initially, click/praise and treat as soon as the dog lies down. As he becomes fluent, though, you'll increase the amount of time the dog lies down. Teach him to wait for a release before getting back up. Do this in very small steps:

1. Cue the down and go back to using the treat hidden in your fist with your fist on the ground. When the dog lies down, wait one second, then click/praise and give a treat on the ground between the dog's front paws. The click not only marks the behavior, but it ends the behavior. Once you have clicked, the dog is free to get up if he chooses.

2. Gradually increase the amount of time before you click/praise and treat, working from a few seconds up to 10 seconds. If the dog gets up before you click/praise, simply start over. Work up until the dog can easily do about 30 seconds before moving on.

**Difficulty**. You have already added some difficulty by varying your position to the dog and by adding a moving down. If your dog is performing about 80 percent correctly at the moving down and the 30 second down, you can now add some difficulty in the form of distractions, such as other dogs, animals, toys, or food. With all of these, start easy, with the distractions at a distance or being low level, and gradually increase the challenge while keeping your dog successful most of the time. This is one place where you can use sheep as a distraction for a pup. The pup should be on a long line and the sheep at a distance, such as across the field.

**Distance**. Your dog will have to learn to stop when you tell him to, even 800 yards away. Start teaching distance after the dog is lying down easily without hand signals and with distractions. This can be introduced with the dog on a tether so he can't come to you. Because most early training involves the dog being right next to you, it is common for the dog to want to come toward you when you cue a down. In the dog's mind, being close is part of the exercise. Get the dog used to being on a 4 foot tether, then take one step back from the dog and cue the down. Drop back and use your downward hand motion if needed the first few times. As always, click/praise when the dog lies down. Then, staying at about one step away, vary your position, in front of the dog, off to the right, off to the left, etc. Repeat this for a few training sessions until the dog is easily performing without you having to use any hand signals. Then gradually increase the distance to 3 steps, 6 steps, 10 steps, etc., continuing to vary position and keeping the dog on a tether. At this point, you can usually take the dog off the tether and just practice random "downs" around the house and yard.

## Recall /come/that'll do

Many people struggle teaching the dog to come when called. That is because the recall is a very complex maneuver. You are asking the dog to:

- hear the cue even in the face of interesting distractions or at a distance,
- stop what he is doing,
- turn toward you,
- come toward you (while ignoring any distractions),
- continue toward you until he arrives next to you,
- and let you take him by the collar and put on a leash.

Added to that is the distance the dog is asked to come, distractions that are enticing and competing reinforcers, like sheep or squirrels. Finally, people often fail to reward the dog when he does come, or even punish the dog for coming because they are frustrated. All of this makes teaching and maintaining the recall a challenging task and one you will work on for the life of your dog.

**Step 1. Shape the behavior**. Start in a quiet, low-distraction location. Have a treat in your fist, hidden from the dog. Put your fist with the treat on the dog's nose and take a big step away from the dog, pulling your hand away from the dog with you. When the dog follows your hand, and you, click/praise for that forward motion toward you and give the treat. Repeat 20 times with each hand. The target action that you are clicking/praising for is the *dog's motion* toward you, so watch that you are clicking as the dog is moving toward you and your hand, not after he has caught up to you.

**Step 2. Increase the distance**. Stay in your quiet, low distraction location. Repeat with bigger steps away from the dog and in different directions from the dog (step to the dog's right/left/ahead/behind, etc.). Continue to click/praise as the dog is approaching you, then giving the treat when he gets to you. Repeat 20 times in three sessions. If the dog is following you and you can't create distance, drop a treat or two on the ground and move away from the dog while he is searching for or eating the treats.

**Step 3. Add the cue**. Using "that'll do" is a good choice. Most sheepdog trainers avoid using "come" or "come here" because "come or Come-bye" is the common cue to flank clockwise. They also don't use the dog's name because that is the cue for "pay attention to me." Repeat step 2, but this time give the cue just before you step away from the dog. Timing is important. The verbal cue should come before you start to move away. So, standing by the dog, say "that'll do" once, then quickly move away from the dog and click/praise as the dog follows you. The quicker and more exciting you are as you move away, the better this works. Give the treat when the dog catches up to you. Repeat 20 times over three sessions in your quiet, low distraction location.

**Step 4. Add easy distractions**. Because distractions are such an issue for most people in teaching the recall, add one early in the training. In your low distraction environment, add a wire dog crate and put some treats inside of it, where the dog cannot reach them, but obviously knows they are there. Go back to step 3. Give your cue once, then lure the dog away from the crate with the treat hidden in your fist. Click as the dog comes toward you, give the treat, then go back to the crate, open it, and allow the dog to get the treats out of the crate. The dog needs to associate leaving the treats in the crate with being allowed to go back and get the treats. Start with something not too exciting in the crate, like kibble, while your treat is something tasty such as a hot dog slice. Repeat for 20 repetitions over three sessions. Then switch to the same treats in the crate as you are using for your rewards. Next, make the treats in the crate actually better than the reward. Be sure you click for the dog leaving the crate and approaching you. Approaching you is what will predict him being allowed to go back and get the treat in the crate. This is a really important concept you will want the dog to learn early in his training.

**Step 5. Start to generalize the action of "that'll do" to real life**. To do this, add a long line for the dog to drag. While the long line is rarely used to force the dog to come to you, it is frequently used to prevent him from rewarding himself for not coming (and doing other things like chasing animals or sniffing or digging). You can use the long line for recall just as you did in the name/attention exercise. If the dog clearly misses a cue to come to you, hold the line and take off suddenly and quickly away from the dog and then reward the dog when he is forced to catch up to you by the line he is attached to.

Start off in an area with minimal distractions. Call your dog and move away from him. As he starts toward you, praise/click and then give the treat when he is by your side. Use the long line to give a gentle tug and release if needed to orient the dog to you, but don't yank on him or drag him to you. Practice dozens of times each day in various places and with various distractions.

The key to the recall being reliable is how much you have practiced.

As you continue to add distractions, things get a little complicated. Continue to cue the dog to come and use food treats as a reward, but in some cases, the best reward will be something the dog wants besides a food treat. This is where your previous training of the dog to leave the treats in the crate in your earlier sessions will pay off. For example, your dog really wants to go chase a squirrel. Starting with a super high value food treat and the squirrel far away (maybe outside while you are inside), call your dog. When he comes, he gets the treat and is allowed to watch the squirrel. Later, as the dog becomes fluent in this action, you can call the dog very close to the squirrel and he will come to you because he has learned that coming to you predicts freedom to watch the squirrel. Being allowed to do what he wants is always contingent on doing a recall first. Yes, this takes time, many small steps, and a lot of practice, but it is worth it.

When you first take your dog to sheep, start with doing a recall on the way to the sheep. If the dog comes, praise and move closer to the sheep (his reward). If he doesn't come, move further from the sheep and try again. Teach the dog that getting to the sheep is contingent on his coming to you first from the start and your training will be much easier at every step.

# Appendix B:
## Daily Training Log

---

Dog:                    Plan/Goals for Today's Training:

Date:                   First Few Minutes Plan:


Time of Day / Weather / Length of Session:

Equipment Used:

Location / Stock:


Behaviors worked on / Number of Repetitions / Percentage of Correct Responses

1.

2.

3.

4.

Comments:

Distance / Duration/ Distractions for Each Behavior:


Corrections Used / Rewards Used / Effectiveness:

Handler Skills/ focus / timing / consistency /clear cues / corrections / what I did well / what I need to improve on:


What is going well:

Need solutions for:

Plan / Changes / Ideas for Next Training Session:

# Appendix C:
# Flow Sheet for Solving a Training Issue

### Step 1. Identify the Issue

- What exactly is happening?
- What is the dog doing or not doing?
- What is the situation where/when the issue occurs?

### Step 2. Evaluate the Issue

- What is the dog's body language when the issue occurs? Is the dog emotionally upset–showing extreme arousal, fear, stress, or anxiety?
- Is the dog showing any signs of a physical problem-lameness, stiffness, slow or awkward motion?

If the answer to the questions in Step 2 are "yes," then stop and evaluate the dog's mental and physical status carefully. There is likely a behavioral, relationship or medical issue that needs to be addressed.

If the answers are "no," proceed to Step 3.

### Step 3. Analyze the Issue

- What happens right before the training issue happens? This is the "antecedent" and is often the real cause of the problem.
- What happens after the training issue? What does the dog "get or avoid" for doing the action? This is what drives or maintains the behavior. This will have to be changed to fix the problem.

### Step 4. Isolate the issue

- Take the problem issue out of the rest of your training and work on it separately. Make sure to incorporate the antecedent so that it is addressed and make sure to change the outcome so the dog is not getting a reinforcement for performing incorrectly.
- Set the dog up to perform correctly by moving closer to the dog, changing the training set up, or making the situation easier for the dog.
- Make sure the dog is performing the sequence perfectly in isolation dozens of times. Set the dog up for success and get the muscle memory of the correct behavior well established. Don't use a correction until you've set the dog up to perform correctly multiple times.

### Step 5. Reintegrate the issue

- Once the dog has successfully performed multiple times, put the issue back into the training sequence.
- Expect the issue to return so stay closer to the dog or be ready to help/correct the dog.
- Plan on maintenance for a long time. Training issues are often related to a particular dog's strength or weakness, so training touch ups are sometimes necessary for the life of the dog. Plan to have to isolate and work on certain issues on a regular basis.

## An Example of How to Solve a Training Issue

If a dog is gripping the sheep, this is how you would solve the issue.

**Step 1. Identify**: The dog is gripping on the lift.

**Step 2. Evaluate**: The dog is excited, but his body language does not indicate fear.

**Step 3. Analyze**: The dog is tight on the top of his outrun and approaches the sheep from the wrong angle. He also does not slow down when approaching the sheep. This causes the sheep to scatter, and the dog bites a sheep as they run past him. The real problem is that his outrun is wrong (too tight) and his lift is wrong (too fast). This causes the sheep to escape. The dog bites the sheep from excitement and an attempt to control them. The reward for the dog is that grabbing a sheep is fun. Because he is too close to the sheep to flank correctly, biting is the only way he can stop the sheep from escaping.

**Step 4. Isolate**: First, check the dog's flank shape. It's likely the flank is tight and that his outrun is also tight. Open up the flanks by working closer to the dog and sheep, stopping the dog and then pushing the dog out. Second, the lift is fast and hard. This also needs to be addressed at a close distance. Step through the sheep and correct the dog for a fast approach to the stock. Incorporate a solid "down" before the dog is allowed to approach the sheep (this provides control over the approach). Third, address the outrun. Shorten the outrun to an easily controllable distance and move to stop and correct the dog at any point if he starts to cut in.

Practice all three behaviors, the open flanks, the slower lift, and the wider, deeper outrun, dozens of times while the dog is close at hand (100 yards or less). Gradually increase the distance on the outrun while walking out to meet the dog at the top of the outrun every time. Make sure the dog is nearly perfect on multiple repetitions up close before increasing the distance. As the distance increases, plan to walk out and meet the dog on top. Do NOT let the dog practice being wrong. Multiple successful repetitions can install and maintain the correct action.

**Step 5. Reintegrate**: Now that the dog has had multiple successful repetitions of the problem area at hand or close by, continue to increase the distance and add in the rest of normal training exercises. The problem will most likely come back as the distance and difficulty increases. The time spent working on this will depend on how long and how many times the dog was allowed to perform incorrectly before the issue was addressed. If it's been going on for months, then it's an entrenched behavior and will pop up from time to time, usually with stress or excitement. Just keep addressing it every time it happens. The worst thing to do is allow the dog to be wrong sometimes, and then corrected at other times. Be consistent. Every dog (and every trainer) has faults that need to be worked on constantly and consistently.

# References and Recommended Reading

*Animal Training 101: The Complete and Practical Guide to the Art and Science of Behavior Modification*, Jenifer Zeligs, 2014.

*Anybody Can Do It: A Sheepdog Training Manual*, Pope Robertson, 1979.

*Behavior Modification in Applied Settings*, Alan E.Kazdin, 1994.

*Beware the Straw Man: The Science Dog Explores Dog Training Fact & Fiction*, Linda P. Case, 2015.

*Click for Joy! Questions and Answers from Clicker Trainers and Their Dogs*, Melissa C. Alexander, 2003.

*Dog Smart: Evidence-Based Training with the Science Dog*, Linda P. Case, 2018.

*Dogs: A Startling New Understanding of Canine Origin, Behavior & Evolution*, Raymond and Lorna Coppinger, 2001.

*Don't Shoot the Dog: The New Art of Teaching and Training*, Karen Pryor, 1999.

*Excel-erated Learning: Explaining in Plain English How Dogs Learn and How Best to Teach Them*, Pamela J. Reid, 1996.

*The Farmer's Dog*, John Holmes, 1960.

*Fired Up, Frantic and Freaked Out: Training Crazy Dogs from Over the Top to Under Control*, Laura VanArendonk Baugh, 2013.

*Handbook of Applied Dog Behavior and Training: Adaptation and Learning*, Steven R. Lindsay, 2000.

*How Dogs Learn*, Mary Burch and Jon Bailey, 1999.

*How 2 Train a ___*, Patricia Barlow-Irick, 2015.

*Inside of a Dog: What Dogs See, Smell and Know*, Alexandra Horowitz, 2009.

*Lessons From a Stockdog: A Training Guide*, Bruce Fogt, 1996.

*The Natural Way*, Julie Hill, 2014.

*On Behavior: Essays and Research,* Karen Pryor, 1995.

*One Man's Way: The Interviews*, Austin Bennett, 2006.

*The Other End of the Leash: Why We Do What We Do Around Dogs,* Patricia B. McConnell, Ph.D., 2002

*Plenty in Life is Free: Reflections on Dogs, Training and Finding Grace*, Kathy Sdao, 2012.

*The Power of Positive Dog Training*, Pat Miller, 2001.

*The Power of Reinforcement*, Stephen Ray Flora, 2004.

*The Science of Consequences: How They Affect Genes, Change the Brain, and Impact Our World*, Susan M. Schneider, 2012.

*76 Exercises to Improve Your Stockwork*, Kelly Malone, 2016.

*The Sheep Dog*, Tim Longton, 1989.

*Sheep for Sheepdogs: A Sheepdog Handler's Practical Guide to Sheep*, Michael Neary, 2019.

*Talking Sheepdogs: Training Your Working Border Collie*, Derek Scrimgeour, 2002.

*Temple Grandin's Guide to Working with Farm Animals: Safe, Humane Livestock Handling Practices for the Small Farm*, Temple Grandin, 2017.

*Top Trainers Talk About Starting a Sheep Dog: Training a Border Collie on Sheep and Other Livestock*, edited by Sally Molloy and Heather Nadelman, 2008.

*Train Your Dog Like a Pro*, Jean Donaldson, 2010.

*A Way of Life: Sheepdog Training, Handling and Trialling*, Barbara Collins and H. Glyn Jones, 2002.

*When Pigs Fly! Training Success with Impossible Dogs*, Jane Killion, 2007.

*Working Sheepdogs: Management and Training*, John Templeton, 1988.

# Index

# About the Authors

**Kay Stephens, DVM, MS**, is veterinarian, animal behaviorist and dog trainer who has been training and competing with herding dogs for more than 30 years. She owns and operates Puppy Love Dog Training, a dog training school that specializes in sound, positive learning principles and techniques for both people and dogs in College Station, Texas. She regularly competes in major sheepdog competitions including the Soldier Hollow Classic, Meeker Classic, Bluegrass Classic and the USBCHA National Finals. She has served on both the Texas Sheepdog Association and USBCHA boards.

**Beth Kerber** is a professional writer who began competing with herding dogs more than 10 years ago. She competes in USBCHA competitions, including the Bluegrass Classic and the USBCHA National Finals. She lives in Ohio where she raises a commercial flock of Katahdin sheep and regularly uses her dogs for farm chores.

# Dogwise.com is your source for quality books, ebooks, DVDs, training tools and treats.

We've been selling to the dog fancier for more than 25 years and we carefully screen our products for quality information, safety, durability and FUN! You'll find something for every level of dog enthusiast on our website, www.dogwise.com, or drop by our store in Wenatchee, Washington.

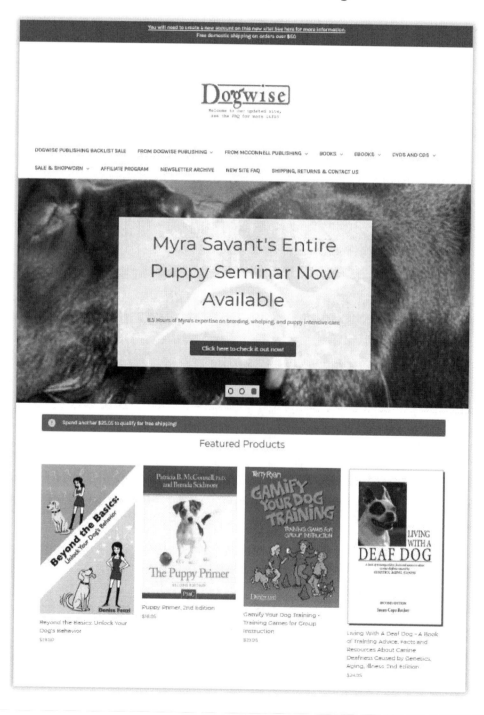

Made in the USA
Middletown, DE
15 September 2024